Ignite35

For more visit: kellyferral.com

Ignite35:
My Life in the Sex Fetish Community

Kelly Ferrall

While I have taken some creative license and some precautions, this story is based on truth. Names and other identifying details have been changed. Also, for the sake of privacy and brevity, some characters have been merged with others. Some events did not happen in my community specifically, but rather in neighboring ones. Those, I have included to give a more, well rounded depiction of what it is like to be in one. Regardless, everyone in this story exists in one form or another and this is how they live. For a while, so did I.

Kelly Ferrall

PROLOGUE

They call me Ignite35. I am a man who carries, not just my own, but many people's secrets. In light of popular media, those secrets are losing some of their power to surprise and shock. However, I believe that is simply the result of overly romantic flights of fancy and haphazard marketing. If there's one thing I learned in the lifestyle that I led for some time, it's that curiosity can open doors to worlds that, even the most imaginative, will find hard to believe actually exist.

The whole thing started for me when I came home to find my girlfriend gone. When I say, "gone," I mean she had packed and cleared out all of her belongings, leaving nothing behind but a note that simply read, "I can't do this anymore." At first, I was in shock. I never saw it coming and was having a hard time figuring out why. I was also heartbroken. I loved Brooke, deeply. Even if our intimate life had been utterly bland, the romantic side was, at least for me, very real.

CHAPTER ONE

I sat at the bar at the Blackstone, a drab neighborhood restaurant staring into my beer. I hadn't said much since I got there. All that ran through my mind was that my relationship was over, I was recently unemployed, and due to my lease ending, soon to be homeless. Depressed didn't begin to cover it. My sadness, loneliness and fear were having a mournful vigil together.

"Hey, Kelly," a voice suddenly rang, pulling me out of my introspection.

I looked up to find Ryder there. She was one of the bartenders at the Blackstone, but she was off of work, experiencing the view from the customer side of the bar.

"Hey," I replied quietly.

"What's wrong?"

"Oh," I nervously laughed, "everything."

"That's not good." She pulled the stool out next to me and took a seat. She was American born of Brazilian parents, caramel colored with unnaturally blonde, short, curly hair and a wonderful body, lean, but with curves in all the right places. I'd always taken special notice of her because she had done the same to me. The first time she served me, she flirted and then expressed disappointment when she found out I had a girlfriend.

Hmm. This could be an interesting opportunity, I thought.

"So, what's the biggest problem on your mind?" she asked.

I sighed. "Brooke left."

Ryder grinned. "That's not a problem. That's a relief."

I scowled.

"Come on, Kelly. She was irritating. You can do so much better. Seriously. You're nice and intriguing and she's...not."

"I still cared about her," I pointed out.

"I know. I'm sorry." She offered me a sympathetic look. "I just didn't like her. She never smiled and she complained all the time."

I gave a conciliatory nod. "That's true. But she was the last thing I had going for me."

It was then that Ryder caught the bartender's attention. "Me and my friend here would like two shots of tequila."

It was not the last shot she bought me that night. As we sat there getting drunk, I filled her in on all the misery.

"I got laid off a couple of months ago. I have resumes at several IT companies, but haven't heard back from any of them yet. I was hoping to wait until I knew where I'd be working to find a new place to live. But, with Brooke gone, I can't afford my place by myself. Everything is completely up in the air right now."

"Which one of the jobs do you want the most right now?"

"The most convenient one is over in Smithtown. The one that is the most attractive is in Franklin. But the one that I'm most qualified for is in Clinton"

"Damn," Ryder exclaimed. "Two of those are really far away. And that's not what I asked."

"I'm not sure."

"Well then, you're just going to have to pester the hell out of all of them."

"Way ahead of you."

"And, for the record, I hope you don't get the ones in Clinton or Franklin," she declared, her inebriation making her frank and brave.

"Why?"

"Because, then I wouldn't see you anymore."

I smiled. The alcohol began to have similar effects on me. "Ryder, would you like to go out some time?" I was nervous, but also proud of myself for finding the courage to be assertive.

"No," she replied.

So much for pride.

"I don't want to date anyone, Kelly, especially one of my friends...*especially* one who's probably about to move away."

"I see." I began to plan my departure from the bar when Ryder gave me an even bigger shock.

"I'd really rather just go back to my place and fuck."

Say what?

I stared at her, looking for any indication that she might be messing with me. It wasn't there. I hesitated, and then smiled, propping my head up on my hand. I looked over at the digital jukebox and got up, programmed in some salsa music and held a hand out to my friend.

"Dance with me first."

She smiled back, shaking her head, but got up anyway. I pulled her to me and we gyrated back and forth to the rhythm, my hand on the small of her back and our hips in perfect unison.

"You know, Kelly, I think one of the reasons I first decided I liked you is that you have such a strong affinity for the same dopey music my parents listen to. Why is that?"

"What? Latin music is passionate and liberating. It's also fun." I spun her around and dipped her as she laughed.

"All interesting qualities." Her smiled beamed. "You're a really good dancer, you know that?"

I pulled her back up and we continued to dance, though our motions slowed a bit.

"So," she said, "what do you say?"

I stopped and summoned the bartender. "You can cash us out."

Ryder's place was small and dimly lit. Her roommate was at her boyfriend's place, so we got started right in the living room. We were kissing and touching each other all over. My hands explored her through her clothes, her denim shirt and jeans providing a thick, coarse cover for a thin, soft frame. I ran my fingers along her ribs and up along the sides of her ideal, B cup breasts, trailing just above the underwire of her bra. I reached up, and as I squeezed a bit, she let out a long breath that turned into a moan. We continued to kiss, sharing air and each other's scent. Ryder's was intoxicating, a subtle combination of lavender soap, booze and natural pheromones. As I breathed her in, I felt my cock press against my pants. I slowly started to unfasten the snaps on her shirt when she stopped me.

"Come on, Kelly. Show me some passion."

I was confused. "What?"

She grabbed her shirt and jerked it open. She put her hands on both sides of my face. "All that frustration you're feeling, take it out on me."

Intriguing. I kissed her again, more intensely this

time. I pulled her shirt off and she shook her arms to help it fall to the floor. After fumbling with the clasp on her bra for a few seconds, I gave up and pulled it over her head. I squeezed her hard enough that a couple of her vertebrae popped and I told her that we were going to the bedroom. She wasn't much smaller than me and I didn't feel confident that I could comfortably pick her up in my arms, so I bent down and put her over my shoulder.

"Oh, yeah," she laughed excitedly.

"Which bedroom is yours, young lady?"

"The one on the right."

I marched her in and tossed her onto her bed where she bounced once. Her smile was delighted and naughty as I tugged her jeans off. I undressed myself quickly before climbing on top of her and kissing her more, beginning at her stomach and working my way up to her neck, relishing her soft, warm skin.

"Hold my hands down," she whispered.

She certainly knew what she wanted and wasn't afraid to ask.

I grabbed her wrists with one hand and pinned them over her head. Then I used my other hand and mouth to work over the rest of her body while she moaned. From the base of her hairline, right at her neck, I kissed, licked and nibbled. I ran my hand across her chest, paying extra attention to her breasts which I pinched ever-so-slightly. My hand began to move, almost of its own volition, exploring every inch of her smooth, light brown skin that I could reach while restraining her with the other, trailing along her shoulders, bumping over each rib, back up to her chest and down again to her soft, yet firm hips. I eventually reached between her legs, slowly stroked up her inner thigh and found her clit, which I began carefully rubbing. As I felt her moisten, I applied more pressure and dipped my fingers into her. The hard little rotations I was making increased in speed and Ryder's breathing and moaning followed suit. She proceeded to push upwards with her hips while her eyes remained shut and her smile thanked me. Within a few minutes, she came, raising her body up off of the mattress more and more and letting out a loud expression of her pleasure. After what seemed like almost half a minute, she exhaled hard and dropped herself back down onto the bed.

"Fuck me, please, Sir," she begged.

How could I refuse?

I reached over to my pants, pulled out my wallet and found the condom in it that I never expected to need. Ripping it open and putting it on, I lay on top of her, pinned her back down by the wrists and buried myself in her hard and deep.

"Ahh!" she exclaimed.

"Did I hurt you?" I asked with sudden concern.

"Not at all," she smiled. "But you should."

"Huh?" I asked intelligently.

Ryder began pushing back into me as she dropped a bombshell. "Hold me down, Kelly. Hold me down by the throat. Pull my hair. Slap me. Bite me. Fuck me mean!"

My mouth was hanging open and not just from the heavy breathing that I was doing. Suddenly, something in me responded. I let her wrists go in order to grab a fistful of her blonde curls and her throat.

"You got it, you dirty little bitch."

She laughed. Then she moaned. At the urging of her little words of encouragement, I slapped her in the face with my open palm. The training of a lifetime, uttered by countless voices, rang in my head. "Never hit a woman." But Ryder didn't react like a victim, she smiled and moaned with desire. When I slapped her again, I found that I was becoming more excited, my heart starting to pound and lust for her increasing. I put my hand around her soft, warm neck and began to choke her a little. Not much, not enough to hurt her. Just enough to feel like I had her, pinned and under my control. I bit her shoulder, licking the skin that was in my mouth, relishing her delicious taste. I did this and everything else that she begged for.

"Oh, God, Sir. Yes, Sir. I'm yours. Use me. Fuck me. My body is only for you to pleasure yourself with. Do whatever you wish with it."

Her scalding pussy was soaked, yet still seemed to tighten around me sporadically, almost tugging. While I didn't ask, I'm pretty sure she came again. Her desire and ecstasy felt like a reward for being the rough lover that she so obviously craved. After a relatively short time, my over excitement caused me to come as well. As I let loose inside of her, I groaned longer and louder than I ever remembered doing, my personal frustrations joining my sexual passion in a scorching, vicious exodus of my body. A one, one, one...two, two, two... three, three, three... ...four... It burst from me, hard and crippling. Once the purge subsided, I collapsed on top of her.

"Thank you, Sir," she cooed, stroking her fingers up and down my back.

"No, no, baby girl," I panted. "Thank you."

When I woke the next day, it was like coming out of one dream and into another one. As my eyes focused around me, the sun blaring in from the window gave me a better look at where I was than I had the night before in the dim light and under my tequila buzz. Ryder was only about five years younger than me, but she still lived a lot like a college student. Her bedroom was small and cluttered. The comforter on her twin bed was a little thin and decorated with bright pink and blue flowers. Her dresser was right up next to the bed in lieu of a night stand and there were a couple of dirty glasses on top of it. The clothes that we'd shed the night before were not the only ones on the floor and her paneled closet was open.

I crawled out of bed, put on my outfit from the previous day and walked into the kitchen to find Ryder sitting at the dining table, drinking coffee and checking social media on her phone. She was fully dressed in clean clothes and seemed no worse for the wear as she gave me a cheerful, "Hi," when I cautiously entered the room.

"Good morning," I replied with a meek smile.

"How are you feeling?"

"Oh, you know," I said, rubbing sleep from my eyes and trying to rub the ache from my forehead. "I'm okay. A little hungover."

"I made coffee." She motioned towards the machine with the mug in her hand.

I immediately fixed myself some and sat down across from her. She looked up from her phone, saw me staring and grinned.

"Did you enjoy last night?" she asked.

"Yeah. Yeah, I did. I've...never done anything like that before."

"Well, you took to it like a duck to water."

I chuckled nervously. I swallowed. "So, what do we do now?"

She barely glanced up from scrolling on her phone. "I'm going to get ready for work."

"No, uh...I mean...what do *we* do next?"

She stopped, the specifics of my question settling in.

"Oh. Look, Kel, don't get the wrong idea. I like you. And I'd love to do the dirty with you on occasion, especially after last night. But, like I told you, I'm not looking for a relationship."

My heart sank a bit, but settled back into place as I accepted the rationale in her words.

She continued. "Plus, you just got out of a relationship. And, frankly, I'm looking for someone with more experience."

"Experience?"

"In BDSM."

"BDSM," I repeated. "That's rough sex, right? It's—"

"Bondage, discipline, dominance, submission, sado-masochism."

"Right. Okay." It was a bit of a blow to my ego. "Is this an active search?"

She contemplated for a moment before replying, "More like a passive one. I've checked out a few websites and answered a few personals, but I have no desire to be part of a community."

"Community?"

"Yeah. The local... I don't know what you call it... group of kinky people who get together and network, have parties, things like that."

I was taken aback. "Stuff like that happens?"

"Apparently." She took a sip of her coffee before continuing with, "Anyway, I like you. But I'm not looking for anything serious with you. Besides, you're probably moving, remember?"

I nodded in agreement. I sipped my coffee. I wanted to redirect the conversation to something completely different, but one thing struck me that I needed to dig for more on.

"Which websites did you look at?"

She shrugged. "There are a bunch of them. Some are better than others. Some bombard you with spam and ads and shit. Others are just blogs. A select few are for networking. I can email you some of the links if you want."

I thought for a second before declining. I'd find them on my own if I decided that it was important. For the time though, I blew the whole thing off like it was just some isolated and special night of crazy...even if I couldn't deny that something had been awakened in me...something wild.

That was just the beginning.

CHAPTER TWO

My apartment complex was re-tiling the floor in the laundry room, so I was forced to go to the laundromat. One good thing about my current situation was that I'd soon be away from the place I was living. Granted, I didn't know where I'd be moving to, but almost anything had to be better than where I was. It was too expensive and the property manager was an ass who was always changing the rules of the lease agreement and doing things like shutting down the laundry room without warning.

I stood in front of the dryers folding my casual shirts and jeans, cargo shorts, socks and boxers. I looked up at my reflection in the glass on the dryer door and examined myself critically. There was very little interesting about me, I thought. Thirty-five years old, Caucasian and the product of a waning middle class. My brown hair was in slight need of cutting. My average build and slightly short stature didn't make me stand out. I had a decent face, but it wasn't one that stopped women dead in their tracks. I was just a guy, an average guy, with an average IT background, living in Chester, one of the most average cities in the country. I sighed.

That's when a little girl of about eight ran past me and plopped down in a chair across from the vending machines. There were band aids on her shoulder, possibly from immunization shots. At least, that might have explained the debate that she was having with her stuffed animal.

"We have to give you a shot, Elmo," she said.

She then produced her own reply in a high pitched voice. "No, I don't want a shot! Needles hurt!"

"But you need it. It's good for you."

"No!"

She then began poking the toy with a pen.

"Ow!" she made it cry out. "Stop it!"

"Don't struggle, Elmo. It will just hurt more."

"Ow! Ow! Ow!"

"I told you to stop struggling. Now you get a spanking." She proceeded to swat the stuffed animal over and over.

This went on for a while and I began to wonder if and how behavior like this might transform over time. Would she grow up to become one of these kinky people that Ryder had referred to, gaining pleasure from torturing and spanking her lovers and not even knowing why?

I set my laundry in the basket and pulled out my phone. I opened a search engine and typed in, "BDSM." All that came up was a series of articles and blogs, so I added other words to my search trying to refine it, words like "dominant" and "bondage."

Bam. Tons of porn.

"Elmo, do you just like getting in trouble?" the little girl asked her toy before hitting it a few more times.

Suddenly, I felt a little weird about the whole thing and decided to look into it at home, away from children and their masochistic stuffed animals.

On my way home, I couldn't shut my mind off. Turning up Chico Buarque on my iPod did nothing to block my wandering thoughts. I kept replaying the previous night. However, eventually my memory reached farther back, to college. At the start of my freshman year, I had almost no experience with women. I had lost my virginity the night of my senior prom, to a girl that I had only been on a handful of dates with. It was an exciting, albeit awkward, experience and it was the last thing we really did together. A few months later, I began working on a computer science degree by day and learning to party and chase girls by night. While I excelled at the first part, the later was always a hit or miss situation. I was never that socially comfortable or confident, so pursuits of my female peers were pretty basic. Also, while many girls were only interested in cheap sex and wild times, I tended to lean towards relationships. I wanted commitment and I did get jealous. The upside is that it made me pretty faithful, though few really found out for extended periods of time.

I did end up dating one girl, Kim, throughout my graduate career and for a few years after that. But, as I thought about it, I realized that I had broken up with her when I turned thirty, not because of a sense of maturity that was coming on, as I had originally thought. What I had done was to walk away from a girl who wanted to get married, settle down in a nice suburb, have two-point-five kids, buy a minivan and have nice, cordial marital relations an average of once a week from there on out. So, I bailed.

Two years later, I met Brooke, at a speed dating event. We liked the same movies and the same kinds of food and we didn't want to even think about kids or suburbia for, at least, another five to ten years, if ever. While the sex wasn't mind blowing, it was a little interesting in the respect that we did it in lots of places other than the bed and in positions other than the one or two approved for people with osteoporosis.

Apparently, that wasn't enough for her. While we did argue a good bit, usually over money or future plans, I began to suspect that, like I had with my previous relationship, Brooke had simply grown bored. By the time I reached my apartment and began hauling my laundry up the stairs, I decided I wanted to make some big changes in my life. I wanted to find that new job. I wanted to find that better place to live. I wanted to live out my fantasies. And, after fooling around with Ryder, most of my fantasies were now about sex.

I walked into my place, dropped my clothes on the sofa and booted up my laptop. The first thing to do was to find employment.

For whatever reason, all of the IT jobs within an hour radius of Chester were being snatched up left and right. Every time I checked on a resume that I had submitted, I was dismayed to find that the job had already been filled. This could have been because eight nearby colleges and IT schools were suddenly cranking out massive graduating classes. It could have been that, like the company that had laid me off, many businesses were downsizing and there were more out of work professionals in the area. Whatever the case, I was having a hard time finding work and my cash reserves were dwindling. I still had a bit of student debt to pay off as well. I was growing desperate.

There was some good news...sort of. One IT company was looking to fill a position, pretty much, right away and they were offering ten thousand dollars more a year than my previous, dinky little job. The only catch...it was over two and a half hours away in the growing town of Clinton. It would be a huge moving expense and I knew absolutely no one there. Still, as my options were beginning to seem more and more limited, I decided that I should, at least check it out.

Wall-Rios Solutions, was a moderate sized operation run by two men who, like me, were in their mid-thirties. Brice Wall had, himself, responded to my resume and met me for an interview with an eager handshake.

"Mr. Ferrell," he smiled.

"Kelly," I told him.

"Of course. Kelly. Brice." He seemed sincere as he pumped my hand firmly a couple of times. "It's great of you to come in. Thank you, so much."

He was tall, well built and energetic, with dark hair and a happy tone that immediately set me at ease. His clothes were very casual, just an untucked oxford and jeans. He kept squeezing and playing with a racquetball, even as he led me to a large, wood paneled office and asked me to have a seat. Before he could take one himself, he was already praising me.

"I gotta say, your resume is fantastic. And I was really impressed with a couple of the posts that you have on your blog."

"My...blog?" I had almost forgotten about the thing. It had been almost three months since I had posted anything on it. During some of my down time at work, I would occasionally write things about particular problems that I would encounter, partially to help others in my field avoid and be prepared to deal with them should they arise in their jobs, but mostly out of boredom. The whole page was now little more than a footnote on my resume.

"Yeah," Brice said. "There was one post in particular

that caught my eye concerning some server upgrades at a law firm that started running into all kinds of bugs. I honestly never would have thought to look at file permissions on a super administrator account. You approach problems with a different angle than we're used to. A lot of the hacks you mentioned I found really interesting." He stood and began to pace and bounce the blue, rubber ball as he continued. "The main reason is because the city, who we have a contract with, is struggling with the exact same thing. A couple of the guys I have now tried to fix it for them, but they kept running into more and more complications. They're more used to working with template systems. They tried to implement some of the hacks from your blog post, but admitted they were out of their element pretty quickly. I think *you* are the man to fix it and to handle our municipal contract from here on out."

I was a little stunned. It was an interesting prospect, certainly one that suggested long-term job security. Still, it was a lot of work, enough that the pay increase no longer seemed that great. Brice could see my apprehension and pressed me to explain its presence. I sighed and, while feeling a little ungrateful, confessed that sixty-thousand dollars a year to cover such outstanding responsibilities, not to mention moving so far away, didn't really make me want to do any somersaults.

"Sixty grand?" he said, looking rather confused. "There must be some mix up in our communication. The job we're offering you starts at eighty."

Okay, now he had my attention. "Eighty...? Eighty-thousand dollars?"

"That's right."

"Uh..." I chuckled. "Well, that does sound a lot more tempting."

"Great!" He smiled as he slapped his hand on his desk. "Here's the thing though, we'd want you to start the day after tomorrow."

"Thursday?" I was suddenly speechless again.

"I know that's soon. But the city is in dire straits and the quicker we can get them taken care of the better."

"I understand that," I told him honestly, "but, I would still need to move. I'm not the least bit prepared to do so. I have to find a place to live—"

"We can help with that actually. My sister-in-law manages a great apartment complex just a couple of miles away. We can get you approved for it by no later than tomorrow. It would be just until you find something more permanent, of course. Unless you just decided that you wanted to stay there. We will also get you some movers and pay your expenses."

"I...I don't know. It's really tempting. It's just a lot to do really suddenly."

He nodded. "I understand. How about this? Start Friday and work through the weekend, just this first week. And we'll make it ninety-thousand, plus a hiring bonus. Say, five grand."

While my responsibility would potentially double, so would my salary. All I had to do was devote the next two weeks to working my ass off, including moving to a new city, which he would help me do.

"I think," I began slowly, "you may have yourself a deal."

Moving was weird and hectic. From almost the moment I walked in the door of my apartment back in Chester, I began packing. This went on most of the night and into the next day. You never realize how much stuff you have until you have to move it. Nor do you realize how settled in you've become. Charming displays on end tables and in foyers have to be broken down and wrapped up. Large wardrobes, dishes, books, old LPs and memorabilia become stacks of boxes all over each room. And the whole process always takes longer than you'd ever expect.

Periodically I would take breaks to read texts that Brice was sending me, telling me when the movers would arrive and that my new apartment had been arranged. However, I also surfed the web looking at various risqué websites. Most of my initial searches just continued to turn up porn or cheap reports by online magazines unrelated to the subject. While the former seemed mildly interesting, it wasn't what I was after and the later was always written by someone as uninformed as me. I continually refined my search with words like "networking" and "education." I still had to scroll past the first couple of pages, but I did begin to run across sites that seemed more aimed at someone like me, someone interested in learning.

There were a number of blog pages devoted to the subjects of BDSM and fetishes. There were also a few sites that asked me to join as a member in order to meet other people who shared my interest. The first one was even free and had good reviews. Still, it wouldn't let me explore without joining. I put the whole task aside and returned to packing and cleaning.

That was my Wednesday.

On Thursday, the movers arrived extra early. As they cleared out my furniture and other belongings, I cleaned more, in an effort to ensure my deposit.

Then there was the long trip to Clinton. The movers

drove at a calm pace, presumably to prevent any damage to my belongings, and the trip following them took three hours. Once we arrived at my new place, a recently built complex aimed at students and young families, the movers quickly got my things inside. I told them not to bother trying to arrange furniture too much or put anything away. I would decide how to do all of that later.

I unpacked my food first and then got started on my clothes. That's when my phone rang.

"Hello?"

"Hey, Kelly. It's Brice Wall. How you doing?"

"Oh, good. I'm moved in, more or less."

"That's fantastic," he said, sounding sincere. "Listen, I know this is sudden and puts more on your plate, but do you think that you could get down to the office today? We need to get you into the system so that you can start tomorrow."

"Uh..." I looked around at everything that I had to tackle in my immediate personal life and it was over-whelming. Then I remembered that I was in my nice, new apartment, which I hadn't had to procure or load anything into because of my new boss and sighed. "I'll be there as soon as I can."

Once I got back home the exhaustion had settled in and I was too tired to try to unpack or anything else. I was hungry though, and prepared a simple meal. While I ate, I dug out my phone, cued up some Jorge Ben and, as the tiny speaker echoed the Latin jazz back up at me, returned to my search on my laptop.

More and more, the free, social networking site that I looked at seemed to be the one that I needed to explore, even if I was apprehensive about starting an account. Finally, I broke down.

The first thing that I did was to set up a dummy email. I figured this would also come in handy whenever I needed to give one to a retail chain or any other source of continual spam. Next, I had to select a screen name. This proved hard as I had no idea what type of handle I wanted to represent me.

I decided that, if I could find a strong word, maybe that word alone would work. I began looking around my new apartment, but as all of my books and other entertainment were packed away, I found little inspiration. I tried an internet search, looking for elemental terms, things relating to earth, fire, the sky...

As I browsed, I was hit with an advertisement for an energy drink inviting me to, "Ignite my day."

Ignite. That had an interesting ring.

I typed it in and was immediately disappointed to find that some other pervert had beaten me to it.

Hmm. Was there something else that I could add to it? My age immediately sprang to mind, the forced rhyme having an interesting appeal.

Ignite35.

I wouldn't always be thirty-five though.

But I was thirty-five when entering this rabbit hole.

Ignite35.

The website accepted the screen name. Next, it led me to a page asking for tons of personal information, my location, a bio, a photo...and my real name.

I froze. I looked over the screen again and found an option to skip everything but my name and a phone number. I took a deep breath and typed the information in. After that, I opted to skip through the rest and just explore. I spent the next hour looking at other people's profiles in the area, as well as back in Chester. The photos, the bios, the discussions on all the member's walls were intense. Not all of it. Some of it was fairly benign and not unlike other social media. But most was pretty wild, shocking even.

There were countless photos of people, mostly women, in various states of bondage, rope predominantly. One woman was posed against a fireplace, wearing stockings and heels. There were small, metal clamps on her nipples connected by a chain, leather cuffs on her wrists and ankles and a collar on her neck. Between the cuffs on her ankles was a metal bar, keeping her legs spread. She also had a blindfold on her face and something shoved in her mouth. Another showed a guy with his hands cuffed to the bars of a cage he was locked in. He was naked, unless you count the large number of rubber bands tightly wrapped around his balls and erect cock. Then there were the many photos of various people with genitalia in their mouths. There were even more of women shoving their naked asses into the camera and men displaying their dicks. There were videos of a variety of outrageous sex acts, including one of a remarkably attractive, fortyish woman being gangbanged by five men.

Not everyone in all of the photos and videos were attractive however. There were plenty of fat guts, sagging tits and aged faces. Many of them seemed to be overcompensating by making sure that they demonstrated the most perverse behavior in their picture, from sucking semen off of toes to gay, anal fisting to one very plain looking woman who had shoved a list of garden tools into her cunt. In some ways, it just got worse and worse. But in others, it got better. For one, everyone seemed to be free to express themselves sexually however they pleased, with no judgment whatsoever. In fact, more often than not, they were praised for it. The other positive way was that people wrote blogs, poems, journal entries and all other forms of posts. That was particularly interesting, especially to someone new like me. A good bit of it was just people expressing their desires for their significant others.

One that caught my attention began, "He calls me by name and I quake inside. There it is. It has become that intimate. I am no longer a thing, an object, a possession committing these acts, I am me. He says it lovingly and it reassures me that, in indulging my desires, I am not filthy. I am not a whore. I am a human being and I have lust. It's okay to have lust. He shows me this. He even rewards me for it.

"He says my name and I am brought to life. I worship him for showing me the truth. There is no shame in my ecstasy."

Intriguing.

I finally signed out and got ready for bed. I would learn more the next day, but for now I had accomplished what I needed the most.

I had become Ignite35.

CHAPTER THREE

I had set my alarm for 6 am, but that time seemed to come extra early. The past two days that I had spent packing, cleaning and moving wore me to a pulp and my muscles were sore, even though I hadn't done any of the heavy lifting. As a result, I found myself hitting snooze for almost an hour. Finally, a voice inside me started calling out.

Hey, it said. *You need to get up and get ready for work. How do you ever expect to earn someone's respect enough to dominate them, if you can't even control yourself?*

I sighed and forced my eyes open before tossing the covers off. I hadn't even put my bed together and my mattress was on the floor, so getting up consisted of rolling over and climbing to my feet. I staggered to the kitchen and found the box that I had packed my coffee maker in, made a pot and stood in the dining room sipping the extra strong, black beverage while looking over the stacks and piles of things that I needed to unpack. As I did, my eyes fell on the arm of the couch where I'd tossed my belt the night before. It was an old, leather belt with various prehistoric looking images, like cave paintings, pressed into it. I'd always liked it because it was so sturdy and unique. I suddenly realized that the stamps could leave some extra special marks were I to spank someone with it.

Another thought occurred to me and I smiled.

Taking out my phone, I aimed it at the threatening looking strap of leather and snapped a picture. Next, I logged into my new account on the fetish website that I'd joined and uploaded the photo. That would be my profile picture for the time being.

Once I got to Wall-Rios Solutions, I was basically given an address and pointed back toward the door. Apparently, the city had been breathing down their necks for relief from their massive computer problems and I was to get right on it. I got back into my car, programmed the address for City Hall into my GPS and was back on the road.

Once I arrived, I walked in, my canvas briefcase over my shoulder. I showed my identification and work badge to the security guard who insisted that he have one of his cohorts escort me to my destination, which was somewhere on the second floor.

We took the elevator upstairs and I was led to the office of the City Planner, a remarkably young man, possibly in his late thirties. He was attractive, even if balding and sporting thick rimmed glasses. His suit was nice but plain and his tie was yellow. He immediately rose and offered me his hand. "Boy, are we glad to see you," he said with a big, politician's smile, matched with a tone that actually seemed sincere. "Jack Pierce. So, good of you to come help us out."

"Of course," I told him amicably.

"Brice Wall tells me you can actually fix this mess we politely refer to as a computer system."

"I'm going to certainly give it my best. Where's the server room? Or, at least a computer with Shell access?"

"Right this way." He led me out of his office. We began walking down the hallway with the security guard shadowing us. As we approached the corner, another man walked out of an office in front of us.

"Mike," Mr. Pierce called out. "This is the new IT guy. " He turned to me. "I'm sorry, I didn't catch your name."

"Kelly."

"Kelly," he repeated. "This is Mike Underwood, Chairman of the City Council."

"Nice to meet you," he said. Unlike the City Planner, he was all business and no smile, very serious. He was tall, blond with streaks of gray and somewhere in his mid-fifties, with a gut that was actively starting to work its way over his pants. The tone in his voice was impatient. "So, you're actually able to do something about this fiasco?"

"As I told Mr. Pierce, I'm certainly going to try."

"The other people you're company sent 'tried.' I need someone who can do it. If that's not you, then I need to know now. This bullshit has placed us months behind, pretty much in every department."

"Well, uh," I began as tolerantly as I could. "I haven't even seen one of your computers yet. We are about to to dig into the logs right now, though. After that, I should be able to give you an initial diagnosis." Normally, I would have been more certain, but I didn't want to promise anything until I could actually look at the problem. Plus, big title or not, he was already getting on my bad side.

He gave me a grunt in return, followed by, "Fine."

After looking through page after page of system error codes, I was reassured that the problem was one that I could tackle. I told them so and Mr. Pierce clapped his hands together.

"That is wonderful news," Mr. Underwood said, sounding only slightly less cold. "When can we get fully functional?"

"Well, it's not going to be quick," I confessed, "certainly not if you want it done right."

"How long are we looking at?"

"Months."

"*Months?*" the council chair snapped.

"Well...yeah. I mean, it's going to require backing up every byte of data before I even *start* writing code. It's a software *and* hardware issue, so I need to find which drives are corrupted or failing, and figure out why the system is allocating all of its resources to—"

"Alright, alright. I get it," Underwood said with the wave of a hand. "Get started. And keep us all appraised." He walked out looking even more frustrated than he began.

Pierce was more understanding. "Well, I for one, am just glad that the problem is being solved. Let us know if you need anything."

And so, that was the start of my new life. I went to work every day at Clinton City Hall and began the process of slowly picking through and cleaning up their computer system. It involved a lot of debugging and following dead ends in spaghetti code. In between all of this, or while I was backing things up or running scripts, I would search the new website I had joined (on my phone, obviously) for information and for people who I might be able to connect with, who might answer my questions, teach me, and mainly, just be my friend.

The later part proved to be harder than I originally

anticipated. In retrospect, I suppose they had a lot to be protective of. However, at the time, I naively assumed that they might be happy to meet like-minded souls, same as me. It started innocently, with me taking bold chances at messaging people, introducing myself in as honest a way as I could from behind a pseudonym with no genuine personal information attached to it. Mostly, what I got was dead air. However, a few were willing to reply.

In the instance of one girl, who referred to herself as a sub, short for sexual submissive, I was taken to task pretty quickly. I had made the mistake of telling her that I had been on other social media, including dating sites, but that this was new to me.

Her reply was rather curt: "First and foremost, I do not consider this a dating site. Second, I do not friend or chat with people that I haven't met face-to-face. The last thing I need right now is an inbox full of suggestive messages from some new creeper who doesn't know the first thing about the lifestyle. We don't just hook up, beat each other and fuck. Get your head out of your ass or get off of this website."

She concluded by saying, "Don't contact me again."

Okay. That was more of a dead end than what I was facing with tracing spaghetti code. I found similar attitudes from plenty of other people who condescended to write me back, women and men both. Then, of course, there were the ones who seemed a little *too* eager to talk to me.

"Glad to get your message. Perhaps we can meet up. There's a great hotel on the edge of town. We can meet for a drink in the bar and then get a room upstairs. I have all kinds of dirty ideas!"

Those people, I decided, were either scam artists, likely to lead me to a room where a couple of thugs waited to beat my ass and rob me of my cash and information, (hardly the BDSM experience I was looking for) or they were even more new to this and less careful than me. I began to get disgruntled.

I decided that, perhaps, my profile was lacking. After all, it had little information on it, outside of a name and photo. A bio. I needed a bio. But what should I say?

I pulled up the screen for it and began to type.

Hi. I'm Ignite35. I joined this website to try to meet people and get involved. I am very interested in BDSM and have found that I love rough sex.

I stared back at what I had written. Then I fought my gag reflex. I moved the cursor back and tried again.

After an intriguing experience in BDSM and much investigation, I have joined this website in order to advance my knowledge and connect with others who share my interest.

Christ. What was I writing? A resume? Delete.

I looked at the blank screen and held my fingers over the keys. What to write? Well, if some thought I was insincere and others thought that I was an easy mark, I needed to defy both. How do I do that?

I thought hard, and then I just typed what I genuinely wanted to say.

I'm new to this. I had an experience that made me really curious, but I don't really know what to do about it. I know what my initial interests are and I have looked online and investigated some things, but, overall, I still feel like I'm wading into the shallow end of a very, very deep pool. At present, all I want is to meet people and make friends. Where that takes me is anyone's guess, most of all, mine. So, if I contact you or if you happen to look at my profile, just understand that I'm looking to learn and make my choices slowly. Whatever I do with this, it's going to be with sober reflection, no selfish libido in play and an honest heart. However, I am not dumb. Be straight with me and I'll return the favor. I just want to find out what this is all about and what place I have in such a lifestyle. I hope that's going to be a good experience and that my presence will return the positive.

I loaded my bio and then began to look, again, at other people in my area and to message a few.

Then there was a ray of hope. It came in the form of a reply from a twenty-five year old "little"—whatever that was—who called herself SeptemberSnowGirl. She was friendly, open and seemed genuinely interested in helping me.

"Hi," she began. "I can appreciate your interest in the lifestyle, as well as the frustrations that you're having connecting with people. It can be a real jungle out there. LOL. What I would suggest is going to a munch. There's one in town every two weeks. That's where you'll meet the people who can really help you and where you can find the answers that you're looking for."

Interesting. I only had one question.

"What's a munch?"

That exchange happened around eleven in the morning. Shortly after lunch, I got my reply.

"A munch is a meeting for kinksters. The local one, like most, is held in a public place. In our case, it's a restaurant on 4th and Pine, in between the gas station and the car lot. It's low impact, meaning that it's casual. No fetish wear, no public play, just people eating and talking. The next one is a week from today at seven pm. Go to the private dining room towards the back."

I read the message several times, just to make sure that I understood it. It was just what I was looking for, a place to really start, to meet people and to learn...even make friends, perhaps.

At about that time, there was commotion in the hallway, right outside of the server room door. I nervously minimized the conversation on my phone. Still, I did so with a little less frustration and a bit more excitement for myself.

I hadn't unpacked my first weekend. Nor did I the following week. Moving, working, adjusting, it was all too exhausting and I allowed myself to be irresponsible in every other respect. I'd usually get home around six, eat whatever I was afraid was going to spoil next in the fridge, clean whatever dishes I had used (few, since most were still packed up) and then settle in front of my laptop. There, I'd check my email and social media accounts and then watch TV or surf the web for my new obsession.

One of the first things that I discovered about BDSM was that it was very involved, convoluted even. There were so many details that, even the basic, 101 stuff confused me at first.

One article on the website began by mentioning that, whether simply looking to spice things up in the bedroom or entering into a 24/7 total power exchange, the basic rules were the same. One must operate safe, sane and consensual.

Okay, well, the last part made sense. But what was a "24/7 total power exchange?" I felt as confused as I did my first day of getting my bachelors in computer science, with all of the terms and details. The only difference was that, when I started my degree, I actually knew a little about computers, enough not to become completely lost right away.

The article continued. It talked about identification, loosely defined as terms to indicate what a person liked to do and the position that they liked to have in a BDSM relationship. Doms and Dommes (male and female Dominants) liked to be in charge, or rather, to "top." Conversely, subs (a term without gender, apparently) preferred to relinquish control, or "bottom."

Control, I thought. That's what I wanted, to have someone submit to me and allow me to have my way with them. I wanted to restrain someone, slap them a little, talk down to them a little, maybe. But also, to reward them and pamper them some. As I glanced around at my packed up life, I also realized that I wanted more control over myself. Perhaps that made me a Dom?

Switches were apparently people who went back and forth, taking control during one encounter with their partner or partners and then submitting the next.

"Partners," plural. That brought me to something called polyamory. Open relationships were apparently common in the community. It was something that I immediately found distasteful, though I didn't really know why. I wasn't brought up particularly religious. Maybe it was because my parents were still together that I found myself attached to monogamy. Whatever the case, the idea of sleeping around didn't particularly interest me. I mean, I had to admit to myself that I had fantasized a few times in my life about that elusive threesome, but never in a way that I wanted to actually make happen. I'd have been too afraid of my girlfriend wanting to know when it was her turn and I would have to be present, seeing all the weird faces some other guy made while he banged her from the other end.

Whatever, I thought with disturbed disinterest. *To each his own.* I moved on.

Apparently, there were subtle differences in some identifications, to the point of causing contention. Masters and Mistresses were Dominant, but Doms and Dommes were not necessarily Masters or Mistresses. Masters and Mistresses had significant training and experience to the point that qualified, outside factors had awarded them these titles. Any aggressive, controlling asshole could be Dominant, the article claimed.

This, of course, was met in the comments section with a variety of disagreements and redefinitions. It seemed, in fact, that many things in BDSM were quite subjective.

However, as I read on, I found that there were many terms and ideas that were pretty steadfast. Vanillas were people who were not in the lifestyle, like muggles in the Harry Potter world. Negotiations, discussions before engaging in BDSM play with someone to discuss safety and what each person wanted, as well as what they were and were not willing to do, were imperative, no matter what. Safe words, words or expressions that could be called out when one partner felt genuinely distressed, were crucial.

Safe, sane and consensual. That was the big theme repeated over and over.

My head was starting to swim trying to wrap it around all of these details. I decided to set the reading aside for a while and see what videos were available to help me. Perhaps a demonstration would help me stay focused on my goal.

I found one video on the website that demonstrated a variety of ways to dominate your partner. It was presented by a couple of switches who called themselves Miss Carla and Dallas Ray. They sat on the edge of a bed and began by stressing consent, negotiating specifics and taking safety precautions.

Miss Carla, a brunet in a leather corset explained. "We can't stress this enough. Talk openly and specifically with your partner. Find out what they want, and especially, find out what their hard limits—the things that they certainly are not willing to engage in—are."

"Also," Dallas Ray picked up, "make sure that you are playing safe. If you're inexperienced, don't tie ropes or restraints too tight. And safe words are critical. Remember, when exploring BDSM, sometimes 'no' doesn't actually mean 'no,' especially when one of you is pretending to be reluctant or unwilling. When choosing such a word, it's recommended that you select something that you wouldn't normally say like, 'banana,' 'elephant,' or 'senator.' That way, you know to ease up or stop, but it doesn't completely break the mood the way it would if you were to sit up and go—"

The screen cut to the two of them playing and Miss Carla holding up her hands suddenly. "Okay, for real. Stop! I don't like that," she exclaimed.

Next, they went through a list of techniques, beginning with psychological domination.

"This, I would suggest, is where you want to start," Miss Carla said. "For example, if you're Dominant, speaking to your partner in a commanding way can put them in a head space that allows them to feel submissive and at your mercy. Addressing them condescendingly or pejoratively and having them address you with terms of respect works well."

They cut to a shot of her on her knees and Dallas Ray standing over her asking her what she wanted.

"For you to take me," Miss Carla told him humbly.

Ray lifted her face by the chin. "What was that, slut?"

"I want you to take me, Sir," came a more desperate reply.

They cut to the two of them exchanging roles, presumably for more perspective. Miss Carla had Ray on a leash with his hands tied behind his back. She was slapping him.

"Say it!" she ordered. "Say it, dog!"

"I'm yours, Goddess. I'm yours to do with as you wish."

Cut back to the two of them sitting on the edge of the bed addressing the viewer.

"Telling them what you're going to do to them is another effective way to set the mood," Dallas Ray continued. "Their mind starts to imagine these things and they become expectant and excited."

Carla added, "It's a form of neuro-linguistic programming meant to lead them into subspace, a mental state where they are wholly submitted and dependent on you."

They cut to Ray circling her as she stood, restrained and blindfolded. He was talking very steadily to her, yet with a tone of authority. "I have a whip here and a vibrator and a whole host of other toys, little girl. I'm going to go down the list, using each and every one of them on you before I ever even touch you with my hands. You're going to feel each of them before I grant you the privilege of feeling me. Would you like that?"

"Yes, Sir."

They switched again, this time with Ray on all fours and Carla up in his face. She had him by the throat. "I'm going to work a butt plug up your ass before I spank it!" she stated harshly. "Are you ready, pig?"

This type of demonstration went on and on. The two of them would explain a technique and then show themselves using it on each other. I watched for a good half hour as the two of them slapped, spanked, and talked down to each other. Ray took a short stiff whip to Carla's backside. She cuffed him to the bed and dragged her nails down his chest. He put her in a large, wire cage and said nasty shit to her. All of it, they claimed, was very basic stuff, leaving me to wonder what the more advanced practices might be, especially after one shot of Carla touching Ray with a metal rod. There was a tiny "click" sound each time she did and he would cry out.

What the hell was that all about? I wondered.

After the tutorial, I thought about SeptemberSnowGirl's recommendation of attending a munch. I searched for the location that she had given me and found a privately owned family restaurant with a meeting room towards the back called, The King's Kettle. I made plans to go and investigate this munch thing. I was a tad nervous at the prospect of presenting myself to a room full of strangers under such circumstances, but I was also excited. This was going to be my next step and it was a big one.

CHAPTER FOUR

The following week, I made my way across town to The King's Kettle. I was more nervous than I remembered being in a long time, more so than any job interview, more than any first date, even more than the one time that Brooke had talked me into trying rock climbing.

I tentatively entered the restaurant, dressed innocuously in a short sleeve, light blue, button down shirt and plain khakis. As I scanned the place, I saw two large, glass doors separating a private room from the rest of the diners. I walked over and peered in, hoping to recognize any faces that I had seen on the internet. As I stood there, blatantly conspicuous to those inside, I was noticed and several heads turned towards me. One of them, a tall, blonde lady in very smart business attire, rose from her seat, came to the door and opened it.

"Can I help you?" she asked with a polite smile underneath a scrutinizing set of eyes.

I swallowed hard. "Uh, yeah..." I managed as I broke into a light sweat. "Is...is this the meeting?"

The lady's polite grin developed a slightly wicked tint. "We're enthusiasts," she returned.

"I'm enthusiastic," I said moronically.

They must have been used to people arriving at the munches for the first time more than a little nervous and unsure. She merely shifted her stern smile back into a friendlier one and invited me in.

"Who are you?" she asked as she directed me toward

an empty chair.

"Uh...I'm Ignite35."

"Is that what you'd like to be called?"

I considered the question. Was she suggesting that I could offer my real name? Or was she asking if my user name was merely what was available despite how I preferred to be addressed by those that I slept with? Should I tell her that I wanted to be called, Master Apollo or something equally as contrived? After quick consideration, I decided to just let my screen name represent me for the time being, just in case the whole thing turned out to be a bad idea.

The entire room greeted me simultaneously with an array of friendly smiles, suspicious glares, curious gazes and condescending once-overs. I took the empty seat I had been motioned toward. Directly across the table from me sat a well-dressed man, slightly older than myself, and about my size, though a bit thinner, with two pretty, young women, one on each side.

"Is it okay if I sit here?" I asked.

"That depends," the man said as he sized me up. "Are you going to behave yourself?"

"Oh, of course," I assured him. I glanced at each of the girls and took more from his meaning. "I'm cool."

He smiled. It wasn't unfriendly, but it was slightly cautionary at the same time. "Then you're fine."

"Okay, everyone," the tall blonde lady said. "The server will be back in a moment to take our orders. Until then, just for the couple of new people, why don't we all introduce ourselves? Be sure to give your screen name. Real name is optional. And, ideally, tell us all how you identify."

Everyone took turns telling me, and another, apparently new, guy wearing a biker jacket, who they were, rattling off odd internet pseudonyms with the occasional touch of kink, names like Sluttypixie, Lord Solomon, The Ghost of Christmas Fuck, Mother of Creation and Gentlista. Each followed their names with a title which defined their sexual interests to some extent: slave, Dominant, hedonist, switch, sadist and a few others I wasn't completely certain how to comprehend. When it got to the trio across from me, the girl to the man's right introduced herself as Tinkerbrat. She had light brown, bobbed hair and fidgeted a lot. She was petite, cute and in her early twenties. The man went next.

"I'm known as Dramatic Comedy on the website. You can call me D.C. I'm a Dom, and Tink is my girl." He then turned to the young lady on his left and added, "And so is this one."

In extreme contrast to Tinkerbrat, the other girl was painfully quiet and still. I noticed that she kept her eyes focused on the table, refusing to look at anyone. She looked shy and nervous, uncomfortable even. She was beautiful, pale, with long blonde hair, svelte and appeared to be barely eighteen, though I would later learn that she was actually twenty-six.

"Go ahead," D.C. told her.

"I'm Posie," she said softly, her eyes still locked onto the table.

The tall blonde commandeered the floor again, saying, "I'm Mistress Christina." She then emphasized an alternative spelling of "Xina," after which she changed track, noting that the server was on their way back to the room and that we should employ some temporary discretion.

As the server entered and began taking everyone's orders, I examined my neighbors. Both Tinkerbrat and Posie wore the same necklaces, black chokers with silver charms dangling from them. As I continued to study them, Tink gave me a big, overly-amused smirk, while Posie continued to, steadfastly, focus on the table. I began to wonder if the blonde was there against her will. D.C. just continued to stare at me with a friendly smile that was still, somehow, unnerving.

It was at that moment that the waiter caught my attention and asked for my order. As I had yet to look at the menu, I decided to keep it simple for the purpose of expedition. I ordered a burger and a pop. The waiter next addressed his attention across the table. Before Tink could answer, D.C. told the waiter that he and both of the girls would have tomato basil pasta.

"But I want a cheeseburger," Tinkerbrat protested.

D.C. glared at her.

"Fine," she whined.

Posie said nothing.

The waiter said that our orders would be up as soon as possible and then exited. The moment he was out of the room, D.C. took the opportunity to demonstrate how discipline worked with his girls.

"Are we going to have a problem?" he asked Tinkerbrat.

"I don't know," she replied in a catty tone, "are we?"

"Okay, that's one," he said. When she grunted, he asked, "Do you want to go for two?"

She gritted her teeth, but said nothing. D.C. looked back at me and shook his head. "Subs," he said.

I tried to agree with a smile, but wasn't fully sure if I knew what it was that I was agreeing with. I also couldn't help but to keep glancing over at Posie. Finally, I couldn't contain my curiosity any longer. "I'm sorry. I don't mean to pry, but...is she okay?" I asked D.C.

"She will be," he assured me. "She's just in trouble.

Her punishment is restricted eye contact."

"I beg your pardon?"

"She's not allowed to look anyone in the eye tonight."

"I see." I struggled with the information for a bit before continuing my inquiry. "If I may ask...what did she do?"

Posie noticeably blushed and Tinkerbrat chuckled loudly. D.C. shot the brunette a dirty look before telling me that his other sub had been receiving behavioral training and that she had broken the rules.

I nodded and tried hard to pretend like I understood. Neither D.C. nor Tinkerbrat were fooled for even a moment and both displayed expressions of amusement at my novice responses to their strange little games. Tink began looking like she was going to burst, until finally letting out an explanation, far louder than was necessary.

"She isn't allowed to masturbate right now and he caught her doing it!"

I looked over at Posie, whose pale skin was now the color of an apple. When I looked back at Tink and D.C., she was laughing and he was giving her a withering glare.

"That was not the original cause for the punishment and you know it," he told her. He turned his attention back to me. "Posie is trying to quit smoking. She cheated and so I took away a privilege. She broke that restriction and now here we are."

"She was baaaad," Tink sang sarcastically.

"She wouldn't have as hard of a time with it," he told her, "if you would stop doing it in front of her."

"Uh, doing which in front of her?" I heard myself ask.

D.C. started to answer, but then stopped.

"Hey, if she just had more self-control—" Tinkerbrat broke in.

"Tink..." D.C. said as he held his palm up, his fingers

spread. His sub looked like she wanted to say something, but then slumped back in her chair, arms crossed and an irritated pout across her face.

I looked back stunned. "What was that?"

"She's not allowed to speak for the next five minutes."

"Wow. How do you manage that?"

"You have to train them right." His mischievous grin remained firmly in place while Tink scowled. He went on to explain to me that "Tinkerbrat" wasn't just a name, it was how she identified. When I asked for more details, he told me that a brat was a sub that acted out despite full knowledge that they would be disciplined for it. "In Tink's case," he continued, "she acts like a bitch because she is one. Or rather, she doesn't always know how to express herself well, so she just misbehaves to get attention and test boundaries. Still, she is aware that she will pay for it and secretly enjoys it."

The sour look on his sub's face seemed to contradict this conclusion, yet she did remain silent.

"And her?" I nodded toward Posie.

D. C. ran his fingers through her hair. "There are all kinds of names for Pos. Some use words like acolyte sub, but I'm not too fond of that, because it implies too much of a god-complex on my part. Another term I've heard is kajira. But I don't like that term either. Kajirae have no life of their own. Posie has a job, her own money, possessions and rights, like anyone else, even if she is domestic in her servitude and excessively reverent." He addressed her directly. "Right, baby girl?"

"Yes, Sir," she replied in a quiet, dutiful voice.

D.C. returned his words my direction even as he continued to pet Posie. "I'd say she's a loving sub. A slave, really. She's formally collared and she's mine." He reached over and lifted the charm on her necklace. He turned his attention to Tink and touched hers, adding, "They both are."

Tinkerbrat swatted his hand away. D.C.'s response was to reach under the table and do something invisible to myself, but that elicited a silent expression of pain on Tink's part.

"Are you done showing your ass?" he asked her.

She continued to bite her lip and clench her eyes closed. D.C. applied more of whatever he was doing to her and her eyes and mouth opened. She still didn't make a sound, but it was clear from the sudden, serious look on her face that she was ready to give in. She bit her lip again and nodded furiously, causing her Dom to relent.

"They're a handful," he said to me.

My head was starting to swim. I was already starting to wonder if I could fit into a community like this or if I was simply someone who had a secret desire to hold a willing party down by the throat while I fucked them. Before I could pick his brain for more details, a very large woman came to our end of the table...and I do mean large, in both width and height. Her hair was black and wavy and she bore a pleasant smile.

"Hey, kids," she said cheerfully. "I'm gonna come talk to you all for a while."

"Cathy," D.C. greeted her. "How are you?"

"I'm good. How are you?"

"Doing well. Just chatting with..." He paused as he struggled to remember the name I had given.

"Ignite35," I reminded him. "...Or just Ignite, I guess."

"Hi," the lady said. "I'm Cathy. Mother of Creation. Most people around here call me Momma C."

"It's very nice to meet you."

"What's going on here?" she asked, as she laid a hand on Posie's shoulder. She immediately pulled it away, almost like she'd put it into scalding water. "I'm sorry," she said to D.C. "May I touch her?"

"Of course, Cat. You can always touch the girls. You should know that by now." He stroked the blonde's hair and informed Momma C. that what she was witnessing was punishment.

"Aww. What'd she do?"

"She's just having trouble showing restraint."

"That's unfortunate." She leaned down and gave Posie a hug. "You doing okay other than that, honey bunch?"

"Yes, ma'am." Posie said quietly, with a soft smile.

Momma C. hugged her again before noticing Tinkerbrat. "Let me guess. Sammie, over there is in a time out."

"It wouldn't be a munch if she wasn't at least once."

Tink continued to sulk. Momma C. went to hug her too and then gave D.C. one of his own. She sat at the end of the table and addressed me, asking what had led me there.

"I just moved here," I told her. "I was in a...not so good, I guess...relationship where I was living. Among other things, very...vanilla?" I waited for a look of confirmation from her, that I had used the word correctly. "It fell apart and things weren't going too well in my life, so when I was offered a job out here, I took it."

"Can I ask what you do?"

I thought for a bit. This woman had allowed me to learn her real name, so obviously there was some level of openness within the community. Still, I decided that it wasn't wise and declined to answer. Momma C. respected that decision and moved on to the question of how I identified.

"Oh, uh...a Dom," I told her. I immediately felt like the term didn't fit. At that moment, control and authority were things that I lacked an abundance of.

"That's a shame," she said. "You're cute. I would have enjoyed beating your ass sometime."

That took me by surprise. She and D.C. laughed and I realized that she was teasing me just a bit, but not entirely.

Suddenly, Tink spoke up. "It's been five minutes," she said in a pitiful and regretful tone. Her arms uncrossed and rested in her lap.

"Yes, it has," D.C. agreed. He leaned over and kissed the side of her head. "Think you can behave for the rest of the munch?"

"Yes, Sir."

"Good girl. Make me proud."

"How did you end up with two submissives?" I asked.

Momma C. immediately started to laugh again. "The guys are always so fascinated with you D.C. 'How did you get two pretty girls? Where can I find an arrangement like that?'"

D.C. was amused and decided to mess with me a bit. "Well, first you have to kidnap them. Rohypnol helps, as does chloroform. Then you cage them and starve them until they develop Stockholm syndrome. At that point, you reprogram them into obedience."

I stared. Momma C. almost fell out of her chair as she howled.

"I'm joking," he assured me. "I had Tink first. We met while doing volunteer work for a local charity."

"You were doing volunteer work. I was doing community service," Tinkerbrat clarified.

"Right. Well, we'd lunch together every day and

started hanging out. That community service was the result of a D.U.I., so she couldn't drive. I gave her rides and we became friends. After a while, she began to realize that I was very secretive about some of my down time."

"You wouldn't say hardly anything," she broke in again. "It was all cryptic. I thought you were a mobster or some shit."

"Be that as it may, I eventually trusted her enough to let her in on my involvement in the community and she became very interested and very insistent that I teach her about the lifestyle. We discussed it for a few weeks, and I decided that it might be good for her and that she could fit in."

"And she has...quite well," Momma C. added, reaching over to pat her hand.

"I see. And Posie?"

"She was a gift," Tink beamed.

"Sorry. What?"

D.C. picked up the explanation again. "By some miracle, Tink managed to behave herself for a few weeks. I told her she could have whatever she wanted for her birthday. She said that she wanted another girl. We started advertising. We met and interviewed a few women, played with a couple... Eventually, we found Pos here. I actually knew her already, but only in passing, and had no idea that she'd gotten involved in the lifestyle. Regardless, we talked about it for a long time, experimented a bit until, finally, the three of us made it a formal arrangement."

"Okay," I said, surely appearing, at that point, like a kindergartener in a physics class. I turned to Tinkerbrat. "Why did you want another girl?"

The tone in her response implied that I might be an

idiot. "Because I wanted pussy and didn't have any."

Everyone smiled, even Posie.

Momma C. decided to direct the conversation back to me. "So, what brought you here tonight?"

"Uh, lots of things." The room was a bit cold, and yet I could feel myself sweat.

"Like what?"

"I spoke to someone named SeptemberSnowGirl on the website and she told me that I needed to attend a munch." I looked around before asking, "Is she here?"

"No," Momma C. shook her head. "SnowGirl doesn't actually come that often."

"Oh."

"So, what else brought you here? I mean, why try and get this involved?"

I glanced over at D.C. and Tinkerbrat who were staring directly at me. It felt like an interrogation, which, in retrospect, I suppose it was.

Momma C. continued with a not-unfriendly smile, "What are you hoping to find?"

I thought for a moment before admitting, "Control."

"Control over what?"

"That's a good question," I confessed. "I discovered, after an encounter with a friend, that I liked controlling someone else in bed. I liked the thrill of being in charge and making her do what I wanted. Maybe, I also liked giving her what she wanted, now that I think about it. Regardless, it was pretty exciting. I also began to feel like, if I could take on a role like Dominant that I might be able to control myself more, take charge of my life. Does that make any sense?"

"It does," Momma C. nodded. "There's some aspects to the lifestyle that can make you feel like you have that and similar things. But not always. In some instances, it can be a bad way to go about it."

D.C. broke in. "There are also plenty of people around here who have a lot to lose."

"I know," I said, considering the notion to be obvious.

"No," he countered, "I don't think that you do. There are people in this community who, if their involvement were discovered, could lose their jobs, respect of their peers, custody of their children... In highly extreme cases, they could even face criminal investigation." The tone in his voice and the scrutinizing gleam in his eyes reinforced his original point. "We may call it 'play,' but this isn't a game."

I was speechless as I considered his words. Finally, Momma C. broke the tension.

"So," she said, warmly, "why don't you tell us what made you want to get involved enough to attend a munch, to actually meet the community itself?"

That was easy. "I wanted to learn and to meet people."

"And?" she asked.

"And, nothing. I just want to meet some people. Honestly, I'm new in town and don't have any friends. Since this is something that I'm interested in learning about and exploring, I figured it was a good way to kill two birds, you know?"

Momma C. and D.C. exchanged glances again that equated into obvious, nonverbal communication. When they looked back at me, D.C. said, "Okay. Let us know if you have any questions or if we can help."

I thanked him.

"And you should also friend us on the website," Momma C. added.

Suddenly, a very energetic, redheaded lady in her mid-to-late thirties approached and introduced herself to me. "Hi. I'm Benji, Electra Jane on the website. Who are you?"

"Hi. I'm...Ignite35, or Ignite, or...whatever."

"Can I call you Iggy?" she asked, her hyperactivity lending an excited and friendly tone to her question.

"Uh, sure. Why not?"

"Okay. Iggy it is. It is *so* nice to meet you." Her enthusiasm was intense and sincere. She pointed down to the other end of the table to a bearded man, approximately her age, with a pleasant smile. "That's my guy down there. We're both subs, which is why we're in an open relationship. We've been together for almost five years, so I guess we're doing something right, much more than anything that I did in my first marriage. Ugh! We're also hedonists. Anyway, I just wanted to introduce myself and meet you, especially since Momma C. and D.C. were both talking to you and neither of them were rolling their eyes or looking like they might hurl. Are you coming to the play party later?" She hadn't even taken a breath throughout all of this and still didn't as she turned to the two across from me and asked, "Is he coming to the after party?"

"We'll see," D.C. said plainly.

"Okay," Benji continued. "Well, it was very nice to meet you. I hope we'll see you at a gathering or event soon. You're good people. I can tell from your body language. You should make friends with these folk." She pointed back and forth between Momma C., D.C. and his subs. "They're good people too." She then directed her attention and her extended index finger right at Momma C. "Talk to me before you leave," she said before bouncing back to her chair.

I let out a deep breath.

"Feeling overwhelmed yet?" Momma C. asked with a

smile.

Tinkerbrat gave a brief laugh and suggested, "He probably needs a drink after that. Come to think of it, I could use one."

"No alcohol tonight," D.C. told her as he rubbed her neck.

"You are so mean," she returned flatly.

"You're abusing your communication privileges," he said to her.

Momma C. asked him with a sarcastic chuckle, "D.C., why do you have such a bratty little thing if you're just going to censor and restrict her all the time?"

"Because I deserve a little amusement in my life," he smiled. He continued to rub his obnoxious sub's neck and back before whispering something in her ear. She smiled and even appeared as though she might blush. He then turned his attention to me. "I don't recommend coming to the after party tonight," he said. "But Cathy's right. You should friend us both. You should also talk to everyone else here, introduce yourself before you leave."

I nodded. "Of course." I looked over at Momma C. who winked.

It was at that time that our food began to arrive and we were all forced to act like civilized adults for a while. After dinner, I did my best to make the rounds and meet as many other people as I could, struggling to comprehend and remember the names everyone gave. Before long, Mistress Xina cornered me to have a chat.

"What do you think so far?" she asked sounding both friendly and authoritative.

"It's all very interesting," I admitted.

"I noticed you speaking at length with some of our regulars and wanted a chance to get to know you myself. Is this your first event?"

"Yeah. I only recently found out that these types of meetings exist."

"Have you been in the lifestyle long?"

"Not at all," I confessed, feeling like a new student taking to the principal.

"What made you take an interest in it?"

I chuckled nervously. "It was a girl I hooked up with. She liked it rough and I discovered that I liked the same. A little bit of internet research led me to the website. After trying to chat with a variety of very unhelpful people, I contacted, SeptemberSnowGirl, who told me about the munches."

The look on Mistress Xina's face was one of distaste. "Yes, Eleanor is always free with the information."

I furrowed my brow. "You don't sound like you approve."

She shook her head. "Don't misunderstand. You seem sincere, from what I can tell. However, we have a lot of guys come through here that are simply looking to get their dicks wet and SnowGirl doesn't vet people before she invites them. It's caused problems in the past."

I was concerned and even slightly offended. "I promise, I'm not like that."

"Perhaps not. In fact, I don't get that feeling from you. You're too nervous." Her remark hit home rather hard. "But, as I said, she doesn't discriminate and there have been multiple times when we've all had to play musical chairs to keep the creepers away from the girls here."

"That's unfortunate," I told her.

"Well, let's not dwell on it," she said ironically. "Please, continue to enjoy yourself. And feel free to join us again."

With that, she excused herself to talk to the other

attendees.

I decided that it was time for some fresh air. I walked outside where I found several other people, all of whom were also there for the munch, smoking and vaping. I stood nearby, hands in my pockets, staring silently into the parking lot.

After a few moments, a short, slightly chubby girl with an hourglass figure and white and green hair approached me. "Need a cigarette?" she asked.

"Hm? Oh. No, thank you. I don't smoke."

She looked at me like I had admitted to voting for Donald Trump. "What the fuck are you doing out here then?"

I found myself insulted by the question and tone. "I just wanted to come outside."

"Whatever," she shrugged before hitting her cigarette. "So, what was Queen Bitch of the Universe talking to you about?"

"Excuse me?"

"Mistress Xina," she said like the name was a joke. "I noticed she summoned you for a chat. What? She wanted to put the fear of God in you over discretion or some dumb shit?"

"No. She just wanted my impression of the munch."

"Whatever," she shrugged again. "So, what do you do?"

"You mean, like, for a living?"

"No, dumb ass," she returned. "Like, how do you identify? What are you into? What are your hard limits?"

This girl was really starting to annoy me. "I'm a Dom. I'm still trying to figure the rest out."

"Really?" She hit her cigarette again and nodded. "That's cool, I guess. So, you wanna get together and do something some time?"

"Do something?" I asked, confused.

"Play, dumb fuck. Do you wanna get together and play?"

"Like, sex?"

She rolled her eyes. "Jesus, you're stupid. Not necessarily. Just get together, try some stuff, see where it goes."

I was completely off balance by this point. "I don't even know your name."

She stuck out a hand. "Megan," she said. "Sluttypixie, on the website."

I tentatively shook her hand. "Ignite35."

"'K. So, how about it?"

"Um..." I thought hard. Was this how it went in the community? Did people just walk up to each other, even people they didn't know or like and start asking to beat and bang each other? That one response I had received after comparing our social media to a dating website didn't seem to think so.

Finally, I decided that I should see this as an opportunity. I wanted to learn more. If I was going to go down this bumpy road, I needed to gain experience. Plus, I kind of wanted to slap the girl in her smart mouth already. I suddenly grinned. "Why not?"

"Cool," was all she said. She tossed her cigarette on the ground and started to walk off.

"Wait," I called out. "What are you into?"

"Everything," she responded over her shoulder.

Suddenly, I heard another voice behind me. "Man, this was a bunch of bullshit," it grumbled.

I turned to see the biker jacket guy shaking his head.

"What do you mean?" I asked.

"I thought this was where you met willing girls looking for some fun," he said. "These people act like it's a cabal. They don't want sex. They just want to talk about rules and restrictions and bullshit." He let out a frustrated breath. "Man, I am out."

I watched him leave with a dismissive wave. His attitude seemed foolish to me. Yet, as I decided that I'd had my fill of counter culture for the evening, I went inside, made my goodbyes, paid my check and left myself.

CHAPTER FIVE

That following weekend, I finally had some time off. I slept until almost ten, but finally got up because I still needed to unpack and settle in. After a breakfast of cereal and toast I began the laborious process, first, by getting my bedroom and bathroom in order. That took much longer than expected and by three o'clock I needed a break. I paused to check my page and was pleasantly surprised to find several friend requests. I also had a message in my inbox. It, like one of the friend requests, was from Sluttypixie.

"What are you doing this weekend?" it read.

I typed my response. "Just finishing unpacking."

I hit "send" and received a quick reply.

"Need some help?"

Intriguing.

"I'd be delighted," I told her.

She asked where I lived and that's when my mind began to race. I didn't know this girl, this girl who'd been so unbelievably rude and then had asked if I wanted to play with her. Now, she wanted my address. Should I tell her? Should I do anything with her?

Maybe her abrasive behavior was just a defense mechanism, it occurred to me. Maybe she was secretly afraid and that was how she forced herself to pursue her desires.

Her desires. Hmm.

Well, if she could be so brazen, I supposed I could do

the same. I typed my address in and hit "send". Within seconds, I got her reply.

"I'll be there in half an hour."

Suddenly, I was nervous. I was also struck that I hadn't had a shower. If clothes did, indeed, start coming off, I needed to not smell like B.O. I bathed quickly and changed into some clean clothes. I then returned to pulling things out of boxes and finding homes for them. Ten minutes later, there was a knock on the door. I opened it and there was Megan, a.k.a. Sluttypixie.

"Hey," she said, walking in without an invitation.

"Find the place okay?" I asked.

"Yep. It was a breeze." She tossed a backpack that she had on by the door. Everything else she was wearing was extreme: a leather jacket covered in studs, spikes and band patches over a cut-off T-shirt and shredded shorts. She also wore beat up combat boots. "So," she said, "what are we doing here?"

"Just pulling a bunch of crap out of boxes and finding places for it."

"Gotcha." Without another word, she tossed her jacket on top of her backpack and started opening boxes.

The following process was relatively short. Megan began asking me where I wanted things to some degree, but eventually just found places for most stuff on her own, even going so far as to hang one framed poster without input. After a couple of hours, we were done.

"Thank you so much, Megan," I told her sincerely.

"No problem."

"Can I offer you something to eat?"

"Got any booze?" she returned.

I thought for a moment. "I believe I have some wine."

I went to retrieve it, along with two glasses. I poured the cheap red and handed her one, tapping my glass against hers.

"Too you," I smiled.

She lifted her drink. "To your fucking health," she said, before draining the entire glass.

"Damn," I said as I slowly raised mine to my lips.

"So, we gonna fool around or what?"

I choked on my wine. She seemed unfazed.

"Um..." I began eloquently, "What did you have in mind?"

A wicked tint sparkled in her eyes. She went to her backpack and opened it, producing a pair of handcuffs and a small leather strap. She tossed them to me and I missed them. As I picked them up, she continued the direct approach.

"Show me what you got, handsome."

So now I was no longer, "dumb ass," I was "handsome." ...'K.

I examined the items in my hands. All the while, she squirmed out of her clothes until only her panties remained. She held her wrists out.

Okay, so...this very forward girl wanted to see my moves.

My moves.

What were my moves?

"You gonna show me some action or do I need to go find a real man?"

That flipped a switch in me. How dare she? She didn't know me. How could she judge and antagonize me like that? Suddenly, I grabbed her by the hair. I let go just long enough to cuff her wrists in front, before reclaiming her head in my hands and staring down at her. I paused as a variety of scenarios sped through my mind.

I could spank her. I could slap her around and say horrible shit to her. I could tie her up. I could tie her up and beat her. I could tie her up and fuck her. That's when a thought hit me.

"What are your hard limits?" I asked finding an odd comfort with the new term I had learned, perhaps because it made me sound like I might actually had a clue as to what I was doing.

"Don't shit or puke on me," she said curtly.

My mind raced again. So, I could fuck her? I could beat her really hard? I could pee on her?

Wait...why would I want to pee on her?

"What about safe words?" I asked, again, feeling happy to actually know something.

"Just use the stop light system."

My ignorance poked me in the side, like a teacher with a stick, reminding me that a little education was just that. "The what?"

She grunted and rolled her eyes. "'Green,' means go, 'yellow,' means slow down and 'red,' means stop."

"Uh huh." I stood there digesting the information.

"Well?" she demanded.

I slapped her. A little harder than I would consider hitting most people, enough to cause a slight sting in my hand.

She took a second before responding with, "Is that all that you've got?"

I hit her again, repeatedly, never taking too broad a swing, just extra-sharp pats delivered from a few inches away. She clenched her eyes shut, but showed little else in the way of reactions. I turned her around and started beating her ass with the strap, trying not to go too hard since I wasn't familiar with the equipment. Still, the "slap, slap, slap" from it was incredibly loud and her ass and thighs began to immediately pinken. At one point, I did pull her head back and bit her shoulder. Megan still didn't respond outside of an increase in her breathing.

That weird urge in me took over completely. I bit her harder. Even harder, feeling her plump skin sink under my teeth and fill my mouth. Her skin tasted liked she smelled, of cigarette smoke and cheap perfume. Finally, she cried out, her fingers curling into her restrained palms as she did. But she didn't ask me to stop. When I pulled away, there was a deep red print. I spun her around and grabbed her hair again.

"You like that?" I asked sternly.

"Yep," was all she said.

My blood boiled and my hormones raged. I was really enjoying this. I wanted a reaction out of her though. I needed to see it. I really wanted her to give in and I wanted to make her, even if it involved going way too hard.

I suddenly felt a little weird about it and fought to pull myself in. But that urge in me pushed to show itself.

I pressed my teeth together and inhaled hard before releasing that same breath slowly.

"What do you really want me to do?" I asked, punctuating the question with a slap from the strap against her thigh.

"Fuck the shit out of me," she replied plainly.

I suddenly realized that's exactly what I wanted to hear.

I pulled her underwear off rather forcefully and shoved her onto the sofa. I began to unfasten my pants when something occurred to me.

"Shit," I grumbled. "I'm out of rubbers."

"You don't need one," she declared.

That's when I stopped. This young woman, this stranger, who had come to see me, demanding sex, was now saying that we should go about it unprotected.

"I don't think that's a good idea," I told her.

She rolled her eyes and grunted. "Fine. There's some in the front pouch of my book bag."

I looked over to where it still lay by the door and went to it. Reaching in, I pulled out a cheap, unlubricated number and opened it.

"Put it on and get over here and fuck me," she insisted.

I was officially tired of her attitude. I tossed it at her. "You put it on me, you mouthy whore."

She became immediately defensive and raised a finger. "Hey! No. That's actually a hard limit. Call me anything you want, anything at all. But I'm not a whore. That's off the table."

For some reason I found this annoying. I grabbed her hair, really hard this time, tangling the strands in my fingers. "Fine. Put it on me you foul mouthed, nasty, cum slut."

She actually smiled a little and chuckled. "Yes, sir," she said making the last word seem like a joke.

I slapped her. I pulled her hair again and pinched her tit hard, feeling the skin flatten between my thumb and finger. "What was that?"

She cried out, but then, chuckled happily and gasped. "Yes, Sir," she reiterated more respectfully and appropriately.

I let go and she took my pants down, fast, rolled the latex over me and put my dick in her mouth, all with her hands still cuffed. After a few deep and expert strokes, she lay down on the sofa. "Get in me, now."

"Say, 'Please'."

"*Please...*"

"Please, what?"

"Please, Sir. Please, come fuck me hard."

I climbed on top and did just that. I entered her and hammered in, watching as she bucked back into me and offered encouragement.

"Yeah, yeah, yeah, yeah!" she breathed.

With each thrust, her soft, plump skin rippled from her thighs to her breasts. I touched her all over her body, not caressing, but squeezing and rubbing hard, enjoying the sensation of my fingers sinking into her toneless frame. I cupped my hand behind her neck and kissed her roughly. Our tongues moved around passionately like two people drunk on passion. Not passion for each other, but for the carnality we were indulging in. She wrapped her short legs around me, crossed her ankles and started to almost growl. Then, with no warning, she slapped me, with one of her cuffed hands. I was surprised and a little irritated. I slapped her back. She slapped me again and I slapped her harder. I put my hand on her throat and squeezed a little.

"Sorry," she managed. She actually sounded a little sincere.

She put her hands over my head and behind my neck. I felt mixed sensations of soothing and stinging, as the cold, metal chain made contact with my skin, while Megan simultaneously dug in with her fingernails. We slammed into each other harder and harder until she began to look more passive and moan. The intensity, if not volume, of her exclamations increased until she began calling out in quick breaths, "I'm coming! Oh, God, I'm coming! Come with me, baby!"

Miraculously, my body obliged and I let loose with a long moan of my own. She dug her nails deeper into my trapezius muscles, showing me a pain that I could enjoy, for if this was her reaction, then I must have done something right. I must have satisfied her. It was a rewarding feeling as we fell into relative stillness and heavy breathing.

I lay there, recuperating on her soft skin, trying to get my wits and also smelling her. She wreaked of smoke, sweat and sex. I found it intoxicating. It was all so...nasty.

After a brief minute or so, I leaned up. "You're crazy, you know that?"

"Whatever," she panted in a wounded sounding tone.

I lay back down onto her warm, pillowy frame and relaxed, stroking her hair and giving her the occasional, soft kiss. She smiled and cooed a bit. It was comforting.

Then, a few minutes later, she pushed me off of her and got up. Without a word she took the handcuffs off and began to dress.

"Leaving?" I asked with surprise.

"Yep." She finished quickly and leaned over to kiss me. "Thanks," she smiled. "Let's do it again some time." She walked out.

What the fuck?

I knew I had to learn. I couldn't fight that voice inside me that just kept saying, *Learn. Become an expert. Don't let all of these confusing scenarios overwhelm you.*

I tried. I hit the internet hard.

Amidst countless lame tutorials, many designed to interest novices enough that they would purchase more detailed videos, I found one that tried to expand past the rope (something an eagle scout like myself actually had an advantage with) and spankings. It was devoted to sensuality in BDSM play and provided me with a different perspective on kinky sex.

In it, a man of about forty, with a shaved head and a

goatee explained that, through the use of sensory deprivation and tactile stimulation, one could provide an array of pleasure for their partner and elicit all kinds of positive experiences.

He demonstrated by directing the camera, as well as the viewers' attention, to a woman who sat on her knees on a bed, wearing only a bikini, a blindfold and a collar.

"First," he said, "limit your partner's senses. Blindfolding them is an excellent start, though you may also consider headphones or earmuffs to block their hearing. The more that you limit what they can experience, then the more intense their other sensations will become. Their other senses will try to compensate for the restricted ones. Plus, they won't know what's coming and will be less mentally prepared for it."

He demonstrated by letting her bite into a cherry and then a cocktail onion. Her face contorted a bit the second bite. He then noted, "A spanking suddenly becomes even more intense in someone's senses, since it's all they can experience."

He tied the woman's wrists to the bed. "Restricting their movement also adds to their sensations. Remember, you're trying to help your partner feel more. Enhancing their experience is what it's all about. As a Dom you want to give them as much as you can."

He then began to tickle his sub. "If they can't see it coming or focus on other things, then these sensations are intensified."

The confined girl laughed in a panicked state that still seemed entertained.

"She can't deflect what I'm doing. She's totally mine. And her sense of touch is turned to eleven."

Next, he pulled a large bag from the floor and dropped it on the bed with a soft thud. She gasped.

"She knows something is coming because she felt me drop the toy bag down on the bed. But she doesn't know what. Though she does knows that she has no way of seeing or deflecting them, be they painful or pleasurable. In fact, the pleasurable stuff is almost worst. Regardless, she's excited."

The woman's breathing increased as if to punctuate his words.

He unzipped the large bag quickly and audibly. She made another loud gasp and her breathing continued in desperate motions. Next, he began to pull an unlikely list of items out: a feather, a silk scarf, a fuzzy mitten, a soda can—which he claimed was ice cold—a rose, sand paper, a doll with fuzzy hair, a curled extension cord, a soft hair brush..." It continued.

Next came a compilation of video material, scored by slow, sensual pop music as he rubbed all of the items all over her and she panted, moaned and called out.

I couldn't help but be transfixed.

I don't have to just hit them, I thought. *Interesting. I'll have to try all of this.*

"Just help them explore their feelings," the man on the video said before leaning down to the restrained woman's ear and whispering, "Does my bad...little...girl...like that?"

She responded desperately. "God! Yes, Sir!"

Sold.

Suddenly, the screen changed and the dominant was there, standing in front of the camera saying, "If you are new to the community and genuinely want to learn, go to munches, find a mentor and get them to teach you. That is the true way that this community operates."

His delivery sounded a little like an ad for an ambulance chasing law firm, but it still made an impression. What exactly was a BDSM mentor and did I need one? I mean, I wanted to be good at this, right?

City Hall quickly became almost like a second home. Not necessarily in the, "I feel content here," sort of way, but I did feel adjusted and comfortable. My personalized badge got me in and out with no problem and I spent so much of my time there. The system really was a mess and I always had something to clean up. As I sat connected to the server, waiting on another scan to complete itself, I sipped my coffee and contemplated what might sound good for lunch. I also had my phone in my hand, casually looking over information concerning my new hobby.

A mentor, it turned out, was just what it sounded like. They took new people under their wing and taught them how to indulge in all of the passion fruits of BDSM while still being careful and respectful. They also helped them to become more educated in the details and protocols, which was something that I sorely needed. I didn't like feeling like a fool in front of my new friends, much less during intimate moments.

"Who are you and what are you doing in here?" a female voice suddenly asked in a mildly demanding tone.

I looked up to see a cute girl in her late twenties to early thirties wearing a white shirt, buttoned all the way to the neck and a plain, black skirt. Her blonde hair was pulled up tightly on her head and her freckled face was without a smile.

I pulled my earbuds out as I turned the volume of my samba collection down and my kink displaying phone on its face. "I'm IT. I'm just cleaning up your system."

She relaxed, but barely. "I guess that's good news."

She went to a wall of file cabinets and began digging through them.

"Can I help you find something?" I asked, not knowing what else to say.

"Doubtful."

"What are you looking for?"

She sighed. "I work in records. Because our computer system is so messed up, we can't always locate what we need. Overflow of our hard copies is in here."

"Oh," I said. "Well, I could try digging it out of the system for you if you told me what—"

"It's okay. I think I know where it is." With that, she bent over to look into one of the bottom drawers, giving me a perfect eyeful of her ass. It was round and tightly contained under her narrow skirt.

Suddenly, I began having some very impure thoughts. An overwhelming urge to spank her consumed them. My eyes dropped, and then trailed up the back of her stocking clad legs until they rested back on her incredibly inviting behind. It was about then that she glanced back and caught me staring.

I quickly focused back on my computer screen and tried like hell to appear both busy and nonchalant. The cute blonde just stood up quickly, a file cradled in her arms and shoved the drawer closed loudly. When I shot glances her way, I could see that she was giving me a harsh look while she made her way out of the room, the loud click of her high heels seeming to scold me repeatedly.

"I'm really starting to become kind of a perv," I mumbled aloud to myself.

On my way out of work, I got a text. When I checked my phone, I was surprised to find that it was from Megan.

"DTF?" was all it said.

Am I "down to fuck?" How charming. I almost ignored her. However, it occurred to me that I might like to try implementing some of the techniques and ideas that I had been learning. Perhaps I could allow myself a few cheap thrills. Plus, I was finding myself more and more sexually frustrated as of late.

Why not?

I texted back. "Seven o'clock?"

Her reply only took a few seconds. "Sounds good."

When I arrived home, I ate and showered. As I washed, rinsed and repeated, I ran down the list of new ideas to try. Once I was clean, I turned off the water, jerked open the shower curtain and stepped out. While toweling dry, visions of restraints dancing in my head, I glanced up and noticed something interesting.

My new apartment was just that, a relatively new complex and sturdily built. As I examined the curtain rod, I began to wonder if it fell into the same category.

Tentatively, I reached out and gave it a tug. While I didn't dare swing from it like a chimp, I did feel suddenly confident that it would probably take doing so to pull it down. My imagination continued hard at work.

I quickly dressed before going about setting the stage. I placed a series of candles all over the apartment, followed by spraying a lavender scented deodorizer everywhere, designed to help someone relax. I gathered together anything and everything that I could think of that might be useful for my encounter, including the belt for my bathrobe which I dabbed with a tiny amount of my aftershave. By six-thirty I was ready and waiting.

Not long after, there was a knock at my door. I went

and answered it, finding Megan there in all of her punk rock glory.

"Hey," she said without a smile.

"Hey." I stepped aside and let her in.

Once again, she dropped her backpack by the door and tossed her jacket on top. She looked around before turning to me and starting to say something, but I was ready. I grabbed her by the chin, though I didn't squeeze. I smiled.

"You really looking to get fucked?" I asked.

She smirked. "That's the plan."

"You got your hand cuffs?" I asked.

"Yeah. They're in—"

"Get them."

I let go, closed the door and she scrambled to pull them out of her bag. She also had a second pair.

"One is—" she began.

"I'm not interested," I told her as I took them both from her. "Take your clothes off."

She continued to give a sarcastic grin as she squirmed out of her tattered pants and old t-shirt. She glanced around as she did. "Place looks interesting. You do all this for me?"

"Something like that."

Once she was naked, I put my hand on the back of her neck and marched her into the bathroom.

"Why are we going in here?" she asked.

"Quiet," I told her. I took hold of her wrists and pulled them over her head. I put each of the cuffs on her wrists and locked them on the curtain rod. "Don't move," I told her. Then I pulled out my bathrobe belt and blindfolded her. Her breathing increased just a bit.

After that, I went into the next room where I had an array of stimuli waiting in a bag. I put a collection of flamenco guitar on the stereo and made my way back into the bathroom. As I walked in, she jerked my direction, the clink of the handcuffs on the rod punctuating her movement, and gasped. I suddenly reminded myself that she didn't know me anymore than I knew her. Brazen as she was, there had to be a part of her that might wonder if I was a serial killer. I almost considered playing that up a bit just to mess with her, but decided better of it.

I dropped everything that I had on the shelf in the bathroom, allowing it to make a loud thud and clatter. She gasped again, but then clearly tried to calm herself quickly. I assumed that she felt she needed to appear tough.

Tough, huh? I thought to myself that I might have a way of breaking that and it didn't include any whips.

"What is this music?" she asked.

"Quiet," I told her. I pulled a feather duster from the bag I brought in. As she hung there, sightless and unaware of what my plans were, I slowly began trailing it across her skin. I didn't tickle her with it, just teased. I trailed it across her torso, over her breasts, down her thighs... I ran it down her spine and across her broad, curvy ass.

She didn't react right away, other than to become still and silent. As I moved it down her naked body, she arched her back and let her head fall backwards. I rolled it slowly around her belly button, pressing just enough to caress her. She let out tiny moans and soft grunts as she weaved back and forth and her breathing rose at a slow, but steady pace. Her movement increased as I trailed it up the inside of her legs and thighs. She even whimpered, lifting one leg quickly before placing it back on the floor. Next, I pulled out a loofah and rolled it down her body, lightly scraping her skin with it, all over. She began to squirm a little.

"Are you going to fuck me or what?" she asked.

I slowly put my hand over her mouth. "Patience, girl. Patience."

Her weaving back and forth increased, as did her emoting, though she did press her lips together, clearly fighting the sounds she was making. I suspected she was also struggling not to surrender. As I scraped it against her nipples, she moved back away from me, rattling the cuffs. When I dragged it between her legs, particularly between the crack of her ass, she surprised me by pressing into it more and more.

I continued to run things all over her: a satin pillow case, a piece of string, ice, even the edge of a kitchen knife which I turned sideways and slowly grazed down her shoulders and the small of her back, barely touching her with it. As she was blindfolded, I can only imagine what she thought each thing was, but her breathing was all over the place. Finally, after I snatched the leather strap from her bag and began moving it up and down her skin she demanded of me, "When are we going to fuck?" in quick, desperate breaths.

I slapped her on the ass with the strap and she called out.

I hit her again, and then, one more time. Each time with a loud "crack" and a deep gasp from her.

I put my hand in her unnaturally-colored hair and pulled her head back. I leaned in to her ear and inhaled deep. As I did, so did she, though hers seemed more excited. I turned her around, crossing her cuffed arms, so that her back was facing me. I squeezed her ass cheek and ran my fingers down her spine and then up the backs of her thighs. Slowly and delicately, I trailed all my digits up and down from her knees to just below her ass, down from her shoulders and across her hips, back and forth. Reaching around her, I cupped her breasts, strumming her erect nipples in between my fingers, before gliding my hands down her plump stomach and across the front of her thighs. As I reached this point, I eased my touch between her legs, on either side of her pussy and paused...before finally...softly...cruelly pulling my hands away. The whole time, Megan whimpered and squirmed.

I pulled a condom out of the bathroom drawer, where I had stashed them earlier and opened it, not even trying to be quiet as I bit into and tore the package. I pulled it out and put it on. With both hands on her hips, I maneuvered her in place. I positioned my cock right at the opening of her pussy and carefully rubbed it there. She moaned and gasped over and over.

"God, put it in me, for fuck's sake," she begged.

I squeezed her ass again. Starting by trailing my fingertips from the inside of her knees and up her thighs, I resumed reaching all over her fleshy body and touched, squeezed and stroked, trying to get her more worked up, all the while with the head of my dick lightly grazing her clit and opening. She kept pushing back into me and I would move away.

Finally, I put a hand on her hip, holding her hard. I didn't use the other hand to guide myself. I just jammed. She was so excited, it went right in, all the way.

Uuugghhh," she exclaimed.

I paused. That is to say, I stopped and waited, motionless.

I pulled out and shoved myself in again.

"Ugh!" she returned to me.

I paused.

"God, please just fuck me!" she cried out as she

started shoving her ass back into me.

I firmly wrapped one arm around her chest, the other around her waist and placed my lips in her ear. "You need to be more patient," I said. I then pulled out and jammed myself in hard again.

"Aagh!" she exclaimed.

I paused.

"This is supposed to be a sensual experience," I told her. I pulled out and forced myself back in.

"Aagh!"

I held still. "Don't you want this to last and be something that entertains you on many levels?"

I repeated my motion. She gritted her teeth and snarled before starting to grind back into me.

"No," she growled. "I want you to fuck me. Just fuck me!"

I continued my thrusts. After each, I would wait a few seconds, pressing but refusing to move. But those seconds quickly decreased. Push into her, hard. Wait six seconds. Into her again. Wait five. In again. Wait four... My speed increased, gradually. Soon, I was just pounding into her as she moaned. I stroked her smooth, ample skin and she shoved back into me. Before long, she started calling out. Eventually, it was evident that she came, as her exclamations increased in volume and length.

I, however, wasn't done. I continued to hammer into her, tasting her skin with my fingers all over and kissing, licking and biting her shoulders. Finally, I rounded that corner and felt the burn inside of me.

The dirtiness, the power, the urge...

I moaned hard and loud as I let loose, my fingers curling tight against the flesh above her hips, her literal love handles.

We stood there awkwardly, both our legs tense and

tired, nowhere to collapse except against each other. I clung to her and we wobbled on our unsteady feet and trembling legs.

Finally, I pulled out and discarded the condom in the convenience of the waste basket next to me. Megan hung there panting.

"You okay?" I asked out of loss for anything else to say.

"Whatever," she gasped, before managing, "That was pretty cool."

I slowly released her and lowered her onto the bathroom floor. I held her there as she caught her breath and we both recovered on the chilly tile. All the while, I continued to stroke her hair and enjoy the warmth of her soft, thick skin.

Eventually, she sighed long and very hard. "I liked that," she confessed.

I chuckled. "Good."

A few more minutes went by, even a couple where she nuzzled into my chest for a bit. After that, she stood.

"I got to go," she announced.

"What?" I asked.

"Yeah. I got school work."

"Um... Okay."

She went to the other room, dressed, came back to where I was still recuperating on the bathroom floor and kissed me. "Let's do it again real soon."

She left.

CHAPTER SIX

My hectic work week had resulted in my neglecting or forgetting quite a few details of getting adjusted to Clinton and my new job. I needed to hit the grocery store, badly. I still needed to replace a couple of only moderately significant things that Brooke had taken with her, like the hair dryer. I also had another errand, and that was that I needed to go to the bank. The deposit refund from my previous apartment had come back, though not all of it. It seems that the property manager had found a few things that he considered issues, such as a few small holes in the walls where I'd hung pictures, and had withheld a portion of my money. He was nice enough to send an inventory of all the so-called damages in a letter.

I entered the local branch of my bank, not really paying a great deal of attention to where I was going. I was scrutinizing the letter and getting frustrated with some of the reasoning in it while I made my way to the desk with the deposit slips and filled one out. I kept examining the paperwork in my hand as I took my place in line and waited. After telling myself that there was nothing that I could do at the moment about the amount of my deposit refund, I looked up to see how many people were in line in front of me, as well as how many tellers were behind the counter.

That's when I got a shock. There, among the three tellers, was a familiar face. It was Posie who was quickly helping people with their transactions, a bright smile in place. As the people ahead of me in line moved forward, I timed it out, even letting a couple of people in front of me, so that I ended up in her cue. She called out for the next customer and I happily marched forward.

"Hey, Posie," I said cheerfully. "I had no idea you worked here."

Her expression became extremely anxious.

"It's okay," I said at a low tone. Remembering that she hadn't been able to look at me, I informed her, "Ignite35."

"I'm sorry, sir," she said, the usual reverence that she applied to the words conspicuously absent. "You must be mistaking me for someone else." The muscles in her jaw flared as she tensed it. Her eyes took on an urgent glare.

It took a dull moment, but I picked up on what she was trying to tell me. I glanced over at the name plate resting formally next to her window. "Oh. I see. I'm sorry, Heather—" She promptly pushed the plate down on its face before I could make out a last name. "Sorry," I said sincerely.

"How can I help you?" Her tone remained formal and stiff.

I slid my check over and said that I wanted to deposit it. She accepted it from me and began typing into her computer at an insane pace. After the thirty seconds that it took her to enter everything, she slid a receipt over to me.

"Thank you," she said. "Have a nice day." She called out for the next person in line, still acting like she had no idea or concern who I was.

I accepted my proof of transaction and thanked her with a slightly embarrassed and less ignorant smile, before walking out.

The following day, I had a similar, and yet, polar opposite experience. I was on my lunch break, standing in a different line at a deli. It was there that I noticed a woman in front of me with a familiar face and frame. I tapped her on the shoulder and politely asked if she had the time, careful to acknowledge her without crossing a line. It turned out that I didn't have to worry.

"Hey, you!" Momma C. smiled big. "Can I give you a hug?"

"Sure."

She embraced me warmly and asked how I was.

"Ah, beginning to get adjusted to my new job. For the most part, good," I said with relief.

"Well, excellent. Are you sticking around here to eat?"

I looked at my phone to check the time that I hadn't actually needed to be told. "I can."

"You should join me for lunch, then." She suddenly looked a little concerned and leaned in to be discrete. "I mean, if you can without a problem."

I smiled. "Absolutely."

After we ordered and found a table, she asked, "What's been going on?"

"Uhhh..." I said with a furrowed brow.

"That doesn't sound good."

"I just had a weird experience yesterday," I confessed.

"What kind of weird experience?"

I told her about seeing Posie and how she, not only pretended like she didn't know me, but did her best to get rid of me.

"Oh," she replied with a sudden look of recognition. "That's just the White House."

"The what?"

"The White House. That's what some of us playfully call D.C.'s house."

"Where he lives plays a factor in their secrecy?"

She laughed. "No. Not his 'house.' His *house.* Him, Tink and Posie and the way he runs things. He feels like he and the girls have a lot to lose professionally—he and Posie especially—if they don't keep their shit on the complete and total down low. It took me almost a year before I learned the girls' real names. Longer to learn his. In fact, I think I'm one of the only ones in the entire extended community who knows it."

"Really? What is it?" I asked.

She smirked. "You know I can't tell you that."

"No. Of course not," I said, silently punishing myself for not using my brain. "It's just weird," I added, "because I was thinking of asking him to be my mentor. It'd be nice to know who I was really trusting so much to."

"Oh, really?" she said. "Well, you actually know who he is, Iggy."

"I do? Who?"

"He's Dramatic Comedy."

I chuckled nervously. "So, Tinkerbrat," I said. "You called her Sammie at the munch. Is that her real name?"

"Oh, no. That's a BDSM term. SAM, a smart ass masochist. It's a submissive who mouths off or breaks rules in order to get punished. It's a form of topping from the bottom." She shook her head. "Don't be fooled. That little girl has more control in that house than you may think."

"Really?"

"Oh, yeah. She has D.C. wrapped around her little finger."

"Interesting." I switched gears to my other weird experience that I had recently had. "So, how common is it for people in the community who don't know each other to mess around together?"

She shrugged. "It's not unheard of. People borrow other people's subs and slaves at the Scene Shop for various purposes. They don't always know each other."

"The Scene Shop?"

She smiled. "It's the local sex dungeon."

"There's a sex dungeon in town?" I asked in utter shock. "Those places actually exist?"

"Oh, yeah," she chuckled. "There are tons of them all over the world. The one here in Clinton, it's really nice. It's big, it's clean, it's safe, it has really nice equipment... And you can actually fuck in there. Lots of dungeons won't let you go that far. Get naked, beat each other, pierce and cut each other... But, God forbid, you actually fornicate... That's just going too far."

"Have you been there?"

"Of course. Lots of times. We'll get you on the list to get in some time. It's an experience."

I let the possibilities of such a visit sink in for a few seconds before back tracking to my original inquiry. "So, people mess around without really knowing each other very well in the community?"

Momma C. finished chewing the bite of food she had in her mouth and followed it with a sip from her drink before responding. "It happens," she said matter-of-factly. "I mean, it's not like we're all a bunch of swingers and free-loving hedonists—although some are. Mostly, you just have shorter courting rituals, more open discussion and expression concerning sex and a more sharing attitude over-all. Why do you ask? You hoping to get it on with someone that you don't know?"

I let out a small, nervous laugh. "I, uh...sort of already did."

"Oh? Do tell."

I was apprehensive about sharing too much right away, but confessed anyway to my encounter with Megan.

"Hm," Momma C. replied. "I don't really know her that well. But what you've described to me isn't totally out of the norm. It's also common place for friends to hook up just for the proverbial benefits around here. Not always, but more frequently than in the vanilla world."

"Interesting."

"You don't seem very comfortable with the idea," she noted.

I sighed. "I've always been a pretty monogamous person and I don't make a habit out of casual sex. Don't get me wrong. I've done it and I think it can be okay. But it's not really something that I view as trivial. I can't see myself making a habit out of it or participating in a free-for-all orgy or anything like that."

"No?"

"Uh uh. I think that if you continually take the meaning out of sex that it ceases to have any value at all. Plus, it's dangerous."

She shrugged. "I suppose. I mean, don't misunderstand. I'm not a promiscuous person necessarily. I prefer intimacy with my partners and to know them well. But I do see the good side of just treating it as a fun time. You help your friends escape the drudgery of their daily lives for an evening. No different than kids playing make believe, except that it's for adults. Benji and I are really good friends and I'm not gay at all, but I have beat the crap out of her and drizzled her with hot wax before. It was just for fun. A gift from me to her, if you will."

"But no clothes came off."

"Mine didn't," Momma C. informed me. "She was topless."

I considered what she was saying. "So, you don't think I did anything wrong?"

"You're both adults, Iggy. You can do whatever makes you happy as long as it's safe, sane and consensual. That's our lifestyle."

Suddenly, my phone buzzed. I looked at it and grunted. "Speak of the devil," I said.

"Sluttypixie?"

"Uh huh. She wants to know if I'm free tonight."

"Are you?"

I thought for a bit and sighed. "No. I don't think that I am. I need some down time. Maybe later." I finished my last bite of food and polished off my drink before saying that I should get back to work.

"Okay," Momma C. replied. "Well, it was good to talk to you. We'll have to do it again some time. My office is just around the corner."

"Really?" I considered a question she asked me at the munch and smiled. "I work nearby in IT. What do you do?"

She thought for a bit before finally admitting, "I'm a therapist."

I smirked. "That must keep you busy, especially with some of the people you know."

"I try never to mix business with pleasure," she kidded. "But, yes, it does."

"Maybe I should make an appointment, you know, just to make sure my head is screwed on straight."

"Seems good from where I'm sitting," she grinned.

CHAPTER SEVEN

The next munch was more fun. I was getting to know people and it made it easier to relax. As I entered the one the week following my bank visit, D.C. immediately caught my attention and waved me over. I went to the chair across from him and his blonde sub and sat down.

"How are you two?" I asked.

"Good," D.C. replied. "Posie has something she really wants to tell you."

She was more animated, and this time, made clear eye contact. "I am *so* sorry," she told me. "I wasn't trying to be rude or mean. I swear."

I gave her a reassuring smile. "It's okay. I ran into Momma C. and she explained everything to me. Frankly, I think I'm the one who needs to apologize. I just wasn't using my head. This is a lot to get used to."

She smiled in return. "I appreciate it. I didn't want you to think I was being hateful."

"Well, I don't really know you, Posie. But something tells me that's not possible." I waved a hand at her. "We'll just pretend like it didn't happen and I'll know better next time."

"Thank you for being so understanding," she said.

"Yes," D.C. added. "Thank you."

"So..." I moved to change the subject of the conversation. "Where's Tinkerbrat?"

"She had to work," D.C. informed me.

"Yeah," Posie confirmed. "She's a bartender and

works a lot of nights. We don't always get to see her that much. Sometimes she doesn't even come home."

"Really?"

D.C. was silent for a moment while Posie let out a slight gasp. He then said, "Yeah. She gets off really late. Occasionally, she has a little to drink afterward and she's not supposed to drive when she does. So, she'll just stay with friends." He followed this by staring at his sub who was present and looking a little concerned all of a sudden before continuing. "But, of course, that was not information that, necessarily, needed to be shared with someone that we only recently met. Was it?"

"No, Sir," she said quietly.

"It's alright," he said before kissing her temple. "At least Iggy can feel better knowing that he's not the only one who doesn't always use his head. Even the veterans make mistakes sometimes. Right?"

"Yes, Sir," she smiled.

He pat her back. "It's okay, kid. I'm not going to punish you. It wasn't really important information—other than her occupation. Just remember to always clear it with me first before you tell people stuff about us."

"Yes, Sir."

As they picked up menus and began to look them over, I noticed Megan, or Sluttypixie, enter. She looked at me and then immediately went to the far end of the long row of tables and sat with some other people. I tried not to read too much into it and just began trying to decide what I wanted to eat myself.

Still, it was odd. Maybe she was mad at me for not hooking up again.

"So," I said to the two friends across from me. "As I said, I ran into Momma C. She was telling me about some place called the Scene Shop."

"Ah, yes," D.C. grinned. "Quite an interesting place. You'll have to check it out some time. In fact, the Shop's anniversary is soon. That would be a good night to begin. It's kind of a free for all."

"As opposed to?" I asked with a cocked eyebrow and a smirk.

"Well, a lot of nights are for specific kinks. There are also lots of seminars and classes on different kinds of play, as well as strictly gay nights, Big and little nights..."

"Why is it called the Scene Shop?"

"It's mostly a theatrical term," he informed me. "A scene shop is traditionally a place for stage crews to build scenery and props and stuff. But, in the kink world, a 'scene' is when people perform whatever acts on each other or themselves. It can be a Dominant disciplining a submissive or someone tying up a rope bunny—"

"A rope bunny?"

Posie filled in, "Someone who allows themselves to be experimented on or put on display by being tied up."

"Yeah," D.C. continued. "It can be something as simple as someone spanking their partner or as intricate as a bunch of people caging, piercing and running a train on a slave. In the case of a dungeon or play party, it's basically anything done for the benefit of the exhibitionists and voyeurs. Although, the term still applies if you do it in private. From the beginning of play to the end of it is a scene."

"I see."

D.C. went on. "We considered calling the place something like Black Snake or Sport, but we were afraid that we might attract the wrong crowd."

"Is there a big sign on the place?" I asked with concern.

"No," D.C. chuckled. "It's quite discrete."

"But you had a hand in naming it?"

"He wishes," Posie smirked. She then pressed her lips together and looked meek and a little afraid under her Dom's glare, though she still grinned.

"Snarky. You've been influenced by your sister too much," D.C. quipped.

"Sorry, Sir," Posie said, while still looking slightly amused.

"Sister?" I asked.

"Tink," D.C. informed me.

I was shocked. I looked at Posie. "You two are sisters?"

They both snickered.

"It's just a term," D.C. said. "Just a way for them to express connection. In our house, it means that they have a sexual connection, two subs serving the same Sir. For others it may mean that they are just tight friends. Family."

"Right. Okay." I barely understood.

"If we were to become very close," he illustrated, "I might call you my brother. They are both mine and live the same life in the same household."

"Oh. Okay." I understood a bit more.

D.C. picked up where 'Tink's sister' had left off. "To answer your previous question, I am not involved in the decision making or planning for the Scene Shop, though I'll confess that I would like to be. Naming the club however, was the result of a poll. People suggested things, it was discussed among the community and the board selected one that seemed to be the best fit."

"There's a board for the dungeon?"

I began to realize that my questions were becoming exhausting and decided to relent. It was just as well, as a server came in and began taking drink orders. I ordered a beer. My neighbors simply ordered water. D.C. then said that he wanted to go ahead and order some food.

"You can bring it out when you bring everyone else's, but she and I will both have the grilled chicken salad with lite dressing." They handed their menus back to the server who moved on.

"Trying to watch your figures?" I joked.

"Yeah," D.C. said seriously.

Posie let out a brief, slightly dissatisfied groan.

D.C. continued. "We've all put on a couple of extra pounds lately." He turned to his sub and put a comforting arm around her. "And while I don't mind if you girls have a little extra on you, I don't want it on me. We all need to watch our health."

Posie nodded reluctantly.

"So, you control their diets?" I asked.

"I control *our* diets," he clarified. "We may not like it, but we have to eat as healthy as we can."

"What else do you control?" I asked, curious.

"Everything," Posie said, sounding slightly frustrated.

D.C. snorted. "Yeah, I'm a terrible dictator."

Posie grinned. "No. I didn't mean that."

"I know," he said while nuzzling the side of her head. "But it's true. I do limit us all, right?'

"Yes, Sir."

"Why?" I asked.

"Because we all need it," he informed me. "I like exercising even less than the girls do. But I also don't want to get a fat gut, develop diabetes and die. Someone has to put restrictions on us. Someone has to have a program for our lives. It just happens to fall to me. If I say, 'do it', they have to. And, if I'm going to make them, then I have to make myself just as much, if not more. Otherwise, I'm not worth respecting. I'm just some controlling asshole."

"Interesting," I admitted while remembering a similar thought passing through my head after reading early descriptions of the lifestyle. "What else do you require from your house?"

He smirked and then looked at Posie. "You want to field that one?"

"He makes us keep things clean and organized and be responsible. We have a list of things we have to do each day."

My mind immediately went somewhere weird and it came out of my mouth before I could stop it. "Any of it sexual?"

"Yeah," Posie confessed casually. "I mean, we have to position ourselves properly at certain times and keep a journal of our journey into submission and discuss our fantasies with him and each other regularly. We have a program, more or less, that we have to adhere to."

Before I could pester them more, a short girl in her late twenties and with a wide hourglass figure walked up. She was flamboyantly dressed, but still street-legal, in a multicolored shirt, a clashing plaid mini-skirt, mismatched socks and Mary Janes. She stood next to us, at the end of the table and addressed my new friends.

"Hey, D.C., Posie."

"Greta," D.C. said courteously. "How are you?"

"I'm excellent. I'm meeting a Dom tonight. I'm excited."

"Interesting," he said.

"If I may..." Posie began with a quick look to her Sir, who nodded. "Where is Blissful Penance?"

She shook her head. "He's not coming anymore. Yeah. He decided this isn't for him."

"That's unfortunate," D.C. said sympathetically.

"Ah, he's right. He's really vanilla and just did all this for me. He's better staying home with the kids." She suddenly looked at me. "I haven't met you. Who are you?"

"I'm Ignite35," I told her.

"Hi. Greta. Nice to meet you."

"You as well," I said. "If you don't mind, who are you guys talking about?"

"Oh," Greta said, "my husband."

I was suddenly very confused. "Um...I thought you said you were meeting your new Dom here tonight."

"I am."

"So...wait... Your husband is babysitting for you while you're here to—"

"Iggy..." D.C. said. He looked at me hard with a pause in his words before adding, "Complicated lives here."

"Uh...huh..." I replied with my mouth hanging open.

Suddenly, Greta let out a brief squeal. "Ooo! AmericanDom1986 is here. Nice to talk to you all." She hopped off.

I had an immediate response. "Okay, I don't get it."

"You're not expected to," D.C. told me. "Just be tolerant and happy for her."

"...'K."

I looked across the room where this girl was fawning all over some very tall, very big guy with a friendly look on his face. She rambled on and on while he simply smiled and nodded. I probably just had a look of total confusion and disapproval, but my neighbors didn't say anything as they began some mundane conversation of their own.

Why would some girl openly leave her husband with their kids to go meet some other guy that she was going to have a BDSM relationship with? More specifically, why would her husband be okay with such a thing?

I continued to watch as Greta interacted with her new Dom who smiled and pat her round bottom. This really made no sense to me and even began to make me a little uncomfortable. I could never see allowing my significant other to just run off and engage in God only knows what with strangers and I certainly wouldn't be watching the kids while she did. More likely, I'd be packing them and our things up to head out of state and away from their deviate mother.

Was I missing something?

At about that time, Mistress Xina walked in with a tall, muscular man behind her. He looked like an athlete, or maybe a cop, and smiled like a massage therapist. They approached and the Mistress greeted us. "Hello, everyone."

"Xina," D.C. said. "Good to see you."

"Likewise. How are you, Posie?"

"Well, Mistress," she said kindly.

"Ignite," Xina said to me. "So nice to have you back. Are you acclimating well?"

"Ah..." I glanced back down to where Greta was sitting next to AmericanDom1986. They were talking and holding hands. "I'm...doing my best."

"Excellent," the Mistress replied. She then held a hand out to the man with her. "This is my slave, Wired."

"Nice to meet you," he said happily.

"You as well." I stuck out a hand to shake.

No one responded. Wired simply looked at his Mistress like he was waiting for confirmation of something. Just as my confusion began to settle in, Xina cleared everything up with an explanation.

"He currently has a 'no touch' policy in place. He can't shake your hand without my permission."

"Oh. Shit," I said, drawing my hand back fast. "Sorry."

"It's okay," she replied. "He has it." She nodded at him and he stuck his hand out to me.

"It's a pleasure," he told me in a tone and breath that sounded grateful and respectful.

I shook his hand and returned the sentiment.

Mistress Xina spoke again, addressing her slave. "Why don't you sit with them? Feel free to socialize casually. I need to go speak with the restaurant manager. It's time to renew our reservations for this room."

"Yes, Mistress," he said with polite reverence. As she walked out, he looked at me. "May I take the seat next to you?"

"Hm? Oh! Of course. Make yourself at home."

D.C. chuckled. "Does that mean you're going to strip and lay in a ball on the floor, James?"

Surprisingly, Wired just laughed. "I don't think that would be a good idea."

"It'd be sexy though," Posie teased. Remarkably, Wired...or James...or whoever, blushed.

D.C. leaned towards his sub. "Is that Tink talking through you again?"

Posie suppressed a giggle and apologized. D.C. swatted her playfully on her rump and then the two continued the conversation they'd been having about personal business between them. Because of this, I focused my attention on Wired.

"So, how long have you been Mistress Xina's...slave?" I felt weird asking it because he was so big and built.

He was unfazed. "A little over a year now. She had another at the time, but cut him loose shortly after taking me on."

"So...you guys had a situation like D.C., Tink and Posie's?"

"No. I never engaged with her other slave. She'd engage with each of us separately."

I tried hard to wrap my head around his explanation. "You didn't mind that she had a relationship with another guy?"

"We're in an open relationship," he told me. "It started that way."

"So, you don't completely belong to her?" I tried to clarify. "You can submit to other people."

"Oh, no," he stated emphatically. "But she can own other people or play with them and she can loan me out. If I want to pursue something with someone else, I have to have her permission." I was mystified by this. He saw it on my face and asked, "Hard for you to comprehend, I take it?"

"Yeah. I just... Why would you want to be in a relationship like that?"

He shrugged. "I like being submissive."

"You like being cheated on?" I heard myself ask.

He laughed and shook his head. "Open relationships aren't like that."

"Right," I said, obviously not sounding like I understood, which I didn't.

"Monogamy doesn't work," he insisted. "Human beings are mammals and we have urges and instincts. Also, lifetime commitment is a huge thing. It becomes impractical."

I suddenly felt like the logical one. "Odd coming from someone who has voluntarily given their rights and body away to another person."

He chuckled. "Yeah, well that's another matter."

I sighed and tried hard to understand again. "I guess it

shows a lot of strength in you that you can do it. I never could though."

"Why not? Jealousy?"

"Probably," I confessed. "But it's also dangerous, stds and all."

"That's why you practice safe sex."

I glanced back down the table at Greta who was still fawning all over her new Dom. "That's true." I tried to sound sincere.

"Look," he began. "I was married twice and neither time worked out. Part of that was because we got sick of each other. But another reason was because, in vanilla relationships, nothing is really spelled out. There are no hard and fast rules governing behavior and roles. You're just feeling your way through, blindly, at times. That's one of the things that I find appealing about this. I know where the lines are, who's in charge, what to say or do and when and what to expect. I have my needs met and responsibilities plainly laid out. So much of the everyday worry and nonsense that most people go through isn't a part of my life. In a way, slavery makes me free."

I considered his words with a furrowed brow and nodded. "Well," I said, "that's certainly an interesting perspective."

He smiled and turned the conversation to me. "So, how'd you get into the lifestyle?"

I grinned back. "Banged a bartender who wanted me to slap her while I fucked her."

He laughed. "Excellent."

I chuckled back and found myself proud that I could be so frank and open with a stranger, one who my heart and mind was already telling me, by virtue of his presence and connections, was already like a friend to me.

"What are you into?" he asked.

"I'm still trying to figure that out. I know I'm dominant, but I haven't fully explored everything that that means."

"That could take a lifetime."

"Yeah, well..." I grinned and shrugged. "I got time."

"Are you into bondage?"

"Yeah."

"Impact play?"

"Uh..." I tried to analyze the words for a meaning, but wasn't fully certain.

He clarified. "Spanking, slapping..."

"Oh. Yeah. I like that a lot."

"Are you bi?"

"Am I... You mean am I bisexual?"

He nodded.

"No. I'm straight."

"Are you sure?"

"Pretty sure." I turned it around on him. "You?"

"Majorly heteroflexable," he grinned.

I laughed. "Is that a thing'?"

He nodded again. "Yeah. I don't consider myself completely bisexual, but do find some men attractive and can play with some of them, especially under certain circumstances."

I began to wonder if I was one of them and if that was why he had brought it up. I decided not to ask though. I didn't really want to know.

Suddenly, there was a young woman next us, a dumpy little thing with thick glasses and a slight lisp. "Hey, guys. How is everyone?" she asked.

"Eleanor," D.C. said courteously. "Long time, no see. We're well. How are you?"

"I'm good. Just felt the need to check in."

"Wait," I broke in. "Eleanor? You wouldn't be SeptemberSnowGirl, would you?"

"That's me," she grinned in a confused manner. "Who are you?"

"Ignite35. Good to finally meet you. I owe you a debt of gratitude."

"Oh, okay. This worked out for you, then?"

"It has, so far. I appreciate it. I didn't really know anyone in town and this has helped me relax and make friends."

She beamed. "Well, good. That's all I ever want for people." She greeted Wired and Posie and started to sit at the end of the table.

Suddenly, Mistress Xina walked up. "Eleanor," she said sternly, yet still with a smile. "Your Daddy is at the other end of the table wondering why you're over here."

SnowGirl seemed unfazed and even a bit clueless. "Oh. Okay." She walked off.

I watched as she went to the other side of the room and sat next to a young man who put a hand on the back of her neck and pulled her to his chest. She talked constantly to everyone else around her, while the young man, who was, somehow, still her "Daddy" sat silently.

"I do not like her," the Mistress said.

"Xina," D.C. scolded. "Eleanor is fine. She's just a little hyper and directionless. She could do with your guidance, in fact."

Mistress Xina smiled at him sarcastically. "Yeah, like that's going to happen."

Before I could ask for more information on the source of their conflict, Xina stood up and began to address everyone. Once again, we all introduced ourselves and explained how we identified. There was no one there newer than me, so that's about as far as it went. Next, the server entered and began taking every ones' orders. After placing mine, I felt a sudden urge to go to the bathroom. I made my way there and conducted my business quickly and calmly.

Once I walked out, however, there was something else...or rather, someone else...waiting for me.

"Oh. Hey, Megan," I said as I almost bumped into the little punk girl outside of the bathroom.

"Come here," she said as she grabbed my arm and began trying to drag me into the ladies room.

"What are you doing? I can't go in there!"

"Shut up," she said as she shot quick glances around. "Come on."

She pulled me in and then shoved me into a stall, which she locked.

"What the hell is going on?" I asked.

"Pull down your pants," she insisted.

"I'm not going to—"

But she was already unfastening them and tugging them down.

"What are you doing?" I demanded to know.

"Fuck me really quick," she said.

"Are you crazy?"

She leaned back and got a naughty smile on her face. "What? You never wanted to have a bathroom quickie before?"

"Huh?" I asked like an idiot.

She started stroking my cock and it immediately responded without my input. "You're getting hard," she said, before sticking it in her mouth for a few strokes.

"Christ, Megan..."

She lifted her mini-skirt and pulled her underwear to the side. "You know you want to."

I felt a little accosted. I also felt a little like this was something that I wanted scratched off of my kink bucket list. I suddenly grabbed her by the hair and shoved her against the door to the stall. I put a finger over her lips to silence her as she breathed heavily and I pulled a condom out of my wallet. I put it on and started fucking her, no ceremony, no foreplay, nothing. She bucked back into me and grunted.

"Yeah! Yeah! Yeah!" she said through her teeth.

Suddenly, the door to the bathroom opened and we paused, me with a hand over Megan's mouth. I shot a quick glance through the crack in the stall door to see Mistress Xina there washing her hands and checking her make up.

Is this really what women do? I wondered. *They go to the bathroom for reasons other than having to go to the bathroom?*

Suddenly, she paused. I saw her slowly turn and look towards our stall, but she said nothing. She simply finished freshening up and walked out.

"Fuck me," Megan said as she started grinding into me again.

Maybe it was the urgency, the lack of knowledge of how much time we had. Maybe it was the risqué nature of our act. Maybe it was some hidden kink that I had yet to discover. Whatever it was, I suddenly became super aroused and came really quick as Megan shoved herself into me.

We panted for a few seconds and stilled before I asked, "Did you come?"

"A little," she told me.

We adjusted ourselves and carefully moved out of the stall. As she washed her hands, I quickly exited the ladies room, relieved to find that there was no one there to see me come out. I adjusted my clothes as I headed back towards the conference room. However, as I past the hostess stand, I heard a voice.

"Ignite," it said.

I turned to discover Mistress Xina there, arms crossed.

"Uh...Mistress," I said, suddenly unable to make eye contact.

She approached me slowly. "What were you doing in the ladies room?" she asked.

I couldn't answer. I was too freaked out and stunned. I forced myself to look up to try to meet her eyes, hoping that I could come up with some believable lie by the time I met them. When I got to her face, she was smirking.

"Uh..." I struggled.

"It's okay," she said. "We've all done it." Her smile seemed amused, impressed and even approving as she uncrossed her arms and walked back to the conference room.

About that time, Sluttypixie came out of the bathroom. "What was that about?" she asked.

"Oh..." I said, "Nothing important."

I returned to the meeting room and took my seat. Wired was still there and gave me a funny look, like he suspected something was off. The embarrassed smirk I gave him probably didn't help. However, if he had any ideas about what I had just done, he kept them to himself. Megan just returned to her place at the other end of the table.

This whole time, D.C. was talking to a pretty, young, short-haired girl who was clad in a floral sundress. She seemed a bit shy, but also like she was doing her best to overcome it. They were discussing her recent development.

"I've been trying to take your advice," she told him. "You know, about taking my time and exploring slowly."

"How has that been treating you?" he asked.

"It's...frustrating," she admitted with a nervous laugh. "But I know it's for the best."

"Are you seeing anyone?" Posie asked.

"Yeah, uh..." she looked around. "He went to the bathroom as soon as we walked in. He should be here soon. It's Killer Rabbit."

D.C. furrowed his brow. "The name is familiar."

Posie supplied, "He's the one that was at that party at Benji's, the guy in the hat that you didn't care for."

"Oh, right."

The girl smirked. "Yeah, he does kind of dress like a douchebag sometimes."

D.C. looked at me and smiled. Then he got a sudden look of realization on his face. "I'm sorry, Lolly. This is Ingnite35. He's new."

"Hi," she smiled to me. "Lolly Popper."

"Nice to meet you," I said. My tone still had an uncomfortable tint to it. It was almost as if I was certain that everyone knew what I had just been doing.

As if to confirm this, D.C. got a puzzled look on his face. "You okay, Iggy?"

"Hm? Oh, yeah. Yeah. You know, I was just in the bathroom and I didn't see this person that you were talking about and I just thought it was a little odd. I mean, I must have just missed him, you know." I chuckled.

Everyone gave me weird looks and my laughter disappeared.

"'K..." D.C. replied in a confused voice.

It was about that time that the munch guest in

question walked in and over to Lolly. His shirt was unbuttoned a little too much and had a dragon down the side. He wore several large rings. Other than that...he still looked like kind of a douche, being slightly overweight, pretty hairy and sporting a goatee.

"Hey, everybody," he smiled. "How we doin' tonight?"

"Good," everyone rang in unison.

Suddenly, Killer Rabbit became fixated on Wired. He pointed. "Mr. Blankenship?" he said.

Wired froze for a second before standing and exiting the room quickly.

"Hey..." Killer Rabbit called after him.

"What was that about?" Lolly asked.

"That was Mr. Blankenship. He was the girls' soccer coach at my high school."

"Oh my, god..." Posie looked horrified. "Stop."

Killer Rabbit completely missed her scolding. "I had no idea he was into this," he continued. "That's crazy. He taught my sophomore history class."

"Okay," D.C. broke in sternly. "Enough. You need to stop speaking about him this instant. You just said all of that, out loud, in front of half of the room."

"Hey, relax, bruh," he said with a douchey hand held up. "I'm sure no one here cares what he does."

"But he might," I pointed out. "Seriously, man. This is only my second munch and even I know better. Keep it to yourself."

He looked offended. "Why don't you go eat a dick?"

Suddenly, Xina was right there, looking at him with distaste. "I'm not one hundred percent what you said, Rabbit, but you need to restrain yourself immediately. If you can't, then you will have to leave."

His hands were both up now in a surrender. "Hey,

look everybody, I'm sorry. I was just surprised is all. I didn't mean to cause problems, honest."

Xina took this as sincere, dropped her hands from her hips and let out a sigh. "Alright," she said. "Don't let it happen again."

"Hey..." he said before drawing a cross over his heart.

"Um..." Lolly began, "why don't we order and maybe sit on the other side of the room, so he can comfortably come back if he wants to."

"That won't be necessary," Xina told them. "He's gone. You're welcome to stay where you are, just try to remember that we are in the business of keeping people's secrets here."

Killer Rabbit and Lolly both nodded cooperatively. Xina walked off.

Killer Rabbit spoke tentatively. "I'm going to go smoke. I'll be back in a minute."

"I'm coming with you," Lolly said. They both exited.

"Well..." I said. "That was uncomfortable."

"At least he realizes he messed up," Posie noted.

"Does he?" her Sir asked.

We all sat there quietly few a few seconds before actively changing the subject to something less cringe worthy, like racism or animal abuse.

CHAPTER EIGHT

I was shocked to find that the Scene Shop actually had a web site. On it was an explanation of their mission, "to expand knowledge and awareness of kink and to provide a safe and clean environment to explore it." There were no pictures or an address, but it did have a long list of rules and code of conduct. I immediately tried to familiarize myself with them.

Must be 18+ to enter.

The Scene Shop is members and guests only.

No alcohol or controlled substances. Anyone believed to be under the influence of alcohol or drugs will be asked to leave.

Clean up after yourself. The Scene Shop provides medical grade sanitizer for use.

No food or drink in the dungeon. You may eat or drink nonalcoholic beverages in the lobby and kitchen area.

No smoking. There is a smoking deck for use of tobacco and vaped oil.

Mind your manners! Do not touch anyone without an invitation. Do not approach a scene closer than ATM distance (that distance that you would normally feel comfortable having someone behind you at an automated teller machine). Do not comment loudly on or intrude upon a scene. Do not touch other people's toys without permission.

The Dungeon Monitors are in charge. If they

intervene in your scene, even if you are married to the person that you are playing with, and tell you to stop, you must stop immediately. The DM's are there for your and everyone else's safety.

No solicitation. Pay for play is a big, big NO.

Needle play, knife play and blood play must be conducted in the medical play area only.

Dispose of all needles, razors or other similar objects, as well as condoms and vaginal dams in the provided biomedical disposal bins.

Weapons: Knives must be legal to carry. Guns are not allowed.

Please do not monopolize the equipment provided by the Scene Shop.

No perfumes or fragrances.

No glass of any kind.

No scat, golden showers or rainbow play.

Red is our universal safe word. Learn it, use it, respect it.

Do not discuss anything you see or learn with anyone outside of the confidential community EVER.

If you do not know, ask.

After trying to take all of this in, I was confronted with something else. There was a dress code. It wasn't ridiculously strict, but it did strongly discourage extremely casual wear: sweatpants, flip flops, running shoes... Ultimately, you could get away with anything provided that you could argue that it was related to a fetish that you had. However, the Scene Shop, mostly, wanted to create atmosphere and that meant encouraging leather, vinyl, sexy under clothes, costumes and, ultimately, anything black.

I considered my closet. Most of it was pretty casual. My jobs had never required me to wear anything specific and I liked comfort. I did, however, have a pair of black slacks and a black polo shirt. I also had a slightly worn out, pair of black dress shoes and a relatively nice pair of brown ones. Between it all, I could get past the Dungeon Monitors to eek my way in. ...Surely.

I noticed Momma C. was live on the website and messaged her.

"Hey," I said, "can I get an address for the Scene Shop. D.C. invited me to the anniversary and I plan on coming."

After a few moments I got a response. "Sure! It's 1763 Truman. See you there!"

I leaned back from my laptop and smiled. I was going to a sex dungeon.

I drove clear across the city to a bland and unassuming area of town. As I maneuvered a long, winding stretch of road consisting of package stores and restaurants, health spas and nightclubs, accounting firms and payday advance places, boutiques and thrift stores, shopping malls and pawn shops, a mix of Latin jazz on my iPod provided my soundtrack. After what seemed like forever, the digitized voice on my GPS instructed me to merge onto a less neon decorated road. Suddenly, there were turns every couple of streets, streets that included houses, as well as community centers and churches. Finally, I turned down one with a mechanic's place, a library, a small post office and a series of attorneys' offices. At the end was a cul de sac with a very plain, unmarked office building.

"You have arrived at your destination," my GPS said.

I looked around the street and then all over the front

of the building. Outside of the conspicuous amount of cars in the parking lot, nothing about it even murmured sex dungeon. Nothing. Nada. Zilch. I turned off my vehicle, got out and began a very slow stroll towards the front door. As I made my way, I was encouraged to see a couple of people in trench coats approach ahead of me and enter. I was a mere few steps behind them as the door closed. I walked up to it, slowly still, took hold of the handle and froze.

You sure you want to do this? I asked myself. *This is a huge step and there is no telling what awaits you in there.*

Just do it, I replied to the voice. Taking a deep breath, I turned the handle and went in.

It was not at all what I expected. Nowhere around me were there groups of perverts, beating, licking or screwing each other. In fact, there was no one there at all, save a lone receptionist behind a tall counter. The place was well lit, painted white and trimmed with a very nonthreatening beige. There were two short rows of comfortable looking chairs on either side of the front door and a handful of innocuous magazines on end tables. It looked more like a doctor's office waiting area or the reception room of a financial adviser than a dungeon.

"Can I help you?" the plain, forty-ish woman in casual attire behind the counter asked me.

"Uhhh..." I drew out. I screwed up my all of my courage and walked over to the desk where she was reading a copy of Mary Shelley's *Frankenstein.* In a nervous voice I managed, "Is this the Scene Shop?"

"It is," she replied, raising her pupils towards me, but not her head, no real emotion in her tone one way or the other.

"Oh, good," I said with relief. "I wasn't sure if I'd

found the right place. I mean, this is not what I was expecting to walk into, as I'm sure you can imagine." I laughed and shook my head.

She said nothing. She only stared back at me.

I swallowed again. "Um...I'm supposed to be on the list."

"The list?"

"Yes."

"What list?"

"Well...the list to get in."

"There is no list," she informed me. "Either you're a member or you have a sponsor to get you a guest pass. That's it."

Shit.

The woman continued to stare with no expression whatsoever as I tried to figure out how I could contact someone to get me past her. I didn't have any phone numbers, only profile information and I seriously doubted anyone already inside was checking their account. Still, I guessed that it couldn't hurt to try. I posted that I was in the lobby and needed a way in on my wall. Then I sat down and prepared for a long wait.

I was surprised however as the door next to the reception desk opened about five minutes later and out walked Mistress Xina. She was dressed in a short, one piece, vinyl dress, thigh high leather, stiletto boots and a German officers-style hat. It was an odd contrast to the sleek business attire that she usually wore. She beamed when she saw me. I'm pretty certain I blushed.

"Hi, Iggy. It's so nice to have you here tonight." She came over and shook my hand. "I was on the smoking deck, posting a reminder of tonight's event when I saw yours. I'm sorry you had trouble getting in." She sounded deeply sympathetic.

"Ah, it's okay, you know," I shrugged with a smile.

"I hope you haven't been waiting long." Before I could answer, she turned to the woman behind the counter and said, "He's with me." As she continued to hold my hand, the secret fear that the receptionist might think that I was Xina's slave hit me. I tried to remain open minded though and pushed it aside as the Dominatrix pulled me to the counter.

"Thirty-five dollars," the receptionist told me.

I quickly dug in my my wallet and pulled out what was the convenient total of its financial content and handed it to her.

She accepted it and slid a clip board with a piece of paper on it consisting of lines and signatures. She pointed at the lowest empty one. "Sign here. Your community name is fine." I complied. She took it from me and reached under the counter. There was a buzz sound and the Mistress dragged me to the door which she opened, talking as she did.

"I'm glad you made it out. I think you're going to be completely blown away by the place, as well as the party tonight." She paused and turned to me with a devious smile. "Who knows? Maybe literally."

She continued to lead me down a hallway, it's only decoration, a long series of hooks with coats on them. I started to ask if anyone was ever concerned with theft, as there was no one there attending them, but then I caught a gimps of a couple of cameras in the corners. My immediate concern after that was if there were any sort of cameras inside the dungeon proper. I needn't have worried though. For as we reached the end, we were met with a heavy, steel door with a sign on it emphatically stating, "NO CAMERAS, CELL PHONES, OR RECORDING EQUIPMENT OF ANY KIND!" I also noticed off to my left another door that had a sign that read, "SMOKER'S DECK. IF YOU MUST SMOKE OR VAPE, DO IT UP HERE."

Mistress Xina grabbed the handle on the first door and paused as she turned to me. Her smile grew wicked again. "I hope you're ready."

"Uh, almost." I pulled my cell phone out of my pants pocket and shoved it into my jacket, which I then hung on an available hook. "Ready," I said.

With that she opened the door and I followed her in. Immediately, the drab and quiet facade of the place disappeared and was replaced by sheer decadence.

As I entered, my whole world changed. Heavy, industrial music, blaring through a pa, greeted me and behind the steel door looked like a satanic gymnasium. All around the large room were what resembled red and black monkey bars, jungle gyms and pummel horses, mixed with padded tables, swings and other fixtures. There were also a variety of cages, mirrors and chairs. In one corner of the room was a collection of medical equipment and a couple of examining tables. All about me were countless kinksters, dressed in leather, vinyl, lingerie, formal wear and, in some cases, nothing. Many of them were doing scenes. It was like a perverted cirque du soleil.

"Have a stroll," the Mistress said, as she spun toward me with a coy grin. "Enjoy yourself. I still have rounds to make." And she was off, leaving me to fend for myself.

I was in awe. I began to wander around, trying to take in all that was happening. That's when I found a shock in the far right corner. It was D.C. and both of his subs, deep into a scene and it was intense.

They were in front of a large mirror. Posie was bent over a black padded, table with Tinkerbrat holding her down on one end, while their Dom beat the shit out of her with a flogger, a small handle with multiple leather strips coming off of it, on the other. Both of the girls were naked and every so often he would grab one of them by the hair and kiss them ravenously, before returning to delivering blows to Posie's bare ass and thighs, sending loud slap sounds, as well as her grunts and cries, across the room. At one point he even grabbed Tink by the throat. She opened her mouth and allowed him to spit in it.

I began to feel a bit uncomfortable, like I was invading my friends' privacy on an epic level. I knew that that was slightly silly. D.C. himself had indicated that people who played there did it for the benefit of others who wanted to watch them, voyeurs. But I still felt intrusive and began to look around at the other people in the room.

Off to my left was a woman with a green mohawk, a black t-shirt and platform boots tying a thin, bird-nosed man to, what resembled, a vinyl mattress, suspended from the ceiling. She was using knots that would make the navy proud. In the center of the room was a shirtless man in tight black pants, stuffed into tall cowboy boots. He had a portly woman, in nothing but red panties chained by her wrists to the ceiling. As she stood on a square box that she could barely reach with her toes, he battered her back, ass and legs with various forms of whips. Behind me and to the right were two women in leather corsets and knee high boots strapping a naked man onto a gynecological examining table. Once they had him secure, they clipped several clothespins to his nipples and scrotum. After which, one of them strapped a dildo on herself and slowly worked it up his anus while her co-conspirator slapped and yelled at the man, who just kept replying with loud cries of, "Yes, Mistress! Thank you, Mistress!"

It wasn't a circus. It damned sure wasn't a gymnasium. It was Dante's Inferno.

"Pretty wild, huh?" a voice said behind me over the din of heavy metal music and screams of pain/pleasure. I turned to find Momma C. there, clad head to toe in black and blue. Her enormous tits were hoisted up into my face by a tight corset. She was grinning.

"That's one way to put it," I replied. I then smirked. "Oh, by the way, I had a hell of a time getting in. That list you said I'd be on doesn't actually exist, apparently."

"Oops," she blushed. "I'm genuinely sorry. When I said that, it was just a figure of speech. If I'd been thinking, I would have had you meet me here and I would have gotten you past the gatekeeper."

"It's okay," I assured her. "It worked itself out. I'll just know better next time."

"Again, I'm sorry."

"No harm done."

"Well, get a good look around," she said. "Just don't wander too far off. I want you to meet my sub."

"You have a sub?"

"Oh, yeah. He's just lives three hours away and isn't on the website. He's here tonight, though."

She nodded toward a tall, thin man who was walking out of a well-lit, door-less room in black shorts that appeared to have snaps up the sides. The only other thing he had on was an elaborate dog collar. Momma C. pointed at him with a short crop that she held in her hand and waved him over.

"Yes, Ma'am?" he asked with a friendly smile.

"Scott, this is Iggy. Ignite35. I've told you about him."

"Oh, of course. It's a pleasure to meet you."

"You as well," I said, trying not to seem too uncomfortable. I held out a hand to shake out of habit. He looked down at it and then over at his Ma'am. I was suddenly reminded about protocol. "Oh. Shit. Sorry," I said. I jerked my hand back.

"It's okay," Momma C. giggled reassuringly.

"I almost forgot where I was and what kind of people I was dealing with."

"I don't see how," she continued to laugh. "So, what do you think?"

I noticed that the woman who had tied her friend to the swinging mattress was giving him a hand job. "I'm not sure where to begin," I admitted anxiously.

She smirked and tapped me lightly on the shoulder with the hand that still held her crop. "Take it all in. Mingle and meet. There's a St. Andrew's cross that's about to be available, so Scottie here and I are going to go play." She hooked a leash to his collar before telling him, "Come on, you."

"Yes, Ma'am," Scott replied, almost cheerfully. As he was being lead off, he said to me, "It was very nice meeting you."

I watched them walk away. Suddenly, I was surprised by a woman, clearly in her early thirties, who trotted up to me in loud Mary Janes. Her hair was in pigtails with ribbons around them and she wore a small pinafore and white stockings.

"Have you seen my dolly?" she asked in a childlike voice.

"Uh...what?" I asked, befuddled.

She held her hands up, palms facing the ceiling. "I can't find her."

Before I could make heads or tails out of the situation,

another woman came over and took her hand. "Adriana," she said, "why are you bothering the nice man? Come over here with me."

"But, mommy," Adriana said, "I can't find Patsy."

"I'm sure she's around here somewhere, under a chair or in the locker room. We'll find her." She looked at me. "I apologize." Her demeanor wasn't one of someone playing a sex game, but of someone apologizing to another customer in a grocery store. She led her "little girl" off.

"Bye," Adriana said as she waved to me.

Okay. That wasn't weird at all.

"Hey, Mr. Ignite," I heard a voice say.

I turned to find Wired there, smiling back at me. I was even more shocked, not by his presence or demeanor, but by the fact that he was completely naked, save a leather collar.

"Oh...uh...hey..."

"Did you just get here?'

I didn't respond. I just tried not to glance down at his junk. He immediately noticed my apprehension and did his best to make me comfortable.

"I guess this is a lot to take in all at once, huh?"

"You could say that," I exhaled firmly.

"Would it make you more comfortable if I put something on? I'll be happy to ask Mistress if I can."

"Uh..." I didn't want to be rude by saying that it would, but I was pretty freaked out.

Rude. Asking a man that I had only met once to put on clothes. Wow. I really had gone down the rabbit hole, hadn't I? Here, I felt bad because he would have to ask Mistress Xina if he could cover his nakedness in front of me. I scavenged fast for more of that courage that had gotten me into the place.

I took a quick deep breath, which I let out slowly, and shook my head. "No, man. I...I'm cool. How are you doing?" I did my best to maintain eye contact.

"Good. You?"

"Pretty fucking overwhelmed," I admitted with wide eyes and a wide grin.

He chuckled. "I can see that. You going to make it?"

I sighed. "Yeah. I just went from having my kink cherry popped to being thrust into a porn set, but I'll adjust." I was telling myself this as much as him.

"Well, good. How are you coming along with your journey, other than that?"

"Man, I'm..." I glanced around in a way that, normally, would have been casual. Everywhere I looked though, was met with crazy. "I'm doing my best."

"Good." He was still cheerful and friendly.

In an effort to avoid looking at Wired's exposed genitalia, I continued to glance around. In another effort to not look at other friends doing odd things, while trying to have a casual conversation, I focused on the people who weren't playing. At one point, my eyes fell on a very authoritative looking man in all black with short, dark hair and a mustache. He wore glasses and had a warm smile on his face, yet there was still something very important and formal about him. My gaze fixed on him.

Wired noticed and glanced over. "That's Master Jon," he told me. "He's on the board and, pretty much, runs this place."

"Really?"

"Yeah. Nice guy. Very knowledgeable and experienced."

Nice, knowledgeable and experienced? That word, "mentor" rang in my head. Maybe I should meet this man.

"He's retired and spends most of his time here," Wired continued.

"Retired?" I said. "What are you talking about? He doesn't look that old."

"He's in his fifties, I think," Wired informed me. "He was in the Marines and left that to start a business of some sort. It must have been successful, because he only did it for a few years before selling it and devoting all of his time to the Scene Shop and the community."

"Marines, huh?" Okay. Kill the mentor idea. I was a computer nerd. The idea of going to boot camp really did frighten me. I glanced back towards the table D.C. and his house were at, catching sight of him holding Posie back against him by her hair, grinding slowly into her, while Tink ran her hands all over her body and kissed her. "What about D.C.? Do you know if he was in the military?"

Wired shook his head. "No. His background is...different. Civilian, certainly." He suddenly looked at his watch, the only thing besides a collar that he was wearing. "I gotta go find Mistress. My down time is up and I have to report to her. It was good talking to you."

"You too."

He smiled, nodded and walked off. I tried not to look at his naked ass, but had trouble, mostly because I suddenly found myself a little envious.

Jesus, that's really tight. Muscular, too. Wished mine looked like that.

Then I started feeling like a high school girl, jealous of a peer. I actually smirked at myself and spoke aloud. "Okay, this is all still weird, but you found a way to be weirder."

I returned to looking around the room. As I did, I got another shock. D.C. had Posie bent back over the table they were using and was fucking her really hard, while shoving her face between Tinkerbrat's legs. Tink played with the blonde's hair while smiling contentedly. It was then that I surprised myself. I walked back over to where three of my friends—new friends at that—were having hardcore, public sex. Standing at about twice the recommended ATM distance, I watched in nervous fascination.

Though Tink kept holding Posie's face in her crotch, the vicious trusts that their Dom was delivering were, I guess you could say, distracting. The pale blonde would occasionally lean her head up and let out loud grunts and groans, her eyes rolling back in her head. At one point D.C. put his hand on her neck and shoved her back down. "Eat your sister's pussy," he ordered. He grabbed Tink by the hair next and leaned in for a passionate, almost animal kiss. As he did, I could see more of what was actually going on in the mirror behind them and I was completely blown away. Apparently, that poor guy strapped to the gynecological table wasn't the only one getting ass fucked. All of those intense, hard, fast penetrations were going into Posie's bottom.

My jaw dropped. Suddenly, Tink began wailing, in the grips of an orgasm. Before she could finish, D.C. had his own. The two of them collapsed over on top of Posie, panting like warriors who'd slain the last enemy in a battle. Mere seconds later, he pulled out, ripped off a condom which he tied and tossed into a garbage can with a bio-hazard emblem on it. He kissed Tink momentarily before sitting next to Posie, pulling her up into his arms and holding her. Tink wrapped her arms around both of them and helped her Dom rock her sister, who was visibly shaking. I caught a glimpse of Posie's eyes, which were tearing up just a bit, causing the small amount of massacre that she was wearing to run.

D.C. pointed and told Tink to go get a towel and some water. She got up, fully naked and walked toward a table with a bag on it a few feet away. She passed me as she did, looked me in the eye and grinned. Then she stuck her tongue out at me.

I had to walk away. I was thunderstruck, to put it mildly. As I left the scene that my friends had finished, I noticed that my other friend, Momma C., had finished strapping her sub to a large wooden "x", a St. Andrew's cross, she had called it. While Scott waited, Momma C. opened a briefcase that looked like something that a secret agent might steal. She began pulling out toys, which she carefully laid on a bench. As a line of crops, paddles, rulers, small rods, household utensils and even a copy of the King James Bible formed, Scott was silent. He even looked a little excited.

I, however, needed a break. I took one quick look back over in D.C., Tink and Posie's direction where they were all huddled together, petting each other, drying each other with towels and drinking from water bottles. Each of them, even Posie, were smiling and laughing.

Yeah. I definitely needed a break.

I walked out with two things ringing in my head, over the din of hard rock and the wailing and gnashing of teeth. One, these people were all nuts. And two...I was really, really excited by the whole thing.

CHAPTER NINE

I climbed the narrow stairwell to the smoking deck, afraid to go out the front because the ever-so-personable receptionist might not let me back in without the Mistresses' company. As I walked out, yet another, heavy steel door, I was met with a broad roof. About fifteen feet away was a small circle of metal folding chairs. Three of them had people sitting in them. One of those people I recognized. It was Greta, who was wearing thigh high, rainbow socks and a beige trench coat. The second person was a man of around forty-five, tall and with a pointed beard and a ponytail. His black shirt and black jeans looked old and a little tattered. His biker boots were square toed. The other person in the mix was a tall, very thin, very attractive Asian girl. She, too, had on a trench coat, but it was mostly open and revealed a corset, garter belt, stockings and high heels, all of which were black, like her long, straight hair. They all turned and looked at me.

I waved halfheartedly, with a nervous smirk. I casually walked over and asked if I could sit with them, the idea of the smoke bothering me not being an issue as they were all vaping various sweet smelling flavors.

"Of course," Greta said. "Pull up a chair."

"Thanks. I'm Ignite," I said to the others, the name still feeling a bit awkward.

"I'm Batlash," the older fellow said. He motioned to the gorgeous Asian girl. "That's Purrterra."

I nodded and smiled. After that, they just continued the conversation they had been having before I walked up.

"This whole damn thing is a circus tonight," Batlash said in a raspy voice, contradicting my previous assessment. "I mean, I'm all for celebrating and what all, but—"

"What's wrong with it?" Greta asked. "I think it's cool."

"Everybody's just going a little too for broke," he continued, displaying what I would discover was a peculiar command of the English language. "Everybody wants to outdo each other and make their presence known and stuff. I mean, doin' scenes is great and all, but everybody wants a turn and they all need to try and spectacle and shit. It starts to look desperate."

The Asian girl spoke up, her voice sounding odd, like it didn't quite fit her. "You're just pissed cause D.C. got to the table you wanted first."

"Oh, God," Greta murmured. "Not this bullshit again."

Batlash scoffed. "Well, that's just it. Even D.C. is having sex in public. He never does that...even though Poise wants to all the time."

"Where do you get that from?" Greta asked.

"She told Benji that, that she wanted to scene more and that D.C. was too much of a chicken shit asshole to do it. But now that it's anniversary, everybody feels need to get into the game and be part of the fireworks. Everybody's gotta show they're loyal, they're kinky, they're part of the goddamn scenery. Hell, Xina offered to pee on somebody earlier. You can't even do that here."

"She did not," Purrterra said.

"I swear. I saw it. It was there and so was I while she

was saying it."

"Are you sure she was serious?" Greta asked skeptically.

"Who knows?" Batlash shrugged. "That crazy bitch is a mystery to me and everybody. And D.C. is her fucking lapdog."

Purrterra spoke up again. "You just don't like D.C. because you thought he was rude to you when the two of you met."

""Well, he was. He was a total dick tool."

I barely caught that last statement. I was too fixated on the fact that it was becoming more and more apparent that Purrterra was not all that she seemed. More specifically, despite the obvious b sized breasts that she was sporting, I was getting the strong feeling that she was not, entirely at least, a woman. I'd never met a transgender person before, not to my knowledge, anyway, and the fact that I had found her so stunning at first, made me a little uncomfortable. Still, as an occasionally outspoken supporter of LGBT rights, I tried to remain open minded.

"A 'dick tool'," the trans-girl snickered in a voice with a tone that sounded like a saxophone. "Can you not just pick one, or is that too tricky complicated for you?"

Greta laughed.

"That dude thinks he's all high and mighty and shit and Mistress Xina is a Nazi dyke who just likes to run people's lives," Batlash insisted. He started listing things off on his fingers. "D.C. thinks he can shut people out of the inner circle around here, while still sticking his tongue up the higher echelon's asses. He didn't want me around cause he saw me as a threat. Xina don't want me involved in any decisions in her community cause she likes everybody in their place—"

"And you don't like being relegated to the congregation," Greta prodded.

"Fuck that!" Batlash shouted. He kept running the index finger of his right hand along the digits of his left. "D.C. disciplines his girls when he's mad. That ain't right. He flies off the fuckin' handle in a fuckin' rage. He's goin' to hurt one of 'em."

"That's not true," Purrterra said with a shake of her head.

"You mark my words," Batlash insisted. "Tinkerbrat's goin' to end up in the hospital, worse or more one day."

"I'm sorry," I broke in. "Are you really suggesting that he's abusive?" I asked, somewhat shocked and concerned.

"I'm suggestin' and sayin' it."

Greta shook her head at me. "They're in a feud," she insisted. "They don't like each other so they say nasty shit."

"What the fuck are you talking about?" the man asked in his continually scratchy voice. "You don't like him either."

"That's not true," she protested.

"It is. You two got into it late last year."

She sighed. "I didn't like some of the things that he posted on the website or some things that he said to me at a slosh. I thought he was being a jerk. That's all. I don't think he's abusive."

"Whatever," Batlash returned. "You told me you thought he was some high handed fucker who took issues with other people's arrangements and shit."

"I said that I didn't like what he said about me dating Mike. And Mike turned out to be a prick. So, even if he wasn't minding his own business, he was right."

"Well," Batlash continued, "would you rather he have

stayed out of it or would you rather he had been right?”

Greta gave a confused, condescending look. “I’d rather he had talked to me a little more diplomatically than he did. He just got up in my business.”

Purrterra piped in. “That’s not true. I was there. He was very respectful and simply cautionary.”

“He was kind of an ass,” Greta asserted. “He took me aside and just started telling me what he thought of Mike and that I should be careful.”

“You mean he warned you,” Purrterra clarified.

Greta scowled in thought. “It wasn’t...quite that... You know what? I don’t want to talk about that situation.”

“Course not,” Batlash snapped. “Cause it means admitting that he’s an asshole.”

Greta shook her head. “No. I mean, he can be a super asshole. But he’s not a bad person.”

“‘Cept when he’s beating his girls cause he’s mad.” Batlash hit his vape.

“He doesn’t do that,” Purrterra corrected patiently.

“Or when he’s social climbing.”

“Well...” Greta struggled, “he does kind of do that.”

“And when he’s shutting people out of the community.”

“He definitely doesn’t do that,” Purrterra said. “Not when they aren’t just creepers looking for quick action.”

“He tried to do that to me!” Batlash barked.

Purrterra lowered her gaze at him and paused. She then held up a hand. “You know what? You need to take a chill pill. And maybe an enema to get rid of all that bullshit you’re so full of.”

“Whatever,” he snapped. “I’m going back inside.” He stood and marched toward the door. The second he was through it, the girls sighed and gave their assessment.

“That man can hold a grudge like no other,” Greta

remarked.

"He is kind of an asshole jerk," Purrterra joked.

No sooner had Batlash made his exit than the door opened again and out stepped Mistress Xina. She smiled cheerfully at all of us as she lit a long cigarette and walked over.

"Hello, everyone."

"Hello, Mistress Xina," my fellow roof dwellers rang in response.

"Ignite," the Mistress said to me, "are you enjoying yourself so far?"

"Well, it's certainly not a Friday night at the roller rink," I kidded.

All three of them tittered, before Mistress Xina adjusted her attention to the trans girl. "Purrterra," she began, "I have someone I want you to meet."

"Oh? Who's that?"

"He's a former member of the community who moved away. He's back though. His name is Jackson. He goes by the name Consummate Tormentor. He's a Dominant, a sadist, experienced, pansexual and a very nice person."

"Ooo," Purrterra replied. "Is he good looking?"

"Very," Mistress Xina said with a naughty grin.

"Hook me up, sister. I've been looking for a good Dom for a while now."

"I think the two of you will get along famously."

"That is some seriously good news," Purrterra smiled. "Until then, though, I need to find some play tonight."

The Mistress pondered for a moment as smoke crept from her lips and nostrils. "I might be able to accommodate you."

"Really?"

"Oh, yeah. Wired had to leave, so I don't have a sub for the rest of the night. And I am still itching for some public play."

"Let's do it." The eagerness in Purrterra's voice was blatant.

The Mistress put out her cigarette and the two of them headed towards the door.

"I'm coming too. I want to see this," Greta said before telling me, "Nice to see you again."

"Likewise," I said half-sincerely, my inherent disapproval of her arrangement, as well as the Mistress' still making me uncomfortable, and perhaps, closed minded.

As I tried to calm my judgment, Tink walked out, passing the trio as she did.

"Tinkerbrat," Mistress Xina said cordially.

"Xina," Tink replied.

The Dominatrix paused and gave her a stern look.

Tink edited her greeting into a very cursory, "Mistress."

The tall blonde didn't respond. She simply gave a more approving expression and went inside.

No sooner than the heavy door shut behind them than Tink amended her address again. "Bitch." She pulled a vape pen out of the jacket that she had over some well-worn, animal print p.j.'s and sat next to me. "You doin' alright, Iggy?"

Having, only moments ago, seen her naked and with Posie's face buried in her vagina, I found it a little difficult to look at her. "I'm keeping it together," I said. I decided to make the conversation about other people in order to avoid my discomfort. "I take it you and Mistress Xina don't get along so well?"

"We tolerate each other," Tink explained.

She said nothing else and so I kept the conversation going, trying to shut images of her nudity out of my mind. "She and that Purrterra girl are going in to play."

"That should be a side show."

"How so?"

"Purrterra is in frenzy and Xina is not above taking advantage of that."

"What's that mean?"

Tink exhaled steam that smelled of cotton candy and sighed. "Frenzy is when someone—usually someone relatively new—dives in head first, playing fast and hard and not always being safe. They're so overcome with all the possibilities in the lifestyle that they can't get enough. Plus part of me believes that Terra really only does this to try and get a reaction out of her parents."

"What?"

She shrugged. "Her parents kind of spoil her and ignore her at the same time. They let her get away with anything, send her money anytime she needs it and they don't really react, no matter what she does. I don't know if they're super open minded or they really don't care. But I'm pretty certain it's one of the reasons she's going crazy all the time. Sometimes I wonder if she got gender reassignment on a whim...or maybe because she's just grasping at straws as to what's missing in her life."

I scowled. "That's kind of fucked up."

"Ya' think?" She then adjusted her comments to add, "Not that there aren't plenty of people who get sexual reassignment for perfectly legitimate reasons. She may even have. I just wonder."

I nodded, trying hard to understand. We sat there silently for a moment.

"So..." I finally said. "What have you been up to?"

"Well, I just had a pretty intense threesome downstairs," she grinned.

"Uh, yeah..." I replied, kicking myself for directing

the conversation back to her. "That was..." I didn't finish my sentence.

"What do you think of the place?" she asked me, bringing some relief.

"It's pretty crazy. I had to come upstairs to catch my breath."

"It's definitely wild tonight," she agreed.

"So, uh... How shall I put this...?" I tread lightly. "Are you ever afraid of D.C.?"

She looked like the question was absurd as she shook her head. "No. Why?"

"Well..." I was having trouble finding the words I needed without being too blatant.

"Just cause he hits us doesn't mean he's actually abusive," she supplied. "It's just playtime."

"You're never afraid that he might fly off the handle on you?"

Again, she shook her head. "Sir is sweet. I mean, he disciplines and punishes us and plays rough sometimes, but he would never actually harm us. He loves Posie and me."

"Okay," I said with relief. I revisited my original idea of seeking his mentorship. "You think your Sir is dressed and can talk now?"

She giggled. "Maybe. He went to the locker room to clean up a little and put his clothes back on."

"Where's Posie?"

"She went with him."

"Into the locker room?" Once again I was stunned.

"It's unisex. Anybody can go in," she told me. "It's just a place to keep your regular clothes, change into your kink gear and freshen up after a scene. But nobody around here cares about being seen naked. Not really."

"So it would seem," I smirked. "Okay. Well...I'm

going to go speak to him and pick his brain a little. Do you think that would be okay?"

"Sure. He prefers socializing to sceneing, actually. He just did all that cause Posie and I begged him to."

Batlash's words rang in my head again. "Really?"

I must have been showing my concern because Tink said, "Yeah. Why?"

"What do you know about this Batlash character?"

Tink scoffed and rolled her eyes. "Jeff? Jeff's an asshole. Never listen to a thing he says, especially where Sir is concerned."

"I see. What happened?"

"Jeff walked into a munch and started acting like he was super experienced in another community in another state and wanted to start planning events and gain a quick position of authority. Sir found out where he had come from and spoke to someone he knew there. Turns out Batlash had only been in the lifestyle for a few months. He's completely full of shit and he demands respect like he's old school. When Sir reported it to Xina, Jeff started his own half-assed munch two towns over. Fuck him."

Well, then...

"Okay," I said. "I appreciate it."

I made my way downstairs and back into the dungeon. The only thing that had changed was who was playing, with the exception of the guy in the cowboy boots who was apparently hogging the spot he had claimed, only now it was with a different girl. Momma C. was also where I had seen her last, only she was smacking her sub up pretty good. As she beat him with a flogger and her hand, he continued to smile and let out expressions of pleasure. She picked up the bible and placed it under his chin before saying something to him up close to his face. Next, she jerked his shorts off, opened the good book, placed his dick in between the pages, shut it and then began slapping the cover while yelling something at him.

"If that's not sacrilegious, I don't know what is," a voice next to me said.

I turned to see the man that I had come looking for standing next to me. D.C. was putting on cuff links emblazoned with a pattern that resembled a "three-teared" yin yang and chuckling. Posie was next to him adjusting the red sundress that she was wearing.

She commented, "Or sacrilicious." Her Sir laughed.

"Hey...guys," I began as nonchalantly as I could. "How are you tonight?"

"Good," D.C. said normally.

"I'm fantastic!" Posie beamed. She kissed him. "Thank you, Sir."

"You're welcome, sweet girl."

"May I go watch Momma C. and Scott?"

"You may," he told her. "Just don't get too excited. I'm not as young as I used to be and you already got, probably, all that I'm capable of tonight."

"That's ridiculous," she smiled. "We both know you can go all night." She walked away, her behind swinging back and forth under her dress, and he watched her with a mixture of lust and pain.

"That girl is going to give me a heart attack one day." He shook his head before turning back to me. "So, what do you think?"

"I think I may have my own heart attack." We both laughed.

"It can be overwhelming your first time," he agreed, "especially when it's a night like this."

I nodded and then changed the subject. "Say, I was wondering if we could get together and talk a bit some time, away from the munches and..." Adriana ran past us with her "mother" chasing her and my eyes followed them. "...Other distractions," I completed. "Would that be possible?"

"Sure. What do you want to talk about?"

"I'll explain it then."

He shrugged. "Okay. Why don't you come by our place tomorrow afternoon? Say, around two?"

I was surprised. "You'll tell me where you live?"

He grinned. "I just let you watch me get it on with the girls, Iggy. I think a cup of tea in my living room isn't unreasonable."

"That's a very good point," I nodded.

He snickered. "Actually, few of these people know anything about me. But you seem trustworthy." He nudged me. "Just don't give me a reason to have you taken out."

He smirked hard. I forced a small, nervous smile.

Suddenly, both of our attention was drawn to a large area that consisted of four posts, all connected by four others across the top and what looked like two trapeze swings hanging in the middle. There, Mistress Xina had tied Purrterra by her wrists and had begun to torture her. She had two long sticks in each hand. One, a thin, flexible number, she used to beat Purrterra across her ass, hard, fast and repeatedly. The other she would just touch the trans girl with occasionally. Both elicited loud screams from Purrterra.

"What is that thing she's touching her with?" I asked D.C. "I saw something similar on a video."

"That," he said, "is a violet wand. It's kind of like a cattle prod. It's a handle with a coil on the end."

"Jesus! So, she's electrocuting her?"

"Basically. It has settings on it, so it doesn't hurt as much as it just vibrates you all over when it's set low." Purrterra called out again, as he continued to explain. "But it looks like Xina has it turned up pretty high. Terra's extremely masochistic."

As if to confirm this, Xina got in front of her and started slapping the absolute shit out of her and spitting in her face. "Quiet!" I heard the Mistress scream. "Shut the fuck up, you fucking whore! You know you like this! So, say it!" She beat Purrterra's thighs severely and shocked her again several times. *Say it!*"

"I like it, Mistress!" Purrterra whimpered loudly, tears forming in her eyes. "I like it!"

Xina grabbed her face. "Fucking right you do!" She slapped her again and then went to her toy bag where she pulled out a menacing looking, ribbed butt plug and started working its way into her playmate's ass. After which, she began pinching and slapping her everywhere before returning to beating the utter shit out of her.

"Mistress Xina is rough!" I observed.

"No kidding," D.C. agreed. "She does not mess around. I've seen that woman bring grown men—big, tough, grown men—to tears. She's aggressive. She can also be very sensual and sweet to her subs. But, when she's dealing with someone like Terra, shit gets real."

Yeah, lots of things seemed to be getting "real" that night. That, my first night in a sex dungeon.

CHAPTER TEN

I entered D.C.'s place around two pm the next day. It was a condo and smaller than I expected, even if it was three bedrooms. It also consisted of a small living room, smaller dining area and kitchenette, all open to each other. It was very clean, but also very populated with books and DVD shelves, an entertainment center, couch, recliner, end tables, coffee table and three bicycles. The dining area was almost entirely consumed by a large round table, chairs and one tall lamp. The kitchen was cramped, but functional.

"Make yourself at home," he said to me, uncharacteristically dressed in jeans and a t-shirt. "I have to send an email real quick and then we can talk."

I agreed and he disappeared into one of the bedrooms. Trying to pass time, I looked around at DVD's on a shelf, curious about the house's taste. There were classic movies like Citizen Kane and Casablanca, as well as tons of Star Trek and other science fiction movies. Toward the bottom of the rack it turned into a collection of children's movies, Harry Potter, both Willie Wonkas and several cartoons.

I wandered over to the bookshelf and found a different type of collection. The top three shelves were entirely nonfiction: history books, psychology, books on business, religion and politics, biographies, countless creative writing texts, books on rock and roll music and, of course, several on the subject of sex. The bottom two displayed fiction, mostly sci-fi, erotic romance and general fiction. One particular author took up almost half of the bottom shelf.

"Hey, Iggy," I heard a voice say.

I turned to see Posie entering the room wearing a floral camisole and pink shorts. Her hair was in two long braids.

"Oh, hey," I said. "How are you?"

"Well. Yourself?"

"Good, thanks."

She smiled and went to the dining room table where she sat with yarn and needles and began to quietly knit. At that moment, D.C. returned.

"I apologize," he said in reference to his making me wait.

"Not necessary," I assured him.

He smiled hospitably before offering me something to drink. I declined.

"Okay," he said, sitting down and inviting me to do the same. "What did you want to talk to me about?"

I cleared my throat and summoned courage. "It's more than apparent to me that I have a lot to learn. I know that lots of people have mentors—or are searching for them—and I thought it might suit me to find one."

"Seems reasonable," he nodded.

"So, that brings me here."

He stopped. He sighed. "I appreciate your having that kind of faith in and respect for me, Iggy—"

"Kelly," I broke in. "My name is Kelly."

"Okay, Kelly." He smiled warmly, but didn't offer his real name in return. Instead, he told me, "You're asking a lot. Mentoring is a big responsibility and I'm a very busy man, especially this time of year."

I sank.

"Have you considered asking Momma C.? She's just as knowledgeable as I am and she's a therapist. She's used to helping people."

I shook my head. "I like the way you do things. I want to learn to institute the kind of control that you have."

"Over my girls?"

"Over your life. You're organized and creative." I continued. "Anybody can just beat another person. You have a program. That tells me that you can teach me what I want to know more efficiently and effectively."

He was silent.

"Have you ever mentored before?" I asked.

"Once," he replied. "He lasted a few months before he moved out of town to pursue a new career."

"Well, I believe in you."

Again, he sat there silently studying me before asking me if I had a sub to train with, to practice on.

"No, actually," I confessed. "I amended my bio on the website to say that I'm looking, but so far, no takers."

"Well, you have to be a bit more assertive than that."

I nodded.

He was silent a bit before calling out, "Posie."

She scrambled to her feet and quickly entered the living area. "Yes, Sir?"

"Fetch my crop."

What little color that was in her cheeks faded and it seemed that she may have wondered if she were in trouble. She glanced at me and then back toward D.C. "Yes, Sir," she repeated. She scurried into the other room and returned with her Sir's crop. She knelt and presented it to him.

He took the toy from her and instructed her to stand, before calmly rising himself. Seeing them in front of me and right next to each other, it was the first time that I noticed that she was actually a little bit taller than her Sir, who handed me the long, stiff whip and asked, "What do you do first?"

I rose to my feet and accepted the high quality leather instrument, but then just froze there, my brain racing, in search of the answer. Hesitantly, I raised the crop. While Posie closed her eyes and tensed up, I swung it toward her shoulder. It didn't connect however, as D.C. caught it.

"Ow," he said calmly. He took it from me and smacked me in the back of the thigh with it, hard.

"Ouch! Shit!" I exclaimed.

"Hurts, doesn't it?"

I just scowled and rubbed my leg.

D.C. then gave me my first instruction. "You talk to her."

I was so nervous, I just waved my hand and said, "Hey. How's it going?"

"Oh, Jesus," D.C. muttered as he face palmed himself. Posie suppressed a smile as he continued. "Iggy, you communicate with her, negotiate. Find out what she'll let you do and won't let you do. Ask her about her interests and limits."

I nodded. I shook off my anxiety and tried to focus on being strong and realistic. "Okay, Posie. What do you think? What will you allow and what won't you?"

As I asked, I realized that I had my own limits in the situation. I wasn't certain what these two had in mind. Would they expect me to screw her at some point? Because I couldn't see myself doing that. Beautiful as she was, my strong feelings about monogamy wouldn't allow it.

"My clothes stay on and I won't sexually gratify you," she insisted, relieving any concerns I had for such matters. "Other than that, I guess it's just the obvious stuff. Don't injure me, no rainbow play or bathroom sports."

"Aw. That's a shame," I kidded. "I was really looking forward to peeing on you."

"No. Only Sir and Tink can do that."

Whoa.

D.C. cleared his throat and looked a bit uncomfortable. "Okay," he said. "We're going to start with what we have." He shifted his attention to his sub. "Posie, would it be okay if Mr. Iggy touches you in places other than your breasts or pussy?"

She thought before saying, "Yes, Sir."

"Can he slap you, beat you and spank you?"

"Moderately."

"May he talk down to you, order you around?"

"Yes, Sir."

"May he give you assignments or restrictions?"

She paused. Finally, she said, "No, Sir. That is, no assignments or restrictions that last longer than this exercise."

"Alright," D.C. said. He handed the crop back to me. "What do you do?"

I took a deep breath. I started thinking about the things I liked to do. I reached up, pausing briefly before grabbing her by both of her long pigtails. Not too hard, but enough to institute some authority and control.

"I'm aware your Sir puts restrictions on you. Have you broken any of them that he is unaware of?"

Her eyes darted around as she thought.

"Hey," I snapped. "Look at me. Have you?"

"No," she replied the usual term of respect that followed it conspicuously absent.

"Have you done anything that you didn't have permission to do?"

"No."

Well, that wasn't working. Suddenly, a thought struck me.

"What about impure thoughts?"

Her eyes widened. "I..." She paused.

"Posie," her Sir said, "answer him."

She was soft, but direct in her response. "Tink wasn't home this morning. When I was in the shower, I fantasized about her...touching me."

"Did you touch yourself?" I asked.

Her breathing increased in pace. Her eyes focused far away for a bit and then began to blink rapidly.

"Pos..." D.C. said.

"...Yes."

"That makes you dirty," I told her coldly. "Even in the shower, you're dirty." I swatted her calve with the crop. Unfortunately, I was inexperienced with it and had it turned, purely accidentally, so that the edge of the little leather flap hit her rather than making a square, flat connection.

"Ow!" she squealed.

There were a couple of moments of silence before D.C. stepped in with, "Okay, let her go."

I did as requested and handed him the crop.

"Not bad," he told me. "Obviously, you're not good with the equipment. You need practice."

Posie pouted and nodded in agreement as she rubbed her leg. D.C. continued.

"You need one of your own, that is, if you're interested in using them."

"I am."

"Okay. Well, don't get one from an adult toy store."

"Why not?"

"Because the ones they carry are crap. They're

cheaply made and don't hold up. Plus, believe it or not, the real thing is often less expensive."

"Really?"

"Yeah. There's a tack shop near here where you can go."

"A what?"

"Equine store. A place to get gear for horseback riding. The owner is completely clueless, so you can go in, swing them around and play with them before buying one and he won't think twice. It'll keep you from feeling exposed, while still assuring that you get what you really need."

I smiled and gave a quick nod. "Cool."

"Now, we'll need to talk about terminology, protocol and etiquette, find where your interests, strengths and weaknesses lie. Then we'll see about designing a training program for you."

I beamed. "Really?"

"Yeah. And, Iggy, for the next two weeks, no masturbating."

"Excuse me?"

Posie grinned.

"Yeah," D.C. confirmed. "If you're going to make someone suffer, you need to know exactly what you're putting them through. No different than learning to use a new toy by practicing with it on yourself. Also, it teaches you control."

I scowled, but reluctantly agreed.

"Well, then," he said. "Let's get started. We'll first need to address your..." He looked me up and down. "...Personal presentation."

Automatically offended, I replied, "What's wrong with the way I look?" I immediately wished that I hadn't asked the question.

"First of all," he began, "you need to stand up straight. How are you to command respect if you slouch?"

I scowled, but took his advice, adjusting my posture.

"Second," he continued, "we need to talk about the way you dress."

I looked down at my checkered, short sleeved shirt and cargo shorts "What's wrong with my clothes? They're clean and they're new."

My mentor looked at me sideways. "I'm sure that you've heard the expression 'the clothes make the man' and 'don't dress for the job you have. Dress for the job you want'. This is no different. How do you want to be perceived a Dom? Do you want your potential subs to see you as some everyday guy with secrets? If so, then, you look great. If you want them to see you as suave, that's another thing. Tough? That definition varies. Sophisticated? Dangerous? Sleek? What is your identity?"

Good question. I wanted to control my life, my intimate life and I wanted respect. I told him this as well as that I wanted to be perceived as trustworthy and knowledgeable. "Even though I'm not," I added.

"Which? Trustworthy or knowledgeable?"

"The later."

"Well," he said, "nothing beats a good suit."

I smirked. "Trying to remake me in your own image?"

He wasn't amused. "Iggy, women respond to a nice sport coat and a tie. One former sub that I had under consideration said that she had to cut out of our first date earlier than she wanted because she was afraid that she'd be wearing my tie before it was over."

I smiled. "That actually sounds kind of sexy."

"Yeah," he chuckled. "I really liked that one. Too bad

it didn't work out."

"Why not?"

"That's not important. What is, is that you need some new clothes. You need to redesign yourself as a strong person. If you don't like the coat and tie, invest in some black t-shirts and well-fitting jeans. Get some nice slacks and some quality knit shirts. Good shoes are a must. Women always look at your shoes, believe it or not. You need to look like you have some strength and good taste. Right now, you look like an Ivy League frat boy. It's like your mom picked out your clothes."

I resisted the urge to grumble and he turned to Posie, saying, "Fetch me a piece of paper and a pen. We need to make Mr. Iggy here a potential shopping list."

CHAPTER ELEVEN

I'd only ever been in a sex shop once in my life. A girlfriend in college and I had gotten drunk and decided that we needed to satiate our curiosity over such things. However, all we really did was wander around gasping in amazement at stuff and making childish jokes until they asked us to leave. This time however, I went with a purpose.

I walked in carefully, almost nervous. The thought that the people there might know what I was up to bounced around in my head, making me shake a little. Then I remembered that the people who worked there were probably used to such things and even found them mundane. I also reminded myself that I had recently been in a sex dungeon and being apprehensive about being in an adult toy store was just plain silly. One deep exhalation later and I was ready to take my visit seriously.

I began looking at restraints, vinyl cuffs, leashes, collars, something called pleasure tape... However most of it seemed cheap and poorly made. I did select a couple of pairs of handcuffs. They had keys, but also featured little switches that allowed a person to get out of them if they needed to. That seemed safe. I also grabbed a blindfold that resembled a sleep mask.

Next, I looked at the crops. I noticed right away that D.C. was right. They were flimsy and didn't seem like they would last long or be very effective. Simply holding one and comparing it to how my new mentor's felt in my hand, I found a massive difference. I looked at the prices and found that the cheapest one was $12.99 and it was pretty much junk.

Then I paused. I examined my realization. Here I was, in a sex shop, scrutinizing the toys and turning my nose up. I smiled to myself. *I guess I am learning some things,* I thought. *I'm probably ten times more knowledgeable and experienced than eighty percent of the people that walk through the door.*

I continued to grin.

Then I found something called kegel balls and paused. The simple fact that I was mystified and had to inspect the package to figure out what they were for, knocked a bit of humility back into me. I still had a hell of a lot to learn. There was a large area packed with adult movies and I considered trying to find one devoted to BDSM, something that I could get ideas from before remembering that I wasn't supposed to be jerking off.

Obviously, the last thing that I needed was porn.

I sighed, cleared my throat and made my way to the counter. My assumption about the staff turned out to be true as the person there seemed very bored by the whole experience and completely unfazed by my purchased.

"Need anything else?" she asked.

"What do you recommend?" I asked.

Without a word or a pause, she reached under the counter, pulled out a twenty-four pack of condoms and plopped them on the counter.

"Good call," I said. "Wrap it all up."

Clinton Horse Supply was a moderately sized place that

looked like it was converted from an old convenience store. As soon as I walked in, I was hit with two things, the intense smell of leather and a friendly greeting from the man behind the counter.

"Hey, there," he said. "Can I help you find something?"

Okay, how could I answer that? I took a deep breath before suddenly noticing that Gary Allen's "Get Off On the Pain" was ironically playing on the radio.

"Uh..." I began discreetly. "I..." My eyes scanned the place looking for a reason that I could give other than needing a riding crop to discipline my sexual partners with. Everything in there was completely foreign to me and I froze up.

"You need riding gear? Feed? Saddle pads?"

"A crop," I finally confessed. After all, my new mentor had called the man clueless.

He pointed to the nearest corner. "There's a bunch of them in those bins over there."

I thanked him and went to examine the merchandise. There were three shiny, metal buckets with a variety of different crops in them. I picked up several and began examining them. The thing was, I didn't have the first clue how to choose one. Some had little leather strings at the end instead of a flap. Others had long strings. The ones with flaps at the end came in a variety of widths and shapes. I was a bit in over my head.

I pulled one out with a short string on it. I bent it a little to test the strength and flexibility. Then I smacked myself in the calf with it. As a loud "slap" sound echoed through the store, so did a brief exclamation of pain from me. I turned to see the owner staring at me from behind the register.

I gave him a sheepish smile. "Seems like that one may

hurt the animal." I laughed nervously.

"Uh huh," he replied in a skeptical tone. "Just what kind of horse is it you got, Mister?"

"Oh, uh, not me," I assured him. "No, it's for my niece. She rides."

"Does she?" He didn't sound convinced. He then pointed towards the next bucket. "Try one of those there, one of the ones with the triangular shaped keeper."

"The what?"

"The little flap of leather at the end."

I picked one up that looked very similar to D.C.'s. It was black and brown, sturdy and constructed from silicone and leather. There was a plastic loop coming off of the handle to put one's wrist through. It felt nice and I gave a few hard swipes at the air with it, a high pitched, "woosh!" sound ringing out each time.

"She planning on hitting her horse pretty hard?" the owner asked, sounding either concerned or skeptical.

"No..." I said as I straightened myself up. I glanced at the price and saw that it was $9.99, three dollars less than the cheaply made one at the sex store. I walked, as casually as I could manage, up to the counter. "I, uh... I think she'll like this one."

The look in the owner's eye was one of amused disbelief. "Uh huh. I'm sure she will." He rang me up, bagged my new toy and handed it and a receipt to me. His slight grin and tone were overtly suggestive as he said, "You tell her...I hope she enjoys it."

I froze briefly before, finally, thanking him and walking out.

Clueless, huh?

I spent most of the rest of my day following D.C.'s advice regarding my appearance. I managed to find some nice shirts and a couple of attractive pairs of slacks on sale. The sports jacket was a different matter. I had to go to a specialty store and spend more than I cared to on a black number with two buttons, dry clean only. I also spent over one hundred and twenty dollars on a pair of dress shoes.

I supposed that that really nice, really big TV that I'd had my eye on for some time would have to continue to wait.

While headed toward home, my stomach began to grumble. I realized that shopping for crops, other sex toys and clothes had kept me distracted enough to not worry about food. Now however, I needed to eat. A sign outside of a bar and grille called Norman's caught my eye as it advertised $5.99 for a cheeseburger and fries. I kind of wanted a beer too, so I pulled in.

The place was small and bleak, but everyone present—mostly at the bar—seemed social, like they all knew each other. It reminded me, in that respect, of the Blackstone and I smiled to myself remembering my last visit there and the pleasant darkness, Ryder had awakened in me. Walking to the bar, I sat and picked up a menu. I began scanning it when I got a surprise in the form of my name...one of them, anyway.

"'Sup, Mr. Iggy?"

I looked up to see Tinkerbrat there behind the bar, smiling at me. "Oh, hey," I said. "What are you doing here?"

"I work here," she said, her normal, condescending tone, more relaxed now that we knew each other a little. "What are you doing here?"

"I'm hungry. Wow, this town really is a lot smaller

than it seems."

"No shit." She pulled a notepad from her back pocket and a pen from behind her ear. "What do you want?"

"That cheeseburger combo on the sign sounds nice. The burgers here any good?"

"Best in this tiny ass town."

"Okay."

"How you want it?"

"Medium. Extra pickles."

As she scribbled, a voice came from the other end of the bar. "Hey, Brittany, can I get another beer over here?"

Tink's catty attitude was obviously one she carried with her to work as she shot back, "In a minute, Gary. I'm taking someone's order, right now."

Brittany. Okay, her real name was Brittany.

"What ya' need to drink?" she asked me.

"I'll have a Bud Light...Brittany." I grinned at her.

She cocked an eyebrow at me and smiled, even as her eyes narrowed. "Don't piss me off, Iggy."

I smiled back. "Yes, ma'am."

Her expression changed only in that it became more intense. "And don't call me, 'ma'am', either."

"So, Tinkerbrat?"

She pondered hard and quick. "You know what? Don't call me anything." With that, she turned in my order, retrieved my drink, and went to appease the other customers before placing her elbows on the bar across from me and asking what I had been up to.

"Oh, just doing a little shopping. Your Sir sent me to a rather interesting tack shop to find a crop."

"He didn't?" she said with a look of shock and amusement.

I nodded while my grin displayed my embarrassment.

Tink laughed and said, "Oh, God. I am so sorry. He

likes that prank. That old dude at the place probably needs to give D.C. a kickback or two."

"Yeah, I walked right into that one."

"Literally." Once she finished laughing, she asked how else I had spent my day.

"Taking more of your Sir's advice. Less humiliating advice. I've been clothes shopping, trying to look more...I don't know. Authoritative?"

"Any luck?"

"Yeah. I found some stuff."

"Cool."

"Let me ask you," I began, "do you think he's right? About appearance? I mean, did his dress style draw you to him, make you respect him more?"

She shook her head. "Not really. When I met him, he was in an old t-shirt, dirty jeans and covered in sweat. We were helping to build a homeless shelter."

"Interesting." I tried to imagine D.C. looking that blue collar and failed.

"Don't get me wrong," she continued. "He does look sexy in his normal clothes. The first time I saw him dressed in his usual fashion, I was impressed. But he already had my respect by that time."

"So, the clothes do not necessarily make the man?"

"Confidence makes the man, Iggy."

Suddenly, the guy at the far end of the bar called out again. "Hey, Britt, you gonna come back down here and entertain us some more or what?"

She looked genuinely irritated. "Fuck off, Gary. I'm talking to a real person right now." She rolled her eyes.

I smirked, realizing that she preferred my company to the regulars'. If I was, indeed, gaining her respect, maybe I could get some more complete information out of her.

"So, can I ask you some questions about the

lifestyle?"

"Sure." She pulled out a vape pen and hit it, right there behind the bar. "Shoot."

"Okay. Well, my first question is, why? Why do you live as a sub?"

"It's exciting."

"Really? Because you didn't seem very excited the night I met you."

"That's just because I kept getting in trouble."

"Yeah, about that..." I furrowed my brow as I decided how to form my question. "Why would you keep antagonizing him if you were just going to get in trouble? And why give someone else that sort of power over you to begin with?"

"Isn't that what you want out of someone?" she countered.

"Tink..."

She sighed. She shrugged. "I think, maybe, I'm just kind of stupid sometimes," she chuckled. "I mean, I don't like being told what to do, not outside of the bedroom anyway. But he does make a lot of hard decisions that I don't want to make and he does take care of me. He also gives me the excuses that I need to be a better person. Maybe that's it. Ultimately though, I think it just turns me on."

"So, that's it? It's just about the sex?"

She pondered again. "You know what? No. I mean, it was at first, but it evolved. I think I just realized how practical it was when it comes to relationships."

"In what way?"

"Well, think about it. You piss off your significant other in a vanilla relationship and that could become a big fight or be really hard to reconcile. You have to apologize over and over. You have to go through a period of mending and healing. But, in our kind of lifestyle, you don't have to do the whole justification dance. You just say that you're sorry, get a punishment and it's all over. You move on, just like that."

I considered her answer. "So, you just think it's practical?"

She nodded as she hit her vaporizer. "Yep. Think about it. I don't have to clean house much. Posie does that. I'm never alone unless I want to be. I have a man when I want one, a woman when I want one, both when I want that... I have someone in charge of me when I don't want to make decisions and someone to dominate when I want to."

"What do you mean?"

"I'm over Posie. I'm the alpha."

"What does that mean?"

"Basically, I outrank her. I like submitting to men, but I like dominating women."

"Interesting," I noted. "Okay. Go on."

"I have a decent place to live where the bills get paid, on time, and I never have to handle the finances. All I pay is my phone bill and the internet bill, and the internet is only because Sir wants me to learn responsibility. Oh, and I pay for my school, of course. Also, I'm a member of a community where I know that I always have friends that I can talk to about, literally, anything. And I'm owned by one of the best Doms in the community, so..."

"Bragging rights?"

"Exactly. Everyone knows who I am and treats me with respect because of D.C. and my relationship with him and Posie. I love it."

I sat digesting everything she was telling me before she added, "And, of course, I get fucked really, really good, in the absolute best ways, any time I want it."

"And that's all you want from sex?"

"No," she said, shaking her head again and blowing steam. "Believe it or not, we have vanilla sex sometimes. But the kinky shit's better." She grinned big. "And both Sir and Posie are really good at it."

"Are they?" I asked with interest.

"Oh, yeah," she beamed hard. "Dude, the first time D.C. blindfolded me and tied me up, I came so hard I was shaking. I was like..." She continued in a pitiful and excited sounding voice. ""...Oh my God! What just happened? That was the best sex I've ever had! How did you do that?"" She laughed again. "It was awesome."

"So, you'd never done anything like that before?"

She shook her head and exhaled vape smoke again. "Uh uh. Most people suck in bed...or, at least, they aren't really amazing at it."

I nodded, but only as a way to respond. Then, a different thought crossed my mind. "So, do you know this girl, Sluttypixie?"

"Megan?"

"Yeah."

"That bitch is nuts," she said frankly.

"Yeah," I laughed nervously. "She is."

"Let me guess," Tink said. "She sent you a few messages and now she wants to bang you."

I was stunned. "Uh, sort of. I met her at the munch and she wanted to get together to play."

"Don't do it, Iggy."

"What? Why?" I already had a feeling that I wasn't going to like the answer.

"Because she's crazier than a bleached asshole."

"Yeah, I—"

"And she's a nymphomaniac."

That stopped me. "You mean she wants it all the

time?" It seemed an odd suggestion. Megan hadn't stayed to get more physical attention either time that she'd come over or tried to follow me home from the munch after our bathroom quickie.

"No," Tink said. "I mean, she is a clinical nymphomaniac. She can't be satisfied. She has a regular rotation of people that she sees and has sex with on most days, one right after the other."

I began to feel sick to my stomach. Tink continued.

"It's not at all unusual for her to screw three or four people in a day."

Megan's hasty exits after both of our encounters at my place were highlighted in my brain. I closed my eyes and silently punished myself for being so naive.

"Whatever you do, don't fuck her, Iggy. There's no telling what she has exposed herself to. And she doesn't care who gets emotionally hurt."

I sighed and hung my head.

"Shit," Tink mumbled. "You already did, didn't you?"

I nodded. "I was caught off guard. She came on so strong. She didn't really give me time to put the situation in perspective."

"Well...are you going to do it again?"

"Hell, no," I replied. "I don't want to be mixed up in a situation like that."

"Smart man."

I sighed again and then dismissed my frustrations. What was done was done, so there was no point in dwelling on my poor decision. I'd been smart enough to use protection. Best to just move on.

I decided to backtrack in the conversation. "You said that D.C. already had your respect by the time that you saw him dressed well. How did he earn it?"

She looked surprised, like it was a silly question. She

held a hand out and started listing things off on her fingers. "He was single. He had an interesting career—"

"Which is?" I asked automatically.

Tink wasn't put off. "He teaches creative writing at Clinton University."

"I see. Go on."

"He was attractive, smart, he was doing charity work just to be a good person and give back, he was kind, confident...hot..."

"Hot, huh?" I grinned.

"Dude, one day, while we were painting the homeless shelter, he took his shirt off and I almost went to the bushes to beat off."

I laughed.

"Seriously," she continued. "By the time he picked me up to go to dinner one night, looking all suave in his normal clothes, I was like, 'I'm going to bang this guy...tonight!'"

"You don't mind the age difference?"

"Older men are sexier," she told me.

"That a fetish for you?"

"That's a fetish for most women. Older men have their shit together more often than boys do. An attractive, older man who takes care of himself like my Sir does, especially with that salt and pepper thing he has going... Fuck! Forget it. Sex walking."

I made a mental note to start exercising more often before asking, "So, is he going to be upset with you for telling me what he does for a living?" Momma C.'s comment about he and Posie having a lot to lose professionally bounced around in my head.

"Only if you tattle on me," she said with a glare.

There was a sudden ding of a bell. Tink turned around to find my food waiting in the expo window, grabbed it and handed it to me before telling me that she needed to check on her other customers. I began to eat while wondering if "tattling" was something that my new community, not to mention, my new mentor, required of me.

CHAPTER TWELVE

Back at home, I decided my next step should be to actively look for a sub. My profile page declared my desire to fill that void, but D.C.'s words about being more assertive led me to scan the website for a group devoted to personals. I clicked on the icon for posting and pulled up a blank screen. The cursor blinked at the top and my hands hovered over the keys. Suddenly, my assertiveness was gone.

What do I say? What am I really looking for? What do I have to offer?

I began to feel stupid. Someone as inexperienced as me didn't seem to have any business soliciting the kink-savvy submissives of Clinton. I couldn't think of anything to whet their sexual or interpersonal appetites.

I was about to sack the whole idea when the chat bar on the bottom right of the screen popped up. It was a message from Momma C.

"Whatcha doin'?" it read.

I smirked at her English slaughtering text and replied, "Just trying to figure out why anyone would want me as a Dom."

"What do you mean?"

I sighed as I typed, explaining what I had been trying to do and why I was feeling inadequate.

"That's silly," she typed back. "You're attractive and kind. You're compassionate, too."

"Hardly Dom-like qualities."

"Don't be absurd. They're excellent qualities for a Dom—for anyone to have."

I considered her words, but didn't respond. She broke the radio silence from her end.

"What do you want? Honestly? Sincerely?"

I thought about it before telling her, "Really, I need someone to play with so that I can learn."

"Say that," she told me.

"Wouldn't that turn someone off?"

"Not necessarily. They may want the same."

Could I do that, nothing serious relationship-wise? I mean, I suppose if neither of us were screwing other people, I might be okay with it. Momma C. caught my attention with another message.

"Not all D/s relationships are sexual."

Intriguing. I realized that it was true. Mentors rarely slept with their protégés. Protectors—people who helped to provide a stop gap between new or more vulnerable people and those who might pose a potential threat—didn't always sleep with their charges. Even Momma C. said that her clothes stayed on when she had played with Benji.

She hit me again. "Just tell the truth. The worst thing you can do is to put up a front or be misleading. Don't sell yourself short, but tell the truth."

I smiled and typed back, "Thanks."

I clicked back onto the empty screen and took a deep breath.

Novice Dom seeks a sub to train with. I have a mentor. I am just looking for someone that I can practice, learn and grow with. Boundaries will be respected and negotiations will take place. No experience necessary.

My finger hovered over the "enter" button. Finally, I summoned the courage to hit it.

"Well," I said aloud, "I guess, now, we wait."

Four days went by and no responses to my ad surfaced. I was becoming disappointed and considering if I should reword my ad, or perhaps delete it altogether. Finally, on the fifth day, I came home from work, booted up my laptop and logged in to find a message in my in box. It was from a thirty-six year old woman just outside of Clinton, who was deeply interested in my ad.

Apparently, she'd had numerous problems with heavily experienced Doms who'd been condescending about the meager four months that she'd spent in the lifestyle. She'd decided to go the opposite direction, after seeing my ad, in the hopes that I might be more accommodating. The message ended with her asking if I wanted to meet for a drink and then talk about the possibility of setting up a play date.

Intriguing.

I clicked on her icon and went to her profile. Her profile photo was some painting of a fairy. It matched the name which was some Wiccan sounding fluff. I clicked on her photo folder and that's when I was immediately turned off. She was not pretty at all, sporting bad skin, sagging boobs, a bad haircut and way too many extra pounds. I groaned to myself.

But then I tried to check my attitude. After all, I wasn't necessarily looking for a girlfriend. Limiting my needs to someone to practice and learn with didn't rule her out.

And yet...she really was unappealing.

It turned out that, were I interested in that type, I'd have been inundated with submissives. The next four that contacted me all fit similar descriptions. Really big, unattractive and unkempt. When that wasn't the case, they were bored housewives looking for someone to help them cheat on their husbands. Also not appealing. One responder insisted that she should be the one to dominate me. Finally, however, I got a different response.

Daisy Darkheart, she called herself. And she was ideal. She was twenty-eight, lived two towns away, new to the lifestyle and she was adorable. She barely reached 5' 4" and weighed a whopping 113 lbs. She had curves in all the right places, a perfect c cup and a pretty, almost childlike, face. Her curly red hair was shoulder length and neatly groomed in all her photos and her fashion sense was casual, yet in good taste. There were no up close pics of her vagina or ass, which I considered a plus.

But the best part was her message.

"Hello...Sir? Is that right? Hell, I don't know. I'm new to this and these super-experienced people that keep hitting me up are intimidating, and occasionally very crude. When I saw your ad, I also saw a small ray of hope. You obviously don't think ridiculously highly of yourself and you want to learn. That's me. I became interested in the lifestyle in the most mundane of ways, through popular literature and seeing a couple of movies. However, after learning about the reality from a couple of websites—including this one—I decided that I wanted to explore a little deeper.

"Actually, I guess that's a little redundant. This is all about exploring fantasies, right?

"Anyway, I was wondering if we could chat. Would that be okay?"

I leaned back in my chair and felt a smile inch across my face. This one seemed like a real possibility.

I responded to Daisy, saying that I was pleased by her response. I then, at the advice of my mentor, suggested that we exchange a series of questions, some vanilla, some kinky. This worked well as I learned a lot about her and her interests in a remarkably short period of time. By the end of the week I had discovered that she liked animals a lot, worked at a cash advance place, loved science fiction and classic literature, hated shopping and doing laundry, watched lots of cooking shows and was originally from Boston. I also learned that she was interested in being spanked and, as she put it, "being treated like a princess by day and a whore in the bedroom." I found all of it to be right up my alley.

We continued sending emails back and forth and settled on a routine of two vanilla questions for every two kinky ones.

"What's your favorite book? What's your favorite music?" I asked followed by, "How do you feel about anal sex? What about role play?"

She answered back. "I'd have to say that the Handmaid's Tale is my favorite book. I also really enjoyed the Sleeping Beauty series for obvious reasons..." (reasons that I didn't comprehend, much less find obvious until my mentor later explained them). "As far as music goes, that's tough. Maybe The Doors, as well as Pink Floyd." She switched gears to more personal questions. "My asshole is exit only. Role play sounds fun, although I've never tried it. I guess, it would depend on what we were playing. Nothing too rape-y."

She then turned my questions back on me.

"I really dig both The Visible Man and Downtown Owl by Chuck Klosterman," I replied. "And I have a perverse addiction to Latin music. It just makes me happy. As far as anal sex goes, I've only tried it a couple of times. Once was unsuccessful and awkward. The other time was interesting. But I'm not attached to it, necessarily. I guess the naughty factor is what's most appealing. Role play is something that I'm inexperienced with, but highly curious about."

Then I had an interesting idea. In addition to more questions, I asked her to tell me one of her fantasies, one that might be translated into role play. She was accommodating.

"I have one recurring fantasy about meeting a stranger. I usually imagine that I have an abusive or unpleasant boyfriend, one that I want to get away from. While I'm on the run, he finds me and tries to drag me back home with him. He grabs me and starts to try to shove me into his car while I, only semi-successfully, resist. Another man witnesses it and intervenes. He knocks my boyfriend out and gives me a ride to a hotel in another town. He pays for my room and intends to leave, but I talk him into staying, telling him that I'm still afraid and don't want to be alone. He agrees, but promises to be a gentleman, to keep his hands to himself and to sleep on the floor.

Halfway through the night though, I decide that that isn't what I want. I call to him, still maybe only knowing his first name. He surprises me by being awake. I offer to let him share the bed and he agrees. I curl up next to him and he wraps his arms around me. Slowly, we start to kiss. He begins to move his hands all over my nightgown and to peel it off of me. He touches me everywhere, very sensually. Having been in such a bad relationship, it's the first good physical attention that I've had in a really long time. We begin to make love, the intensity of which increases until he's completely having his way with me and I surrender. After which, we fall asleep in each other's arms.

"When I wake up the next morning, he's gone. There's a little note next to the bed wishing me luck and saying that he enjoyed the night, but I never see him again."

Intriguing. I began to wonder at the prices of hotel rooms in Clinton.

Daisy then asked me to share one of mine. I was reluctant to confess that most of my recent ones had been about taking a woman forcefully after her "nothing too rape-y" comment, so I chose another.

"I think it might be intriguing to be a teacher or principal who has to discipline an unruly student," I told her. "Not that I have pedophile tendencies, understand. But there is something very tasty about a grown woman dressed like a teen and the power play involved. The authority over her, is something I find sexy. Maybe she has been truant repeatedly. I call her into my office and have a stern talk with her. Sometimes, I think it might be kind of fun if she is disrespectful while I'm scolding her or starts trying to give me a peak under her skirt to try and rattle me. I just respond by bending her over the desk and giving her a spanking. Maybe then, she confesses her true desire and I give her what she secretly wants, teacher's cock."

While I wondered if this was too much, I still sent it. She replied that she thought my description was both humorous and titillating at the same time.

This went on and on. I began to look forward to every email. She, in turn, told me that mine were the highlight of her day. After about a week and a half, I felt that it was time that we met face-to-face and told her so.

"What did you have in mind?" she asked.

I messaged D.C., asking what would be a good idea.

"Coffee," he insisted. "That way you'll be able maintain your faculties and you won't be dropping ninety-eight dollars on dinner and drinks only to find out that you aren't right for each other."

I took the suggestion and handed it off to her. She accepted and we made plans to meet at a place halfway between our two locations, one neither of us had ever been to, neutral ground.

I smiled. I couldn't wait.

That Saturday, I rose early and showered. As I did, I was filled with anticipation. I thought of the cute photo that Daisy had on her page and began imagining all of the wicked things that I could do to her, stripping her down, blindfolding her, tying her hands behind her back... I pondered running my fingertips all over her tiny form while she squirmed. I was already longing to try my new crop out on her bare bottom and I imagined her skin growing slightly red as I popped her with it a few times. I wondered what kinds of sounds she would make as I caressed her, struck her, went down on her... Would she moan? Whimper? Scream? Would she make any noise at all? Or would she be one of those women that was so entranced by the experience that all she could do was remain so silent that her heartbeat could almost be heard?

The next thing I knew, my hand was on my dick and I was gratifying myself while the warm water poured over me and thoughts of Daisy's submission urged me on. The two weeks I hadn't been allowed to do this had made me extra sensitive, like a regular drinker laying off of the booze for a bit, only to find that their tolerance had quickly gone down. When I came, mere minutes later, it was hard and with the picture of her bent over the kitchen table granting me the aggressive use of her pussy in my head.

I stood there, knees wobbly and breath heavy for a few seconds, my free hand on the shower wall, propping me up, before turning to let the water hit me in the face. I collected myself, turned off the shower and got out. After toweling off and shaving, I put on my best jeans and a clean, button up shirt, a black one. Finally, I picked up my phone and emailed Daisy.

"I'm headed there. See you at noon?"

I jumped in my car and hit the road, an excited, eager feeling in my heart and a nervous feeling in my stomach.

I arrived at the coffee shop that we'd agreed on, ordered an espresso and sat down. I checked my inbox, but found no reply. So, I waited.

After about forty-five minutes and countless checks of my inbox, I still hadn't heard from Daisy. I began to worry. Was she okay? Was she just not a punctual person? Had she decided to forget the whole thing? Was she actually sitting at the restaurant across the street watching me?

I messaged her. "Everything okay?"

Another ten minutes went by before my phone finally pinged. I eagerly scooped it up to check it and found her reply.

"I'm sorry. I can't do this. I'm totally freaked out. Maybe this isn't for me after all."

I stared at the response, reading it over and over and becoming disappointed and angry. It felt like a weird spell of double-double-toil-and-trouble was being stirred in me. Then I relaxed. I sent back the calmest message that I could.

"If it's not for you, then it's not for you."

That was the last exchange we had.

"That was such a huge waste of time," I told D.C. during our next session. "Two weeks and eighty-seven emails back and forth."

"It happens, I'm sad to say." He shook his head. "People—women especially—think this sort of thing is so fascinating until they are faced with actually having to try it."

"Did it ever happen to you?" I asked.

"Oh, yeah. A few times, especially when Tink and I were looking for Posie." He sighed and smiled. "You can't let it get you down. The only thing worse than wasting your time looking is wasting your time having."

I was still aggravated, but nodded.

"Okay, look," he said. "Let's see what all you have learned from the study material I sent you."

"You mean like a quiz?" I asked, remembering that he was a teacher.

"Basically. BDSM stands for what?"

That was pathetically easy. I sighed and replied, "Bondage and Discipline, Dominance and Submission, Sadomasochism."

"What is subdrop?"

"When a submissive, usually after a scene, crashes from the adrenaline rush. It can cause depression, chills, sickness and many other negative reactions, including suicidal thoughts."

"How do you counter it?"

"Aftercare, the definition of which varies from sub to

sub."

"What are some basic methods?"

"Keep them warm, hydrated and hold them. Say nice things, cuddle with them and talk them down."

"Good. What's a DM?"

"Dungeon Monitor. It's usually someone who has some safety and medical training who is present during events and scenes in the event that participants are careless or something goes wrong. Kind of like a referee and EMT rolled up in one."

"Interesting analogy," he said with a nod. "Alright, safety. What are some basic tools to employ and things to remember?"

"Safe words, negotiations, safe calls—meaning, calling a kink minded friend at a set time after playing with someone new, to let them know that you're safe and the new person hasn't killed you or locked you up against your will... First aid kits that include things like bandage scissors... Never play with people you don't know or don't trust... Never engage in play that you have not learned about first."

"What would be an example?"

"Don't tie someone up or engage in breath play with someone if you haven't learned how."

"Good." He began to pace. "Etiquette. What are the basics at a public gathering?"

This one was a little harder, more subjective. "Basically mind your manners, respect other people and their space, never assume anything and don't judge."

"And some examples of protocol?"

"Well, the main things that I've noticed are never to touch or talk to someone without permission or invitation. Also, address people however they prefer, be it by a kink name or gender specific pronoun or title."

"So, if someone insists you call them, Master?"

I paused. "That's a bit tricky," I admitted. "I mean, if I'm not someone's submissive, do I have to do that?"

"You do not," he informed me. "In fact, if someone insisted that I and everyone called them by such a title without being their sub, I would automatically think of that person as being a dim dom."

"A what??"

"Just what it sounds like, an idiot who doesn't deserve respect and tries to demand it."

"I see." I suddenly remembered Mistress Xina's disapproving glare aimed at Tinkerbrat when she called her by her proper name. "So, if Mistress Xina insists that your girls have to—"

He saw where I was headed and immediately broke in. "My girls have to call her, Mistress. But that's because *I* told them to, not Xina. They have to address any Dominant that I respect buy their community title or with a 'Mr.' or 'Ms.' in front of that person's name. Just like you're, 'Mr. Iggy', now."

I was flattered. "So, does that mean you respect me?"

He smirked. "Enough to teach you. We'll see about the rest."

I grinned back before joking, "And what if I want them to call me, Master Iggy?"

"Become one and we'll talk."

I nodded. "And how would I do that?"

"By learning and gaining experience. It's not, ideally, a title you just claim. More properly, it's awarded you by your community when they recognize that you deserve it. From my perspective...I occasionally have a tough time respecting Masters or Mistresses who never spent time as a sub or slave, but I can be kind of a hard ass about some things."

"Did you ever live as a sub or slave?" I asked with sudden curiosity.

"I did my time," was all he said.

"Who did you submit yourself to?"

He smiled and shook his head. "Some other time. For now, suffice it to say, it was for about a year and it was a woman. She's not in the Clinton community."

"Okay. So, why aren't you, 'Master Dramatic Comedy'?"

His smile grew a little more pronounced and he shrugged. "Because I don't want to be. I like being, 'Sir'."

There was a pause. Neither of us spoke for a while and finally he sighed. "I'm sorry your new sub didn't work out."

"It's okay," I shrugged. "Obviously, it just wasn't meant to be."

"Most likely not." He sat and invited me to do the same. "Maybe you just need to flesh out your bio a little more. You're not as inexperienced as you were when you first wrote it...or your classified, for that matter."

I offered him an appreciative smile.

"You have any questions?" he asked.

"Why won't you tell me about your submissive experience?"

"I meant about our training session." I didn't respond. He smiled and shook his head. "It's..." He paused again. "Okay, look... That was something that I did purely because I thought that I had to, in order to learn. I didn't actually find much fascination with it. Or rather, I didn't to begin with and I certainly didn't with her. She was knowledgeable and she was attractive, but she didn't fulfill me in that way. It *was* sexually exciting at times and did teach me a lot. But mostly, it was just like a hard, exhausting crash course from the opposite end. And her limits were different from mine."

"In what way?"

"Shit," he said as his smile vanished. "You think I'm tough on my girls? One of the reasons that I let them get away with so much crap and be so familiar with me and others is because of Ruby. She was the definition of a totalitarian."

"Was that your Domme's name?"

He nodded. "Yeah, Mistress Ruby was very Old Guard."

"What does that mean?"

He scratched his head and scowled as he thought. "Well, 'Old Guard' mostly just refers to the gay biker BDSM scene that emerged after World War 2, but—"

"Wait," I broke in. "There was a gay—"

"Kelly," he said, stopping me immediately with the familiarity of my Christian name. "If we're going to get through this story, you can't be stopping me tons of time to ask for clarification."

I pressed my lips together in a slightly embarrassed, yet understanding smile and nodded. "Sorry. Continue."

"The Old Guard, being from a strict military background had, and often still have, very tight rules and regulations governing their behavior. Their etiquette and protocol make ours look like the dress code at Burning Man. There was also a straight culture that evolved that had very tight codes of conduct. Again, many of those participants were ex-military. Ruby was a former Sergeant in the army and she did not screw around. Honestly, if she saw me let my girls get away with their familiar tones and lackadaisical attitudes—especially Tink—she'd probably try and reclaim me for a refresher course."

"Why do you?"

He sighed and his smile returned. "I'd never tell Tink this—and if you repeat it, I'll deny it—but...I kind of like her the way she is. It's challenging and kind of adorable in an obnoxious sort of way. It also gives me a lot of excuses to do horrible things to her from time to time." He amended his statement. "Though, I must admit, that's not *always* fun, not when she really screws up."

"What about Posie?"

"Posie, too," he nodded. "Ruby never would have allowed me to smirk when she was talking or make snide comments like Pos did in reference to my wanting to help name the Scene Shop or be on the board. She'd have beaten the shit out of me if I pulled stuff like that."

"So..." I considered what he was saying, "You're more lenient, then?"

"Believe it or not, yeah. Ruby did teach me about discipline though. She helped me learn to keep things, myself and my house, in order. She helped me grow. Before Ruby, I was kind of aimless and irresponsible...self-destructive, even."

"Really?" I asked, somewhat surprised.

He nodded. "Oh, yeah. It was because of her that I finally got my graduate degree and found my current profession. Had I not learned discipline that may not have happened."

I thought for a bit and suddenly heard myself say, "Teaching?"

He looked stunned and mildly irritated.

"Tink told me," I confessed. "Don't be too hard on her. We were having a serious conversation where she helped me a lot and I know how to keep a secret."

"Clearly not," he pointed out.

I smirked and shrugged. "I won't repeat it again.

Please go easy on her."

He grunted and smirked himself. "Obviously, I'm too easy on her already." He shook his head and chuckled. "That little bitch. What am I going to do with her?"

"Hey, at least she didn't tell just anybody."

We looked at each other, both smiling, me hopefully and him reassuringly. Finally, he said, "No. I guess not."

CHAPTER THIRTEEN

After rewriting my profile and redesigning my personal ad, things did pick up some. Suddenly, I was getting responses from more experienced people. Not many, but some.

I responded, with interest, to a couple only to quickly discover that we were looking for slightly different things or we were inconveniently far away from each other. There was one however, that really caught my attention.

She called herself Attendant Available and had been active in the lifestyle for around nine months. More than anything, she told me, she wanted to be objectified.

"It's kind of weird, since I'm a hardcore feminist and all. But then, maybe that's why it's a turn on. I get to relinquish control and responsibility, forget my worries. I also get to experience total degradation, all the while knowing that it's not real, like playing out a rape fantasy. I'm certain that there is no one, anywhere, who wants to actually be sexually assaulted. However, it's a wide held fantasy and I happen to have it myself."

The process of getting to know a new person began again. Only this time, her responses were far more friendly and optimistic than Daisy's. When I asked her sexual orientation, she stated emphatically that she liked men and women equally. She was open to threesomes even. But she was looking to be "owned" by one person, someone who knew how to treat her like a princess half the time and like a "slut-slave" the rest of the time. She liked being tied up, beaten and used.

"Used," she stated again. "That's really it. When sex comes down to me being treated like just something to fuck, I really like that."

Her vanilla interests were few. She said she had little time to indulge in movies or cycling or hiking at the present because she worked two table waiting jobs, approximately seventy-five hours a week in an attempt to pay off her student loans and survive at the same time. Even with two roommates, the loans—acquired while working on a degree in political science—ate up most of her money.

"Loans. Yeah," I replied. "I still have some of that to get out from under myself." I explained that I was getting closer due to my new job.

We talked about work. We talked about our degrees. We talked about leisure. And we talked a lot about sex. Even through the mundane parts of it, she held my attention with a confident and comfortable tone in her words.

"You know, I learned in college to be responsible," she said. "I learned to avoid the parties and chaos after a while because I wanted more from life. I discovered that watching people dishevel, covering for them in class and covering for them at work made me want to kick puppies. I needed to move forward and find what gets life done. I learned that I am a good, strong person and that I need to gain from that...before I abduct a teenage, reality TV star and kill them while recording it and the hastily dug, shallow grave I put them in on my cellphone. I need to be an adult and a person who makes something of themselves."

I leaned back from my computer, my fingers covering my smirk. She was really amusing.

Finally, I realized that I didn't even know what she

looked like. I had been so caught up in her banter that I had forgotten to ask. She hadn't asked me either. When I did, she agreed and I got the surprise of my life attached in an email.

Jenny, as I finally came to know her, was a knock out.

She had dark, curly, brunette hair, highlighted with reddish-brown, in all of the photos that she sent me. One had her sitting in a restaurant laughing. One was a selfie in a bathroom, fully clothed in a white, v-neck sweater and black jeans, standing confidently before the mirror, hand on a cocked hip. One was even of her on the beach. Her smile was dazzling and the photo of her sunbathing had her in a string bikini, showing off an emasculate body, slender, yet with luscious curves and a round bottom designed for spanking.

Jenny was gorgeous.

I leaned back from the computer screen with my mouth hanging open. I was entranced. Then it occurred to me that I was expected to send one or more back. How in the hell do I make myself look qualified for such a total beauty?

I thought long and hard. Finally, I messaged my mentor asking him what to do.

There wasn't much of a wait.

"Just take a fucking picture of yourself wearing something besides those stupid ass, fucking cargo shorts and looking happy and you'll be fine, Iggy," was all he said.

I grimaced at the text. Then my phone pinged again. D.C. rephrased his advice. "Seriously though, just send her a friendly picture where you're dressed nice and giving her the look that you want to give her if she just walked in the room. Be nice."

Dress well. Be nice.

Yeah. Okay, that made some sense. Certainly more than pointing my phone towards the bathroom mirror while I stood there shirtless.

I looked long and hard at my wardrobe. I finally just picked out a nice, long sleeved, button up shirt, put it on, combed my hair and pointed my phone at myself. I clicked.

I looked at it and had two thoughts. *Yeah, that's me...looking like I didn't just get home from work.*

The other was, *Yeah...that's you...trying hard to look like you didn't just get home from work.*

I stared. Then I just told myself, to hell with it, and sent it. Minutes later, I got a reply.

"Ohh. You're cute!" it said.

I'm...cute?

I smirked and probably blushed.

Wait. I'm "cute?" I'm not handsome or sexy or... I'm "cute."

I suddenly got another email. "I was a little anxious," it said. "Now, I know I'm lucky."

My mouth dropped again. Cool. A super-hot girl thinks I'm cute. That's awesome, right?

I sat next to the server at City Hall, hacked in with my laptop, troubleshooting their problems. At one point I was looking through a database connected to Jack Pierce's computer. As I scanned through various pages, one memo caught my eye. I wasn't actually reading all of the information, but the words, "sex club," were kind of hard to miss in a municipal letter, even scrolling passed it really quickly.

I stopped. I looked around to make sure no one else

was nearby or in the hallway. I then backtracked to have a little to peek at the information.

Apparently, there was a strange sex club, possibly conducting illegal, and certainly unwholesome, activities at the same address that the Scene Shop was located at. Jack Pierce had discovered this and planned to make it a public issue, sometime in the coming months, due to the fact that there were tentative plans to build an elementary school on the same block.

I stared at the information. It was clearly not good for every one of my friends and plenty of people that I had yet to meet. That's when I was startled by the sounds of people passing in the hallway and clicked off of the memo. I returned to scrolling through the database, looking for problems, or perhaps just pretending to.

What was I going to do? Should I warn someone? I mean, it could put my job at risk. Of course, it could, as my mentor had explained, potentially put many others' at risk if I didn't.

This was one that I was going to have to think about.

CHAPTER FOURTEEN

As I sat in the back room of the King's Kettle, greeting people who entered and passively cruising the internet on my phone, I did my best to remain calm. Jenny had said that she was coming straight from work and that she would, most likely, be there right at seven. That didn't keep me from looking up every time someone entered.

At one point, D.C., Tink and Posie entered with Cat who was telling some amusing antidote about a conference that she'd just gotten back from.

"I swear, the next 'professional' I meet in my field who criticizes sex and extolls Jesus Christ may get prescribed some medication by me," she bitched.

"You can prescribe medication?" Tink asked, seeming almost interested in it herself.

"No," Cat replied frankly. "But I may do it anyway."

The group saw me and I smiled at them. I had done my best to save a few seats and waved them over. I wanted their opinion of Attendant Available when she arrived.

Attendant Available. We'd have to do something about that name if I took her on.

"'Sup?" Tink said as she and the rest of our house and Cat sat across from me.

"Excuse you," her Sir said to her a little harshly.

Tink pressed her lips together, appearing as though she were struggling to suppress frustration. She then addressed me again, sounding only slightly less casual.

"Hello, Mr. Iggy. How are you?"

"Jeez," D.C. remarked. "Don't exhaust yourself or anything." He turned to me and sighed. "Please forgive my disrespectful little tart, here. She left her manners at home. How are you this week?"

I chuckled. "I'm okay." I thought about my response and then amended it. "A little nervous." D.C. smiled knowingly.

"Whatcha nervous about?" Cathy asked.

"I'm...meeting a potential sub tonight."

"Is that right?" she beamed. "That's exciting."

"Yeah." I felt myself begin to sweat a little.

"May I ask who it is?" Posie queried.

"Uh," I chuckled uncomfortably. "She calls herself Attendant Available. She's relatively new." I pulled up the photos Jenny had sent me on my phone and showed them to my friends.

"Damn," Tink said. "She's hot. If it works out, can I borrow her?"

D.C. and Posie both shot sideways glances at her.

"Kidding," she assured them. "Totally kidding."

"Uh huh," her Dom replied. He looked back at me. "She *is* very attractive. Did you two make contact the same way as the last one?"

"Yeah."

"How was that?" Tink asked.

I felt as though I might blush. "Well...actually, I put up an ad for a sub and she answered it." My admission made me feel desperate.

Cathy seemed to pick up on my shame. "Nothing wrong with that," she assured me. "How do you think I met Scott?"

I pursed my lips and nodded. "That makes me feel a little better. I'm still nervous though."

D.C. gave me a reassuring smile. "Part of being a confident Dom is acting the part," he informed me. "When she comes in, stand up, button your jacket and take her hand..." He reached out for mine with his thumb squarely on top. He placed his free hand on top of both of ours. "Like this. Don't let go right away, don't break eye contact and smile. Not too big, but smile."

"And don't forget to unbutton your coat again before sitting back down," Cathy added.

"Yes," D.C. agreed. "That too."

Before anything else could be said of the subject, Greta approached and hugged Cat from behind. "Hey, Momma C.," she said.

"Hey, kiddo. How's your week been?"

"Great! Sir, gave me a massive caning the other day." She peeled the top of her pants down, exposing large, dark black and green bruises.

"Holy shit!" I heard myself exclaim. This elicited chuckles from Posie and Tink. "AmericanDom did that to you?"

"Yeah," she grinned. "Then he made me choke on his cock."

I scowled. A sick feeling formed in my stomach. *How could she do this to her husband?* I wondered. *Doesn't he care?* I shook my head and looked over at D.C. who shrugged.

Greta showed off a couple more marks he'd left on her while trying to sit next to me. Before I could say anything, Tink intervened.

"We're saving that seat."

"Really?"

"Yeah. Mr. Iggy's got someone coming and we need it."

"Okay," Greta said with resign. She excused herself

and went to the other end of the table where she proudly showed her extramarital abuse to other people.

The second she was gone, Tink spoke up again. "I hate her. She is *so* irritating."

"Tink..." D.C. cautioned.

"She gets on my nerves, too," I agreed.

"What's your problem with her?" Tink asked.

I shrugged. "I guess I'm just not enlightened enough to condone adultery."

D.C. shook his head at me. "It's not really adultery if the relationship is open."

"If you say so," I replied. "I just figure that if you can't get what you want at home, you need to move on, break the relationship off and go be with the person you really want."

Cat spoke up. "But she loves her husband. They just aren't sexually compatible."

"I guess. I just have this image in my head of him sitting at home, depressed, while she's out fucking other guys who don't have the decency to leave other people's wives alone."

"Maybe he's a cuckold," Tink offered semi-sarcastically.

"What's that?" I asked.

"Maybe he likes to feel emasculated," she clarified.

"Why?" I was even more mortified.

Everyone on the other side of the table grinned at my naive disgust. Finally, my mentor shrugged again. "It's their life," he said. "And, just out of curiosity, why don't you have an issue with me and the girls all being together? I mean, is it because I'm a man and they're women?"

I glanced at all of them, including Momma C., who was giving me a look that said that she was even more interested in my answer.

"No," I said. "I don't think so. I think, it's because you're all in a relationship together."

"So then," Momma C. said, "if her husband was also here showing off his bruises, that would be okay?"

I clinched my jaw a bit as I struggled to form an answer, knowing full well that I didn't actually have one. However, before I could concoct a response, I caught a glimpse of the munch guest that I had been waiting on entering the room. I pushed my confusion and nervousness aside. "Showtime," I said.

I did as advised. I stood, buttoned my coat and caught her attention with a hand held up. She saw me and smiled, big.

Okay. That's a good sign, I thought.

She was dressed in a white oxford and black slacks. They seemed a tad dirty, indicating her quick exodus from her table waiting job. Her hair was in a ponytail. She walked eagerly around the table and presented herself with a hand out.

"Hey," she said brightly, yet with a mild tone of nervousness.

I did as instructed, taking her hand in both of mine. "It's a pleasure to meet you in person," I said. I then surprised myself by having the common sense to ask, "What should I tell everyone to call you?"

She cocked her head and looked a little impressed at my discretion before saying, "Jenny is fine."

"Okay, Jenny," I motioned to the chair that I had saved and pulled it out for her to sit.

She thanked me while apologizing. "I'm so sorry that I look like something pulled from a dumpster. I just got off of work and I'm...nasty."

"Nothing wrong with that," D.C. grinned.

I cleared my throat and my mentor opened his mouth but, said nothing. He smirked and held his hand up in acknowledgment of his Freudian slip, before apologizing. I sat, feeling a tug across my mid-section from where I'd forgotten to unbutton my jacket.

Shit.

I tried to be nonchalant as I corrected the problem, while introducing everyone across from me. Each of them greeted her happily and I noticed that she didn't offer her hand to anyone, especially the subs. She then turned her attention to me.

"You look nice," she said.

"Thank you," I replied, both flattered and proud. My tone was sincere as I said, "You actually do as well."

She blushed. "No, I don't," she insisted with a grin. "I look disgusting."

"You do not," I told her seriously and with a smile.

"I do."

"You do not and you will stop saying such nonsense right now," I instructed her with kind firmness. "You just got off of work and you're a little dirty, but you look great. Now, take a compliment when it's given." I smiled.

She smiled in return and nodded in a nervous, flattered state. She then admitted that her long day and long drive had resulted in the need for a bathroom trip. She asked where it was.

"It's by the front door," I pointed. "Can I order you a drink while you're in there?"

"Um, yeah. Heineken?" she returned cautiously, almost like she was afraid she might be asking too much.

"Done."

We continued to smile at each other and I stood as she exited. Once she was gone, I sat back down. I looked over at my neighbors, all of whom wore big grins.

"What?" I asked.

Tink replied, "You two are *so* adorable." She sounded mildly sarcastic.

"Yeah, yeah," I said. "Do me a favor and go fuck yourself, Tink." Everyone, including her, chuckled.

She then turned to her Dom. "Are you going to let him talk to me like that?"

D.C. looked upwards as he considered the question, or maybe just pretended to. "Um...yes," he finally said. Cathy and Posie laughed.

"She is very pretty," Poise said. "How old is she?"

"Twenty five...I think."

"You should watch out for the young ones," D.C. joked. "They're very immature."

"Oh, shut up, dirty old man," Tinkerbrat returned. Her Dom reached over and twisted her nipple hard, yet still smiled. "Ow! Shit!" his sub exclaimed. She then acted like she might slap him. He sat there with a look that dared her to. She gritted her teeth before slumping in her chair with an expression that merged her grin with a pout. "Damn it," she muttered.

"I'm not immature, am I?" Poise asked, sounding almost sincere.

"No, baby girl," D.C. said as he put his arm around her. "Except when you poop your pants."

Momma C. and Tink laughed while Posie protested. "I don't—"

"I'm kidding," her Dom assured her, a hand on the back of her neck and a kiss to the side of her head.

I decided to join the ribbing again. "Based on the night we met, as well as our conversation during my first training session, you do seem to have some trouble keeping your hands out of your pants."

She blushed, but also smirked as she told me, "Fuck

you, Mr. Iggy."

"Yeah," Tink agreed with a loud jeer and a middle finger jabbed my way.

D.C. chuckled, but said, "Alright, girls. Behave."

I grinned. "It's okay. I'm glad you guys are all here."

At that point, Jenny returned. She sat down next to me and asked how I had been. Before I could respond however, Mistress Xina commandeered the floor.

"Alright, everyone. Let's do introductions while we have a moment."

We went around the room and stated our names—or what we chose to be called—and how we identified. Having Jenny next to me as I stated that I was a Dom helped me to feel more natural in the expression, as did the presence of my mentor and his house. Jenny went next.

"Hi," she began. "I'm Attendant Available..." She looked at me. "...Or maybe not." She smiled. "I'm a submissive. I usually go to the munches in Fairview, but I had reason to come and check out yours."

I could feel my pride swell, that is, until I saw Tink's shit-eating grin. Then, for whatever reason, I became embarrassed.

The introductions continued to inch around the table until they reached a new guy. He was around forty, tall, very tan, with blond, graying hair and wore a light green polo shirt. There was a smarmy-ness about him, even as he praised us all.

"Hey," he said. "I'm Rick, Natural Defiance on the website. And, I got to say, this seems like a great group. You're all so obviously tight knit. I think it's amazing. So many nice people and so many pretty girls."

You could feel the entire room squirm and internally groan.

"I'm sort of feeling my way through this and I welcome all the help that I can get."

"Not likely," Tink mumbled.

"Right?" Jenny agreed. "I need a shower even more, now. Maybe a Silkwood one."

After a bit, everyone had introduced themselves and Mistress Xina commandeered the floor again. "Okay, everyone. I hope we have a good munch and let's all remember to be respectful." She didn't look at Natural Defiance, but we all, secretly, knew who she was stressing this too. As everyone began to socialize again, I noticed out of the corner of one eye that she sat near him and seemed to be observing his behavior and comments to other guests. I then noticed out of my other eye, Jenny looking at me and smiling. I looked over and felt myself return the good cheer.

"So," she began, "you said that you were a member of a house with these other people?"

"Yeah," I confirmed. "D.C. was kind enough to take me on as a protégé and his girls are also helping me learn."

"How's that going?"

I glanced over at my mentor who gave a supportive nod. "He's coming along very well," he told her. "He learns fast and seems to have a good understanding of everything...." He then added, "If you don't count the fact that he's still struggling with his gender issues and inner sissy-boy."

I gave him a frustrated, barely amused look. "Really? You're going to mess with me right now?"

He let out a quick chortle. "I don't know who's more surprised, you at my teasing or me in response to that question." He then turned to Jenny. "He's a good guy, actually. He's got a lot to learn, but he's a genuinely decent person. He's smart and he's sincere. You could do a hell of a lot worse."

She looked at me and beamed. I felt almost embarrassed at his compliment and rewarded it by telling him, "Jeez, don't exhaust yourself or anything." He and Tink both laughed.

"I have a good feeling about him so far," Jenny said as she kept her gaze on me. "At the very least, I'm reassured that he's not a poser or abusive."

"Speaking of which..." Posie murmured as she glanced down at Natural Defiance who was trying to force his way into a conversation with Greta who was without her Sir.

"Well," I said, "at least he found one of the people who isn't afraid to bang someone she isn't already attached to."

"Iggy..." D.C. and Momma C. both lightly scolded me.

"You're right. You're right," I said in surrender. "It's none of my business."

"What isn't?" Jenny asked.

I shook my head and waved a dismissive hand. "Let's talk about you. How was work?"

"Oh, Jesus," she laughed. "I don't want to talk about work. I want to learn about all of you." She focused her eyes my direction. "Especially you."

"Oh, you already know a good bit about me," I assured her. "The main thing that you don't know is what I'm like around these assholes." I pointed at my table mates.

"That's true," D.C. nodded.

"Yes," Momma C. agreed. "We are assholes."

Jenny laughed. "I don't believe that."

Tink pointed at her Sir. "He's an asshole," she said

with certainty.

Posie covered her mouth to conceal her shocked laugh.

D.C. spoke up. "An asshole who's about to start taking some privileges away."

"Kidding," Tink assured him. "I was kidding...again. That's what we're doing here, right?"

Her Sir laughed. He then looked at me and winked.

"So, uh, Jenny," I said, "what are the Fairview munches like?"

"Pretty much like this. Except we don't do introductions and our leader is a fifty year old, gay sub who speaks like a church mouse."

We all laughed and that's when the server came in. The whole room changed. Everyone seemed to sit a little straighter and talk a bit more politely. And, of course, no one mentioned kinky sex. No one except...the new guy.

"I was considering getting a steak," he told the server. "I'm just curious. Is that stuff tenderized, cause I like my meat beaten real good." He chuckled.

Several throats near him cleared noisily and he seemed to get the picture just a bit as he toned it down and simply requested his meal.

"Fuck," Jenny whispered. "That guy's head is so far up his own ass he's about to disappear. Does this happen often?"

"Less than you might fear. More than we need," Momma C. replied.

For a while after that, things were relatively calm. We placed our orders. We talked casually. We all received our food and ate.

Finally, Jenny nudged me. "Hey," she said. "I'm having fun."

I smiled back. "Good."

"So..." she shifted her shoulders back and forth nervously, "where do we go from here? I mean, what do we do and how do we proceed?"

I looked to my mentor.

"Why don't the two of you come to my place this weekend?" He looked at Jenny. "That is, if you're able." She nodded and he continued. "We'll put the two of you through a training exercise and you can both go from there. Until then, you can just have coffee and talk as much as possible." He smiled reassuringly.

"Cool," Jenny beamed.

"Yeah," I agreed. "I'm okay with that."

My mentor spoke up again. "Jenny, Ignite and I will meet you at the coffee shop at the end of this block whenever you're available."

"I'm off Sunday after three."

"Good," he continued. "We'll take you back to my place—my and the girls' place—and we'll see how the two of you interact with each other. As I said, we'll go through some training and the two of you can bond a little. Sound good?"

"Sounds great," she smiled. "Are you guys going to gangbang me?" she seemed to joke.

Before D.C. or I could answer, Tink asked him, "Can we?" He and Posie shot her irritated, yet tolerant glances again. "Kidding, remember? God! You guys are so serious."

Posie actually spoke up. "Um hm."

"You will not treat Mr. Iggy's potential new sub like a bowl of chocolates on someone's coffee table," D.C. informed her.

"Oh... That's too bad," Jenny smirked.

I immediately wondered if she was sincere about the idea of being ganged up on until I saw her eyes focused on the other end of the table. There, Natural Defiance was trying hard to make the rounds next to everyone female that wasn't very large or over sixty. Regular munch attendants were shifting seats to keep him away from the girls.

Jenny scowled. "It's like watching a cat approach a fishbowl...with its dick in its hand."

I laughed briefly. I knew it was a terrible situation, but she was funny.

I grabbed her attention. "So," I said, "you're okay with me learning with you as an educational aid?"

"Yeah. It sounds fun actually."

"He's not a dumbass," my mentor broke in. "He does know some things. So, you should be able to get something out of it and have some fun."

I knew this was close to bullshit. I also understood that D.C. was trying to reassure her and also make me sound like a valid Dom. I appreciated it.

Jenny smiled. "I can't wait." Her expression changed. "But..."

"But?" I asked.

"I do need to go to the little girls' room again. Will you excuse me?"

I smiled. "Of course."

"I'm coming with you," Momma C. chimed.

"I need to as well," Posie said before looking to her Sir for a nod of allowance.

Jenny got up and I watched her walk.

"She seems like a good one," my mentor smiled.

"Yeah," I said while still watching her ass move back and forth as she walked away. "I wonder what she looks like tired to a chair with her panties shoved in her mouth and tears running down her cheeks."

He laughed. "Sick mother fucker," he mumbled.

"You're one to talk."

He continued to chuckle while nodding.

While Tink went outside to vape and the other ladies made their bathroom visit, I saw an opportunity to let my mentor in on the touchy information I had learned.

"Hey," I began, "while we got a second, there's something you should know."

"What's that?"

"I learned something at work, something that could affect all of us."

"In what way?"

I sighed and gave him a serious look. "My job has me working at City Hall a lot at the moment. The other day, I saw a memo that the City Planner sent out about a sex club on Truman that he wanted to out. Apparently, they want to build an elementary school across the street."

The look on his face became very serious. "What did this memo say?"

"Just that he was aware of the Scene Shop. He doesn't fully know what it is. But he hopes to make its presence public."

D.C. was silent for a bit. Finally, he said, "Find out what you can and let me know."

"Ah..." I began with trepidation. "That isn't exactly easy. I can't just dig for information. I could lose my job. Plus, access to it or not, it's not legal. It'd be like a maid who was charged with cleaning your office, including the desk, stealing a file from it."

"But if you see something—"

"If I see something, I'll tell you. For right now, I just wanted to give you a heads up. Really, that's all I can do."

He thought and then nodded. "Okay. Thank you."

Suddenly, all of our female friends came back. As

Jenny sat down, she took my hand in hers for a brief second. For whatever reason, it seemed more intimate than anything else that I had done with a woman in a long time. Maybe it was because it was affectionate. Maybe it was her adoring smile.

"This place is nice," she said. "In Fairview we all just crowd into the corner of the restaurant. We don't have a room to ourselves."

"Well, we're not actually supposed to be able to use this room," I joked. "But the restaurant thinks we're witches, and so, they're afraid of us."

She tittered. "They should be afraid of us though, right?"

"Well," I replied, smiling myself and squeezing her hand, "we're definitely some strange people." She giggled again. There was silence after that as we both just beamed at each other like school kids.

It was nice.

Then it wasn't. That's because Natural Defiance walked to our end of the table. "Hey," he said. "Who do we have down here?"

"Keep moving," my mentor said casually. Tink and Posie both scooted closer to him and he put an arm around each of them.

"What?" the man chuckled. "You just gonna hog all the pretty girls for yourself, dude. I mean—"

"He's right," I asserted. "You're kind of making everybody a little uncomfortable."

"Hey," he said in a not unfriendly tone. "I'm just trying to be social. I mean—"

"Okay, Rick," Mistress Xina said as she walked up and crossed her arms. "You're done."

"What do you mean?" the man asked.

"This is not for you," she assured him. "Trust me."

"Look, I'm not trying to cause problems. I just want to mingle. I was told to come to this meeting by someone called SeptemberSnowGirl and—"

"Of course you were," Xina said with a sudden and obvious loss of patience. "She's banned too, now. Please leave and don't come back."

The two of them looked at each other for a while. Rick seemed genuinely confused, but eventually threw his hands up and left in frustration.

While it was clear that each of us were glad to be rid of him, D.C. did offer his opinion of Mistress Xina's final judgment.

"Xina, you can't banish SnowGirl for—"

"I just did," she insisted. "This is the fifth or sixth time this has happened. I won't tolerate it anymore. She's done."

"Xina," Momma C. broke in. "Eleanor has also sent other people our way, good people. She sent Iggy to us and he—"

"Irrelevant." The Mistress directed her attention to me. "I'm sorry, Ignite, but it is." She spoke to the group again. "Eleanor is gone." She walked off to the other side of the room to assure everyone that she had handled the Natural Defiance problem.

"That seemed extreme," Momma C. said.

"Well, yeah," D.C. grumbled. "But honestly, Cat...SnowGirl does this. She isn't careful. She tends to assume the best in everybody and that isn't always the case. We have to be cautious."

Momma C. sighed hard and shook her head. "Maybe...but..." She was silent for a few seconds. "I don't know. Mistress Xina shouldn't be able to tell one of our regular, real community members that they can't come around. Not unless they genuinely endanger people."

"You said it yourself," I offered. "SeptemberSnowGirl doesn't come around much as it is. Maybe it won't affect her a great deal." I glanced over at my mentor, trying to back him up, while simultaneously feeling a little guilty. It was true. I might not be there were it not for SnowGirl.

"Um..." Jenny finally said. "Why don't we all change the subject? Would that be helpful?"

Everyone seemed to shake off the whole experience and get back to socializing as comfortably as they were able.

After the munch, Jenny and I stuck around, commandeering a table next to the bar and ordered espresso. "This was all very fascinating," she said. "The Fairview munches don't have this much excitement."

"Yeah, well," I began, "I'd like to apologize for some of that excitement. The whole Natural Defiance, banning stuff was pretty weird."

"It's not your fault."

"I know. But allow me to apologize on behalf of my community. We like to avoid true craziness when we can."

"Think nothing of it." She kept beaming at me, even as a look of curiosity crossed her face.

"What?" I asked.

She shook her head. "I was just wondering why you haven't tried to touch me yet. Other guys I've met with would have put their hands on my legs or crotch under the table or at least put an arm around me or something."

"I just met you," I pointed out.

"Yeah. Still, in this lifestyle, a lot of people think they

can just charge into physical stuff, I've noticed."

"Me too," I said, remembering my experiences with Sluttypixie. "I don't know if that's healthy or not and I certainly don't consider it safe. You have to gain each other's trust first, prove yourselves. Plus, there are things like stds to consider."

"True. When's the last time you got tested?"

"A couple of months ago, right after making a very poor decision that involved me moving too fast with someone," I confessed.

"I take it everything turned out alright?"

"Yeah. I got lucky. But I also used protection."

"Ugh. I hate condoms," she said, causing some concern on my part. "I get regular tests though, usually right when I meet someone who seems promising."

"When was your last one?"

She smiled again. "A week ago. My results come in tomorrow or the next day."

Her flattery was touching. "So," I said, "you like to be used."

"I want to be with someone who will tie me up, rough me up and take advantage of my...openness." The suggestiveness in her response was intense.

"Really?"

"Really."

"All of it?"

"*All* of it. I just want to be a thing, a...toy, used horribly, but not cast aside."

We stared into each other's eyes, the sexual tension building at an alarming rate. As I felt my dick move in my pants, I had a quick flash in my head. I wondered if I could talk her into coming back to my place right then. However, I stopped myself. We had just met and she was still waiting on test results.

I snapped myself out of my longing by changing the subject a bit. "Jenny, I want you to do something for me."

"What's that?"

"I want you to select a new kink name," I told her. "In fact, I want you to select three. Try and think of some that might sound like actual names, so that if someone heard me calling you that in public, they might think it was real, or at least a nickname or term of endearment. Can you do that for me?"

She considered my request and nodded. The tone in her voice was still suggestive as she said, "Yes, Sir."

I felt my smile grow more approving. "Good girl. Pick carefully. I'll decide which one you're going to be. I expect the suggestions to be...presented to me by no later than the day after tomorrow."

"As you wish...Sir."

CHAPTER FIFTEEN

I didn't have to wait long. The following morning I found a message that she had sent me listing off ideas for her new kink name.

"I thought about what you requested and these are what I have come up with. Of course, if you don't like any of them, I'll be glad to think of more. And, just for the record, while I understand the need to keep my real name off of the website, I'm still perfectly fine with being Jenny in public. But again, I leave the final decision up to you. ...After all, I'll just be calling you, 'Sir.' Am I right?

Here they are:

Sermonette.

Sweet Eloise

Going Knots (I guess, I would be Knotty or K)

And just for fun: Cum Guzzling Lap Whore.

I smirked. Crazy girl. Dirty girl. Funny, pleasant, exciting, good girl. Well, I considered her suggestions.

"I like the first one. Sermonette. That's you from now on."

I didn't receive a reply. Rather, I just noticed that when I looked later in the day, Attendant Available was no more. She had been replaced by Sermonette. I did respond to that.

"Good girl."

I sat with my mentor in an outdoor cafe, sipping coffee and discussing the plans for my training session with Jenny.

"First, we'll talk to her a little," he told me. "Set her at ease."

"Sounds good," I said.

He continued. "Once we're all ready, we're going to put her in the car and blindfold her."

"Blindfold her," I asked in shock. "Why?"

"Well, we've only spoken to her once. I don't want her to know, specifically, where I live," he pointed out. "But, more than that, it's to put her in a good head space to explore."

I nodded while doing my best to understand. "Okay," I said. "I guess that's not the worst idea I've ever heard. What are we going to do once we get her there?"

His response was clinical in tone. "Mostly, we're just going to explore negotiations. But, keep in mind, while we're doing all of this, I'll lead you a little, answer questions and help. However, you're going to need to ultimately take charge."

"How do I do that?"

He cocked an eyebrow. "By not being a fucking idiot, for one thing."

I gave him a frustrated smirk.

"Seriously, Ignite, just be assertive. You are in charge of this exercise. I can guide you, but you are the one making the real decisions...based on her desires." He paused. "Don't do or try anything over your head, and once we get started, lead the exercise yourself. Think you can do it?"

I nodded. "Yeah, I'm pretty sure."

"Don't be pretty sure. Be certain. Be in charge."

I nodded again. "I got it." I then asked, "Are Tink and Posie going to be there?"

"Yeah," he assured me. "I told both of them that we might need their help for demonstration purposes. I'd prefer to avoid it too much. As I said, you need to focus on and dominate Jenny. But they'll be available if you need them."

I became curious about something. "How'd you start Tink off?"

"Oh," he began with a smile, "basic shit. Tied her up and blindfolded her. Restricted her speech."

I remembered Tink's recollection of her first experience. "What came next?"

"She did," he grinned.

I returned a look that expressed a recognition of his joke, but that, also, wanted him to be serious. He chuckled and continued.

"Position training, mainly."

"What's that?"

"Teaching her different and specific ways of sitting, kneeling, standing... I also set her schedule so that she was up at a certain time and in bed before a certain hour. I put her on a diet and an exercise routine."

"Same diet and exercise routine as yours, I take it."

He confirmed this with a nod, but added, "I had to institute some specifics for her that were different. What she was willing to do," he clarified. "I did adapt them to myself as best as I could, though."

"Did you run into any problems or resistance?" I asked.

He cocked an eyebrow. "What do you think?"

I took that as confirmation. "How did you deal with it?"

He collected his thoughts before saying, "Well, you

can't mold someone to your ideals when they have different ones. Don't even try. You'll suffer for it." He took a sip from his latte. "Regardless, to genuinely dominate a sub on a long term basis, you have to understand them on a psychological level. You have to analyze their behavior and the things that they say in order to learn to see the things that they keep hidden. You have to read between the lines of their words."

He paused for a moment, contemplating before he continued. "Tink is a tough, determined young woman. She's headstrong and opinionated. She's a creature of habit. She also suffers from a degree of low self-esteem. Despite acting, and genuinely feeling, that she knows better than most the majority of the time, she also knows that she's not perfect. Still, she also secretly strives to be. She wants to be the most impressive force to be reckoned with anywhere. The fact that she's not makes her get really down on herself. Now, while that can repeatedly motivate her to be better, it also makes her a bit rebellious. She knows that she's trying and when I or other people take issue with her shortcomings, she wants to spit at us and point out all of her efforts and accomplishments. Not to mention, since she's already punished herself for many shortcomings, she secretly feels like more from outside sources is unreasonable."

I tried to follow him as best as I could. "That's what makes her rebellious?"

"Mostly," he said. His smile turned sympathetic. "I also believe that she secretly doesn't feel worthy of love, especially from two very disciplined people like Posie and me. I think, perhaps, that she acts out to prove to us that our love for her is misplaced."

I shook my head. "I still don't understand why."

"Always understand your sub, Iggy," he smiled. He

sighed again and had another sip of his coffee. "You've got a pretty self-deprecating sense of humor. Why do you think that is?"

I considered his question. "I think, maybe, I just want to cut people off before they criticize me. Let them know that *I* know that I'm not perfect and that I'm already addressing the issues."

"And when someone scolds you for something that you're already trying to fix?"

I scowled. "It kind of pisses me off."

"Uh huh," he said. "Of course, you'd get more respect if you embraced your strengths. I mean, you told me that you feel confident in your job, that you didn't let people push you around."

"That's different," I asserted.

"How?"

I thought for a second. "Well, I know what I'm talking about better than most."

"You also know how to be Kelly, as well as Ignite, better than anybody else on the planet. Why not embrace that?"

I considered his words before asking, "How does that relate to Tink's behavior?"

"She wants to be right," he told me, "even when being right is bad for her. She wants to beat me and Posie to the realization that she's not perfect. If she can do that then she shows us that she's not completely bad by virtue of being able to see and embrace her faults." He paused. "You do something similar. Stop," he instructed. "Don't confirm people's worries about your shortcomings or faults. Go with your strengths."

His words settled in my head and I examined them like a map that I was trying to understand. That's when we heard footsteps and a familiar voice.

"Hey, guys," Jenny said as she walked up, shifting her sunglasses from her eyes to her head. She smiled big. "How are you?"

We both stood. D.C. was silent, allowing me to respond first. "Hey," I replied cheerfully as I gave her quick, yet firm, hug. "Good."

I held a hand towards a chair as I pulled it out and she sat with us. She looked dazzling, dressed in tight jeans, a form fitting, baby blue shirt and red flats. Her hair was down and flowed over her shoulders. I was profoundly attracted to her and grinned big as I asked, "How are you?"

"Great. My test results came back yesterday," she beamed.

"Yeah," I said. "I take it the news was good."

She cocked her head and held a hand up. "All is well."

"That's wonderful news," I replied with a smile which she returned.

"Yes," she agreed. "No penicillin or maximum security quarantine for me."

I laughed. She continued to smile back.

"So, what's the plan for today?" she asked.

My mentor and I exchanged knowing, wicked glances.

"Well," I began, "I hope you're prepared to offer some trust. Because the first thing that we're going to do may seem a little scary."

She looked concerned, and yet, amused. "How so?"

"You, little girl," I smiled, "are going for a ride."

The three of us walked up to my mentor's place, me

leading my blindfolded new friend who held one hand out in front of her cautiously. D.C. quickly unlocked the door and we walked in without ceremony. It may have been that factor that contributed to Tink and Posie's unpreparedness. Tink was lying on top of Posie on the couch. While they were fully dressed, it appeared that they may have been making out.

"Hey," Tink said, startled. "We didn't expect you guys back so soon."

Posie pushed Tink off of her and sat up, looking a little bewildered.

"Clearly not," their Sir said as he shut the door behind us. "We may have company, but it's kink friendly company."

Posie said nothing. She just got a sudden, knowing look on her face and dropped to the floor on her knees in front of D.C., her hands on her thighs and her eyes on the floor. Tink's reaction wasn't nearly as generous. She simply looked inconvenienced as she slowly climbed to the ground, grunting like an old man condescending to get on his knees in front of a large group of family members in a photo. She placed her eyes down and her hands on her slightly spread thighs, as well.

As I removed the blindfold from Jenny's face, D.C. said sarcastically. "Jeez, thanks girls. I appreciate you troubling yourselves and all." He paused before telling them to get to their feet, stand at attention and that he felt a reminder of their position was in order.

The girls stood and glanced at each other. Tink looked tolerant at best.

"Let's hear it. Both of you together," D.C. said.

Suddenly the girl's tone was reverent as they recited, though Tink smirked a tad.

"I am the sole property of you, Sir. I will honor, serve,

obey and worship you at all times and in all ways. Pleasing you is my purpose, my duty, my privilege and my joy. I will never hesitate in my obedience and there is no greater shame or sadness to me than when I have displeased you. For you provide me with and allow me to enjoy many things to be thankful for, be it a bed to sleep in, food to eat or the joy of complete sexual exploration. In addition, I am fortunate to be a member of and to serve a great house. I will honor it and the others who belong to it always. I am a strong woman and a submissive of great value, and though I have much to learn, I trust that you, Sir, will guide me and protect me. I will wear my collar, as well as the marks you leave on my body proudly, for in submission, bondage and discipline, I shall be set free.

I am grateful to you, Sir. And I am yours."

As Jenny and I both stood there in awe, D.C. snapped his fingers and pointed to the floor in front of the sofa. Tinkerbrat and Posie immediately went to the spot and knelt there with their eyes on the floor and their hands behind their backs.

There was a brief moment of silence before Jenny chimed in with, "Okay...that was kind of cool."

"I'm glad you approve," D.C. said. He then turned to the two of us. "Now, let's establish just what sort of arrangement the two of you want to put together."

"Well..." Jenny began, her focus on him. I cut her off.

"Hey," I said calmly, but with a bit of an edge. "I'll tell you what the first thing that we're going to put in place is. And this is nonnegotiable. You direct your questions and responses to me." I reached into my toy bag, pulled out my crop and put the keeper up under her chin. "Understood?"

She smiled and flushed, while her breathing visibly increased. "Okay."

I pushed up with the whip. "Come again?"

"Yes, Sir," she replied reverently.

"Something else. Unless asked a question that requires a more detailed answer, the only thing I want to hear out of you is, 'Yes, Sir,' 'No, Sir,' and 'Sorry, Sir.' Agreed?"

"Yes, Sir."

"I'm impressed, Ignite," D.C. said. "So, what do you do next?"

I released the pressure I was applying under her chin, dropping the crop down her shoulder, caressing her arm with the leather. "I determine her hard limits for the purpose of this exercise."

"Good. How do you do that?"

"Well, first, I'm going to find out how she'll allow me to address her. I kind of like, 'dirty girl'." I spoke directly to Jenny. "Would that be alright with you?"

"Yes, Sir," she panted.

"Excellent. Next thing, dirty girl, eyes on the floor. You don't look at me or anyone unless you are given permission. Understood?"

Her eyes dropped. "Yes, Sir."

"Very good." I suddenly realized that I had no idea what D.C. had planned for the lesson, so I just asked him as I twirled the crop in my fingers. "What do you recommend next?"

"Well, I was hoping to go through some basics of her requirements, things like what you expect from her when you walk in the door, what she can and can't wear, can and can't do..." He looked over at me. "Go over what those will be, see what she'll consent to and see how much is reasonable to do here with me and the girls present."

"You heard him," I said to Jenny...or, to the dirty girl

(heh). "I'm going to list what I would like to find when I walk into a room where we are free to express ourselves and you tell me what you'll agree to. Then we'll go back over it and see what you're willing to do here."

"Yes, Sir."

"First," I said, "when I walk in, I want to see you naked, with the exception of a training collar, one that I'll get for you once we've established all of our parameters. How does that sound?"

"Yes, Sir." Her response seemed eager and excited.

"Good. Next, I want you at my feet, kneeling, prostrate before me."

"Yes, Sir." She giggled a little.

"Hey," I snapped. "Are you not taking this seriously?"

Her response was quick and nervous. "No, Sir. I mean, yes, Sir. Sorry, Sir."

That brought up another question. I put the crop back under her chin. "Can I discipline you right here with this thing?"

"Yes, Sir."

I swung it at her hip. As I had been practicing with it, hitting myself, my bed, my couch and anything else around the house that could take it, my technique had improved and the moderate "slap" sound indicated a proper blow. Not too hard, not too soft and effective. Jenny gasped and I returned the keeper to under her chin. "No laughing."

"Sorry, Sir."

"Now, where were we?" I paused because I had actually forgotten and D.C. had to remind me.

"She's to be naked, with the exception of a collar, to be provided at a later date and to present-down in front of you."

I looked at him quizzically.

"Prostrated," he clarified. "On her knees, bent over, face down, arms above the head, maybe with wrists and ankles crossed." He snapped his fingers at his girls and they demonstrated quickly.

"Yeah," I agreed. I redirected my attention to my potential new sub. "When I say so, you will sit up and ask if there is anything that I need or want. Can you do you that?"

"Yes, Sir."

I continued. "That may be anything from a glass of milk, to dinner, to a massage, to a blow job."

"Yes, Sir." She continued to blush and fought a grin.

"Wipe that *fucking* smile off of your face, dirty girl," I insisted.

It quickly disappeared. "Sorry, Sir."

"Alright," I said. I paused, considering my next question before asking it. "Answer specifically. How much of that are you comfortable with trying here?"

I expected to hear that she'd get face down on the floor, and maybe, ask me if there was anything that I wanted. I got a surprise, however.

"All of it, Sir."

I was stunned. "All of it?"

"Yes, Sir."

"So, you'll take off your clothes and suck my cock right here if that's what I expect of you?"

"Sir. Yes, Sir. In fact..."

There was a pause. Her breathing continued to increase.

"Go ahead," I urged her.

"Sir, the thought of being objectified in front of everyone, is...is actually *really* turning me on."

I looked over at my mentor.

"Hey, it's up to you," he told me. "The girls and I

have already seen most of our friends naked at one time or another and many of them were performing all kinds of sex acts on each other at the time. Hell, I may even let them get involved by holding her down for you or something. All I ask is that you don't get cum on the furniture or carpet." He thought for a brief second. "Or Tink or Posie, for that matter."

Here I was with a big decision to make. Do I throw caution to the wind and perform an entire scene with a sub, whom I had only recently met, in front of my friends? Or do I keep it restrained and risk disappointing Jenny?

I looked back at her and she was starting to sweat a little. It was pretty clear what she wanted me to do. But I'd never engaged in public sex before. Still, if I was going to commit to this lifestyle, then I had to overcome some of my apprehensions and I knew it.

"You heard the man," I said to her. "Strip. Now."

As Jenny began pulling her clothes off, I glanced over at Tinkerbrat and Poise, both of whom D.C. had allowed to sit up. Though their eyes were still looking down, they were both wearing small, but eager, smiles and seemed highly entertained. When I looked back at Jenny, her shirt was off and she was tearing open her pants.

"Hey," I said sharply. "Slow down, dirty girl. Never rush a good thing."

She did as she was told and began to disrobe in a slower, more sensual, teasing manner. D.C. actually snickered a small amount and pat me on the back before crossing to the couch and sitting behind his girls. I heard him instruct Tink to fetch something. With a reverent, "Yes, Sir," she got up and walked out of the room.

I kept my eyes on my new treasure as she inched out of her jeans, kicking her shoes off in the process. She slowly reached behind her back and unfastened her bra. As she let it creep down her arms, she exposed her nicely shaped breasts, the nipples of which were hard and pronounced. She dropped her garment on the floor before tucking her fingers on each side of her white panties and decreased her speed even more as she gradually pushed them down her thighs to her knees before letting them fall. She stepped out of them, providing us all with a marvelous view of her delicately groomed pussy, the hair on it, just a thin triangle above her lips.

There she was, in all her glory, and I was enchanted and highly aroused. Her lightly tanned body was perfect...thin, yet curvy, soft, yet toned. She was magnificent. She carefully knelt down and bowed towards the floor at my feet, her arms over her head. I couldn't help but smile in approval and pleasure.

"Sit up," I commanded.

She did.

"Look at me."

Her eyes slowly, nervously, yet with clear excitement, moved up to meet mine. Her voice was soft, trembling and seductive as she breathed heavily and cooed out, "Does Sir, desire anything?"

I was entranced. Suddenly, all I wanted was to fuck this girl right then and there while the others looked on. I felt my cock grow so rigid that it hurt, straining against my pants.

It was then that Tink walked back into the room and over to me. She knelt and held up a plain, black, leather collar in her hands. "Mr. Ignite," she said respectfully. "Sir, offers this to you for your use today."

A lascivious smile curved my mouth. "Thank you," I said to her. "With your Sir's permission, I offer you the honor of placing it on..." I looked over at Jenny, put the keeper back under her chin without pressing and felt my smile turn even more devastating. "...This."

D.C. agreed with a nod and Tink crawled behind Jenny. "Hold your hair up, sweetie," the experienced sub whispered to my new one. Jenny did as instructed and the small leather belt was cinched around her neck.

I stepped closer and looked down at my prize. I caressed her cheek with my index finger as the rest of them held the crop, the strap at its base moving across her forehead during the process, and she closed her eyes and gasped. "I am a member of this house," I said. "If you please me, you will be as well and that is a great honor. Learn well, with me, and we will start our own house, where pain and pleasure are the blessing and the law."

I paused, considering how far I would take it next. I knew what I wanted. My shyness and fear were leaving me. Jenny had made her desires known, but I felt that they needed to be expressed again.

"Tell me what you want, dirty girl. Tell me the truth."

"Sir," she panted. "Sir, I want you to please fuck me."

It was tempting. I could also feel Tink behind her and Posie off to the side squirming with anticipation at the prospect of a show. But I decided that it was too soon. Still, I was so aroused that I had to give in a little. "No, dirty girl. Not yet. But we will stick to the original plan." I turned to my mentor. "Are you still willing to let the girls hold her for me?"

"Hey, why not?" he grinned. "I'm getting a pretty big kick out of watching all this. Might as well let them perform a little too." He shoved Posie lightly. "Girls, hold Mr. Ignite's sub for him. Make her do whatever he tells you to."

"Yes, Sir," they eagerly said in unison.

The two of them scrambled to each side of Jenny and

took her by the arms. Tink grabbed the back of her hair.

"Ugh," Jenny grunted excitedly.

"Unfasten my pants," I told her, before thinking. I mean, the other subs had her arms pinned behind her back and her head motionless. They started to let her go, but my oversight gave me an idea. "Keep holding her. The dirty girl will just have to find another way."

Jenny leaned forward, straining to get close enough until her mouth was right at my fly. She fumbled exorbitantly with her teeth attempting to get a hold of my zipper. As she began trying to lift the slider with her tongue, the stroking against my cock through my slacks was amazing. She began having a buildup of saliva that she smeared all over my crotch in her efforts.

I was loving it.

She kept lapping. Finally, she got the slider in between her teeth and slowly, carefully, pulled it down. Next, she bit into my belt, actually having a much easier time unfastening it, though the drool was becoming pleasantly excessive. The dirty girl managed to get my pants open and tugged them down just enough that she could, next, pull down my underwear, still using her teeth, tongue and lips, releasing my cock. It sprung forward with a frantic zeal.

"Suck me off really well and I may grant you an orgasm. Alright?"

"Yes, Sir!" The tone in her voice and the look on her face were hungry, almost inhuman.

"And another thing," I added as I reached down and lightly grabbed her by the chin. "You heard Sir D.C. My cum doesn't get on anything. Do you understand?"

Her breathing was at a point just below hyperventilation as she earnestly agreed. With that, Tink shoved the girl's head forward and onto my cock, while still being keen enough not to choke her. Jenny decided that it would be fine if she did, however, and slowly pushed further and further onto me until I was all the way in her throat. After a few seconds, she pulled off with a load gasp and a thick trail of spit hanging between her lower lip and my dick. She then went to giving me proper, sensual head, moving back and forth, sucking with her mouth and rubbing with her tongue.

I heard Tink whisper to her, "Oh, that's excellent, baby girl."

"Yeah," Posie agreed. "Suck off your Sir. Show him how worthy you are."

Between the intensely risqué nature of the situation and my extreme arousal, I didn't take long. In fact, I did my best to hold my orgasm at bay, so as not to appear like a minute man. But it wasn't much more before I felt it building in me and I started to moan.

"Get ready, baby," I warned my sub as I stroked her head.

She increased her speed and seconds later, I let loose in her mouth. She pushed forward and clamped her lips around my cock so as to prevent any spillage. Several hard, hot bursts ripped through me and I groaned over and over. Then, once I was done, she slowly eased off, while running the tip of her tongue underneath and along my urethra, squeezing out every last drop. That last move actually made me cry out a bit. It was incredible.

I stepped back and pulled up my pants, quicker than I had intended, a tad delirious and off balance. I got down on my knees, put a hand on Jenny's cheek and looked deep into her eyes, my own breathing now chaotic. She swallowed hard and gazed adoringly back at me, panting. It occurred to me that I hadn't even kissed her yet. I rectified this hard, with no concern or apprehension about any remnants of my own semen that might be in her mouth. Then I pulled back and shoved my hand between her legs and my fingers in her pussy.

"That was very good. The dirty girl was a good girl and she now gets a reward."

She was soaking wet. D.C. might not have had to worry about my fluids on his carpet, but I was definitely about to break my promise with regards to Jenny's, because she was dripping as I fucked her with my hand. She cried out and squirmed as Tink and Posie continued to restrain her.

I grabbed the back of her hair. "Do it!" I commanded. "Come."

A few seconds later, Jenny became quiet and tense, her mouth still open but no sound or breath coming out. There were a few quick gasps from her, followed by more silence each time. Finally, she leaned forward and let out a shrill cry that surely alerted the neighbors. I just kept hammering away into her pussy, digging hard into the moistness with three fingers, until she collapsed against my chest, breathing like a shipwreck survivor who had finally crawled out of the water and onto a beach.

I pressed my hand into her pussy and hugged her tight while the girls let her go and began petting her.

"That was awesome," Tink smiled.

I suddenly heard D.C. who I had almost forgotten was watching calmly from the couch. "That was...pretty cool."

"It was!" Jenny gasped. She beamed. "Thank you, Sir! Thank you!"

I smiled and kissed her on the forehead.

D.C. suddenly spoke up again, breaking the mood a good bit with, "So...who wants take out?"

Everybody paused, even Jenny whose heavy

breathing stopped for a moment. Then...we all started laughing.

CHAPTER SIXTEEN

If you ask anybody who works in IT what their jobs are like, they will usually just tell you that they spend a lot of time at a keyboard. What they're less likely to tell you about is all of the dumb questions and out of touch people that they encounter. It's almost as if the pros are the only ones who have any idea how to get from point "A" to point "B" and everyone else is just driving in circles with no idea how to use a turn signal, much less a clutch.

I was walking back from the bathroom at City Hall, hands in pockets, when I heard a loud exclamation.

"Damn it!"

I looked to my left and saw, in the records department, the reserved blonde who had come in search of hard copy files, slam her fists down on her keyboard.

"Hey, hey, hey!" I said as I instinctively charged in, a cautious hand out. "You don't want to do that!"

She sighed and rubbed a hand back across her forehead.

"What's the problem?" I asked, like the computer was an animal that she was abusing and I was a member of the ASPSA.

"The stupid printer won't print out and now the stupid cursor won't even move on my computer. The stupid thing just stays in one place!"

I looked around and followed the cord from the mouse. As it turned out, it had come loose from the computer itself. I plugged it back in.

"Try it now," I said.

She moved the mouse around with a sigh. "Okay, well, that worked."

Next, I examined her printer. I leaned over her shoulder and typed. "Your computer is defaulting to an awkward page size and your printer doesn't have that size loaded."

"Why would it do that?" she asked.

I remained with my arms around her, not in a claiming way, but just trying to reach the keyboard in order to fix the problem. I typed and found the original setting. "You obviously hit the other option by accident," I said as I leaned up. "It should work now."

She tried printing and got nothing. I touched the power button on her printer, rebooting it. All of the copies, plus the extras that she had requested out of frustration, started spilling out.

"Problem solved," I said tolerantly.

"Thank you," she said quietly, not looking me in the eye and clearly embarrassed.

I found myself frustrated. "Never hit your computer. It doesn't solve anything. It's just a machine."

"Sorry," she returned. "I just got, I don't know...aggravated."

"Yeah, well..." I replied as patiently as I could, "save the abuse for people. They're the only ones who respond to it...and then, only if they consent to it."

She looked up at me curiously. I gave her a serious expression, meant to let her in on my disapproval of her technical abuse. This was work. And play was far from my mind at the moment. She paused briefly before turning her head back to her computer.

"Thanks," she said, almost dismissively.

"Next time you have an issue," I said, "come get me.

I'm just down the hall."

I walked out and thought to myself, *That's how I want to feel in the kink world, like I have it all down and everybody else's problems are just dumb.*

I suddenly stopped. Wait. That wasn't even close to true. If everyone in the kink community were as clueless as my tech clients...there would be a lot of people in the hospital. Just because I wanted to feel informed did not mean that I wanted everyone else to be dumb. Wanting to know more than most was not necessarily a good idea.

Arrgh. I gritted my teeth. *Learn first, teach latter and keep it all separate from your vanilla life*, I scolded myself. I went back to the server room.

My phone suddenly rang. I looked at it to find that D.C. was calling me.

"Hey," I said. "What's up?"

"What are you doing Friday night?" he asked over the receiver.

"Uh...nothing planned. Why?"

"There's an important P.O.P. and I wanted to know if you wanted to go."

"P.O.P.?" I asked.

"Play optional party," he clarified. "Haven't you been doing your homework?"

I smirked tolerantly. "I do have a life outside of our world, you know?"

"No, you don't," he said sarcastically. "So, how about it? Interested?"

"What's required?"

"Just look your absolute best and be on your best behavior. It's a big party and a lot of important people are going to be there. You can bring Jenny, if you want."

"I'm pretty certain she has to work. But maybe she can meet us there. Would that be okay?" I asked.

"I'm sure it will be fine. Just tell her to clean up and look nice and introduce her to the hostess when she arrives," he said. "I'm texting you the address."

I slipped into my coat and cinched my tie up as I looked at myself in the mirror.

You look good, I told myself. *D.C's advice was quality.*

I moved back and forth in front of the mirror. I looked like someone with class, someone powerful and secure in life. It produced an intoxicating confidence in me as I admired the subtle "v" shape my torso and waist formed. Gone was the immature appearance and apathetic air produced by my regular, casual dress. In their place was an aura of authority, style and sophistication. I was a professional, a shark, an alpha. I was James fucking Bond.

I tugged my lapels and ran my fingers down my thin, black tie, practically fondling myself. It was almost impossible not to feel dashing and self-possessed...not to mention, sexy and I smiled.

Then I farted a little.

I paused. *Let's hope that's the only time that happens tonight,* I thought.

I took a deep breath. After a quick, reassuring nod to the mirror, I went to my car and headed to my mentor's place.

I followed D.C., one step behind him. Posie and Tink were on each of his arms, both decked out in beautiful, yet simple, dresses. We approached the house and my mentor told me to get the door. I moved ahead and held it opened as the rest walked through, the girls thanking me as they passed. As we entered the foyer, I took the girls' coats and purses and hung them on a long coat rack on the wall. When I turned to see our next destination, I found D.C. and the girls just standing there looking like customers waiting to be seated at a restaurant.

A few seconds later, an older, matronly looking woman in a tight, leather—yet, somehow, still tasteful—dress and opera gloves approached on her tall, shiny high heels. "D.C.!" she called out cheerfully.

"Lady Nessa," he smiled and the two of them took each other's hands. "You remember Tink and Posie?" he said as he motioned to them.

"Of course. So, nice to see you again." She eyed them mischievously. "Have you girls been good?"

"Yes, Ma'am," they chimed in unison. Each of their smiles seemed campy and tolerant.

"And," D.C. continued, "may I introduce my protégé, Ignite35."

I almost stuck out my hand to shake, but quickly thought better of it. The rapid tactical thinking caused me to get nervous and I spat out, "People call me, Iggy," perhaps a little more quickly than was appropriate.

Everyone grew quiet for just a second and Tink and Posie suppressed giggles.

I adjusted my demeanor and followed my dumb comment with, "Thank you for having us. It's an honor."

My mentor smirked, but still looked approving.

"Nice to meet you. Welcome to my home," Lady Nessa said hospitably. She addressed us as a group. "Please, make yourselves comfortable. I only ask that we limit the amount of bodily fluids that get spilled and that you use the sanitizer that is provided in each room if it does. Otherwise, mingle and have fun."

We all thanked her and she walked away to attend to other hostessing duties. D.C. adjusted his cuffs, looked at each of us and said, "Well, shall we?"

For the next half hour we just walked around saying our hellos to people and checking out the scene. Lady Nessa's house was enormous, all hardwood and very tastefully decorated. There wasn't a single room in the house, not even the kitchen, that didn't have a book shelf. Few walls had more than one painting or picture on them, though each were big. The furniture was all brown and red and quite posh. The curtains, which hung on every window, some open, some drawn, we're of the same yellow, floral print. There was an upstairs, a large back porch and an even larger, perfectly groomed backyard.

Everywhere we went, in or outside of the house, there were people gathered. Some were plainly dressed. Others were in various forms of kink attire. Corsets were in abundance, as were black pants. Some men wore very tasteful suits, though there were few ties. Many wore black shirts under their coats. I spotted countless pairs of super-high heels and a few outfits that resembled cliché, yet risqué Halloween costumes like school girl or French maid. Most of the attendees were older and all they really did was talk. Every few feet we walked we'd encounter another person that D.C. wanted to introduce me to, though none of the conversations lasted long.

We continued to check the party over until we'd made all the rounds, returning to the living room, at which point my mentor turned to me and said, "I'm going to go find a couple of people. Why don't you mingle on your own?"

I looked around and realized that we'd shed the subs

who were headed to the back porch.

"Oh. Okay," I agreed nervously.

He turned and left me to fend for myself. I stood there awkwardly, glancing around at all of the people who seemed to know each other really well and felt a bit thrown to the wolves. My expert tactical move was to do absolutely nothing but freeze there with my hands in my pockets and with, what I was sure was, a vacant stare on my face. I turned to find a tall, broad shouldered, black man standing next to me.

"Hi," he said in a very friendly tone.

"Hello," I replied affably.

"Are you new or have I just not met you yet?" His voice was soft, but secure.

"I'm still relatively new, I guess."

He put a hand out. "Hi. I'm Mac."

"Iggy."

"Iggy?"

"Ignite35." I shook his hand. His grasp was limp.

"Oh, I see. I'm Spirited Wheels on the website. Of course, I'm thinking of changing that."

"To what?"

"I'm not sure," he confessed. "What do you think of Cabin Boy Fever?" He grinned and I laughed.

"That's...that's certainly telling," I said.

"So," he continued, "are you here with anyone?"

"Yeah. Yeah, my mentor and his subs brought me."

"Who is your mentor?"

"Dramatic Comedy."

"Oh, really?" He looked impressed. "M'k. He's got an aura I wouldn't mind bathing in. I bet his cock tastes like romantic English literature and the tears of virgins."

"S...sorry?" How should I respond to that, I wondered.

"He's fine," Mac sang. "So, does that mean that you're a Dom, too? Or is he teaching you how get on your knees and behave?"

I was genuinely speechless. "Uh..."

"Mac, why are you always freaking on the cute, white, *obviously straight* boys?" The question came from a young, short, round, bespectacled, black girl who'd walked up.

"Because I saw him first and he hasn't asked me to stop yet." He smiled flirtatiously at me.

I chuckled nervously, flattered, yet uninterested, while fumbling for a response.

The girl chimed in again, this time to me. "You have to excuse him. He thinks he can persuade any man to switch teams for a night."

"No," Mac corrected. "I just use a shotgun method to find my play partners. And you'd be shocked how often I hit something."

"I doubt it," the girl said, implying that his reputation as a quality marksmen may have often preceded him. She turned to me. "Hi. I'm Zee Zee."

"Ignite. Nice to meet you."

"Are you new?"

"Iggy, here was just telling me that he's D.C.'s new protégé," Mac told her in a sassy voice.

"Really?" She seemed excessively interested. "So, you're a Dominant?"

"Yeah, yeah." As usual, I didn't feel much like the term fit in that particular situation. The upper hand seemed pretty foreign at that moment. But I remembered my mentor's words and stood up straight. I tried to appear confident. "Dominant."

Zee Zee scooted closer to me. "You need a sub?" she giggled.

"Girl, now who's freakin'?" Mac asked her.

"Just putting myself out there." She looked me over. "I don't think he's a chocolate lover, though."

"Hey, now," I protested. "I'm not racist or anything like that."

"No one is suggesting that you are," Mac said. "You're only into what you're into."

"You ever been with a black girl?" Zee Zee asked me.

"Or a black boy?" Mac tacked on.

I smirked. "My first BDSM experience was with a Brazilian girl. Does that count?"

Mac shook his head. "Not at all. Although, I do here that they're a bunch of horny monkeys."

Before I could agree, a thought struck me. "I just noticed that there aren't a whole lot of African American community members. Is there a reason?"

"Oh," Zee Zee said with a dismissive shrug. "They have their own community."

"Yeah," Mac agreed. "The local kinksters are about as segregated as this town. Most of the black folks do their own thing. Their community activities are pretty group oriented."

Zee Zee nodded. "Orgies and stuff."

"Yeah and lots of white girl gang bangs," Mac sneered.

"Really?" I immediately realized that my reaction sounded appalled. "Sorry," I amended. "I'm not put off by the whole interracial thing as much as by the sharing. It's not really my bag."

Mac's delivery was deadpan as he joked, "When you've been oppressed for so long, you get used to making everybody's soup out of the same bone."

Zee Zee laughed. I tried to decide if I should join in, but ultimately just stood there. Finally, I offered another possibility.

"I guess it could be understood that slavery wouldn't sound appealing to most black people."

"Depends on the context," Zee Zee grinned suggestively.

"I know that's right," Mac mumbled into his drink.

The girl continued. "This community is different. Most of the black folks around here are blerds."

"Excuse me?"

"Black nerds," Mac supplied.

"Yeah," Zee Zee said. "Most of us are regulars at ComicCon."

I nodded. "I'm learning that a lot of people in the community, regardless of race, are."

"How long have you been in the lifestyle," she asked.

"Actively? About six months."

"Damn!" Mac exclaimed. "You're not white. You're green."

I chuckled nervously. "Yeah, well...I'm learning fast, if it's any consolation." They both just smiled suggestively at me. I tried to switch gears, "So, uh...I haven't seen either of you at any of the munches. Are you just busy?"

Mac got a very distasteful look on his face and grunted. "I used to be at all of them, but I'm not *allowed* to anymore." The emphasis on the word implied some disdain.

"Why not?" I asked.

"Cause of that Xina bitch," he stated flatly. "She didn't like the fact that I had issues with another community member that she was friends with and she just told me not to come back."

I remembered what went down with SnowGirl. "She banned you?" I asked.

"Mm Hm," he confirmed. "Don't ever cross her inner circle. She will do her best to put you out, even if they are the ones who messed up."

I glanced over at Zee Zee who wasn't making eye contact, but also looked annoyed. She shook her head. "That whole incident is why I don't go to munches anymore," she supplied.

There was a moment of silence before we were joined by other guests.

"What's going on?" Killer Rabbit said as he approached with a smile and a swagger, while sporting an acid washed shirt. Lolly Popper was behind him.

"Hey, Rabbit," Mac said with an up tilt in his voice. "I didn't expect to see you here."

"Lolly got an invite," he replied. "I'm her plus one."

"Okay..." Mac nodded. "Still an asshole?" he asked casually.

"Still a fag?" Killer Rabbit returned with a sarcastic smile. The two men exchanged tolerant laughs before Killer Rabbit turned to me and offered a hand to shake. "Ignite," he said strongly. I greeted him back and shook his hand. He squeezed extra hard.

All the while, Lolly and Zee Zee were exchanging friendly greetings. I broke in to say hello to Lolly.

"How are you tonight," I asked her.

She smiled shyly. "I'm well," she said. "How are you?"

"Good, actually," I told her.

Killer Rabbit put an arm around her and tugged her close before saying, "So, what have you been up to?"

"Ah, just making the rounds. My sub—or rather, the one I have under consideration—should be here soon," I told him.

"Sick," he said. "I've never actually gone that path.

Me and all my girls always jumped right into it."

"Mm Hm," Mac said. "We know, Rabbit. Cause every time someone has been to the moon, you've been there twice."

He grinned defiantly. "I can't help it if I have my shit together better than most."

I decided to weigh in. "If you don't mind my asking, why wouldn't you want a courting period of some kind? I mean, what happens if you find out things aren't going to work and you've already dove in head first?"

He smiled and shrugged. "At least I got laid."

"Charming," Zee Zee commented with a sickened smirk.

I started to say something, but my mouth just opened and stayed that way for a moment, no words coming out. While all Rabbit did was grin, I began to feel a little less green, or rather naive, in the presence of someone so clearly arrogant and foolish. I glanced around anxiously and that's when I saw my mentor over next to the entrance to kitchen.

D.C. raised a hand to summon me and I excused myself from the conversation as politely as possible, telling them each that it was nice to talk to them all. I was then led into the dining room where Master Jon stood talking to a woman who appeared to be an adult version of Wednesday Addams. The Dungeon Master's posture was perfect and his friendly manner belied the wickedness inside of him. Off to his left, a foot or so behind him, stood an attractive, slim, forty-ish woman in a knee-length, 1950's style cocktail dress silently looking at the floor with her hands behind her back. As we approached, I caught the tail end of the conversation.

"If the city builds that school there, they may insist that we move," adult Wednesday Addams said.

"That's provided that they do, in fact, know we're there," Master Jon replied.

She gave him a questioning look. "Of course they know we're there, Jon."

"Last I heard, they think we're a social club. And we are."

Her look turned almost condescending. "You're not even remotely this naive. Why are you acting like it?"

He grinned. "Just trying to see if you're paying attention." He gave a conciliatory nod. "Look, some people at City Hall are aware of us. But the others, the ones who would react badly, they have no concrete proof of it."

"We'd still be across from a school. If we want to show that we aren't a threat, then we should be prepared to move before such a thing happens."

He continued to smile and nod. "I told the board the same thing. They are considering it. It would be very helpful if you would share your opinion with a few of them."

D.C. stepped up next to them. "Master Jon, Mekara," he said respectfully.

"D.C.," Mekara said in a friendly voice. "How are you?"

"I'm well. I was wondering if I could borrow Master Jon's attention."

She nodded, "Of course," before getting a wicked smile on her face. "You bring your girls?"

D.C. smiled back. "I did."

Her smile remained mischievous. "Can I tickle them?"

My mentor chuckled. "Be my guest."

Mekara left us to seek out Tinkerbrat and Posie while I watched Master Jon give D.C. a moment.

"What can I do for you?" the Dungeon Master asked politely.

"First, I wanted to introduce you to someone." My mentor motioned me closer. "This is Ignite35. He's my new protégé."

Master Jon turned to me with a smile that offered a degree of immediate respect. "A pleasure to meet you." His handshake was remarkably firm, without crushing me.

"You as well, sir," I replied.

He grinned bigger. "You hoping to be subjugated, Ignite?"

"Uh...no, sir."

"Then don't call me, 'sir.' Master Jon or Jon is fine."

I laughed nervously. "Right. Sorry."

D.C. took over the conversation again. "Jon, I couldn't help but overhear that you may have problems with the Scene Shop's location. I wanted to let you know that we have someone new on the inside of City Hall."

Crap.

"Really?" Master Jon asked, seeming suddenly much more interested.

"That's right," D.C. continued. "Iggy has access to the goings-on there. He's encountered a few things and could be a source of slightly-early information."

"Is that the case?" The imposing Dom looked at me.

"Uh..." I began eloquently. "Yes. But I can't really do a whole lot. I have to maintain a certain level of discretion and professionalism."

Master Jon's eyes looked at me, flashed over to D.C. and then leveled back in my direction.

"But," D.C. pointed out, "you could share information, things that you run across that might affect us. We could have a heads up. Such as the fact that the

City Planner, who is bothered by our risqué nature, is now aware of us.”

I was still and silent. Master Jon saw my demeanor and gleaned my predicament. “Hey, we understand that you can’t break the law or endanger your job. If you come across something that you feel that you can share, great. If not, no one is going to hold it against you.”

I let out a breath. “Thank you. I am willing to do what I can.”

Master Jon’s smile turned grateful. “And we appreciate that.”

Right then, Posie came whipping around the corner, laughing. She dodged Master Jon perfectly. However, Tink, who was chasing her, did not. She collided with the Dom’s shoulder as she pursued her sister. Her laughter vanished and she became still, her head down, hands clasped in front of her and her lips pressed together. “Oh, God... Master Jon...I apologize.”

He simply pulled himself together, raised an eyebrow, ever-so-briefly, and then looked back at D.C. and myself. “Keep us apprised,” he said calmly before leaving the room, the silent woman behind him in tow.

There was a very brief, yet highly tense, few seconds.

I looked at D.C., who was clearly pissed. The glare he gave Tinkerbrat made my blood run cold.

“I’m sorry, Sir,” she whimpered.

He continued to look at her for a moment before suddenly reaching out, grabbing her by the throat and yanking her to him. “Where is your purse?” he growled.

Tink’s lips quivered. “In the foyer, Sir.”

“Fetch it!”

He let her go and she scurried off. He turned to Posie, who was standing by looking embarrassed and scared.

“You,” D.C. said sternly. “Pick a number between one

and four."

Her eyes were on the floor as she whispered, "Two, Sir."

"That's how many nights you sleep on the floor. And no TV, internet, texting or games for that time."

Tinkerbrat returned and held out her purse. D.C. furrowed his brow and she knelt down, head bowed and hands raised, presenting it to him. He took the bag, dug around inside and pulled out eyeliner.

"Look at me!" he commanded.

She raised her view up as told and he began to write on her forehead, spelling out, "Stoopid Bitch." He put the eyeliner back in her purse and handed it back to her forcefully before putting his hand in her hair and slowly guiding her to her feet as he spoke.

"You are going to walk up to every single person at this party and apologize for setting a bad example for all the other subs and slaves. Understood?"

She looked at him a touch horrified, like she thought the punishment a tad extreme. But then, lowered her head. "Yes, Sir," she replied dutifully.

"Go!" he instructed. He turned his attention back to Posie. "You. Go with her. Make sure she does it. Everyone here."

"Yes, Sir."

The girls walked away, heads hung. D.C. sighed heavily.

"That's an interesting punishment," I noted.

"Tink hates being humiliated in public."

"Well, is that...I don't know, maybe a bit much?"

He turned his whole body towards me and pointed after her. "She was running around someone else's home like a toddler and slammed into Master Jon...while we were having a very important conversation with him, no less."

"I wouldn't say that she 'slammed' into him."

D.C. was quick. "Her behavior reflects on me. She knows this. I want her to feel free to have a good time, but there are limits. She acted up."

I was silent. I didn't really know what to say and had trouble making eye contact.

D.C. took a deep breath and slowly exhaled. His response was calm. "She is going to do her punishment, she is getting a beating when we get home and we are going to have a long talk about it."

I paused and then nodded. "Whatever you think is best."

His expression turned slightly pained and he sighed before telling me, "I need a drink. Would you care for anything?"

"No, thanks," I said. "I think I'll just wander around some more. Jenny should be here soon and I want to make sure I know my way around the party when she gets here." He nodded and we parted ways.

CHAPTER SEVENTEEN

I decided to check out the upstairs again, where I had been led to believe that some scenes may take place at some point. It was essentially a long hallway with four bedrooms, two on the right and two on the left. All the floors were hardwood, which I supposed was convenient, should anyone spill any of the fluids that Lady Nessa mentioned upon our arrival.

I peeked into the first bedroom where several people were watching a curvy Domme in a pastel tank top and sagging jeans, repeatedly flog two shirtless men who had their hands pressed against the wall. Every so often, she would lean in and whisper something to one or both of them and they would reply softly back, "Yes, Ma'am." After which, she would caress the reddening welts across their backs and return to whipping them.

After a few minutes of that, I turned and looked in the room across the hall. There a tall, slender woman in a pale blue oxford, unbuttoned all the way to expose her black bra was stepping on a girl with her high heels. The Domme had a crop in one hand and a strap in the other. After digging her heel into the yelping girl's back, she stepped off and began beating the sub's exposed back and thighs. At one point, she pulled the girl's head back by the hair and allowed a drop of spit to crawl its way out of her own red lips and slowly inch down to the sub's face, where she rubbed it in. After that, it was back to beating her.

"You're going to have a very hard time sitting at work for a while," the Domme said very plainly. The girl on the floor laughed, before letting out more yelps and moans.

I looked next to me where another guy was transfixed. Before I could censor myself, I heard the words, "So, this is all they do? Just beat each other for an extended period of time?" come out.

He looked at me and I thought I might get a quiet reprimand, but he smiled instead. "Things are a little more graphic and detailed in the other two rooms," he told me. He then returned to staring at the Domme/sub play.

I inched out of the door frame and moved towards the next room. There, I got a surprise. He was right. It was certainly more graphic. Much more. I found a middle aged woman who was on her knees, naked and surrounded by four men who all had their dicks out. She was servicing all of them with her hands and mouth.

As I watched in shock, I realized that it was the same woman that I had seen on the website when I first explored it, the one who had been the centerpiece of a gangbang. Apparently, that was her thing. It must have also been her Dom's as he, who turned out to be one of the men there, grabbed her by the hair and shoved her face onto one of the other men.

"Don't forget anyone here, you filthy slut," he ordered. "You've got four cocks that all need to be serviced. Keep at it."

"Sir. Yes, Sir," she gasped in between gulps.

Despite my aversion to sharing, I must admit that I was momentarily mesmerized. The events were so extreme that I couldn't help but look on. Still, I eventually began to feel genuinely dirty and moved on to the forth room.

That's where I landed, and happily.

It was the master bedroom. There was a king sized bed there with an iron frame that included tall posts at each corner. At the foot of the bed, a man in leather pants and a designer black shirt had a woman in nothing but her underpants, standing and spread eagle, tied with rope to the posts by her wrists and ankles. He had her blindfolded, with her back facing him and his arm around her chest. As he pressed himself up against her body, he whispered in her ear, just loud enough that I could barely hear him.

"You're going to be a good girl, a sweet girl, right?"

"Yes," she quietly said through heavy breaths. She then asked, "Are there people watching?" She sounded concerned.

"That's nothing for you to worry yourself with," I heard him say as I inched into the room, closer. "You just be good."

He leaned back away from her and held out an elaborate flogger, a thick handled one with red and brown strips hanging from it. He ran it down her shoulders and back, tracing it all over her body as she sighed and moaned. Then he reared back and slapped her back, ass and thighs with it about nine quick, hard times. The girl cried out.

As quickly as he had begun with the lashes, he stopped. He ran the flogger's strips down her skin again before gently caressing each place he'd hit her with his fingertips, all evident from the rapid reddening in her skin. She let out a series of quick, heavy sighs and gasps.

He hit her with the whip again, all across her, perhaps nine to ten more times before returning to barely touching her with his fingers, all over where he had struck. He moved his face close and blew on the new welts. Her emoting grew in volume. The man had made a simple breath overpowering.

He got closer to her again, pressing himself up against her hot, stinging flesh. Again, he whispered in her ear and again, I caught myself inching even farther into the room, closer to the scene.

"You're being very good," he said. "I'm pleased."

"Thank you," she managed. "I'm trying."

He reached up to her wrists and delicately trailed his fingertips along her skin, down her arms, across her shoulders, along her back and ribs, against the fabric of her panties and down the back of her thighs. I could actually see the hair on her body stand up. Each time he grazed a place he had taken the whip to, her exclamations grew. Her breathing stayed intense.

"I'm going to hit you again," he whispered to her.

"Please don't," she begged, almost sounding sincere.

"I have to," he told her.

He struck her with the flogger about four times before resorting to his bare, open palm against her ass cheeks. After a few strikes, he squeezed and then slowly released his grip until he was just stroking her butt.

He leaned in again. "You're on display," he cooed to her quietly.

"No," she whimpered, though it was obviously an act on her part.

"Yes. You're amusement for these people. You should really give them something."

"Please don't," she begged. "I don't want to."

Without another word, he slipped his hand into the front of her panties and grabbed her between the legs. He didn't immediately begin to move, he just held her there. But, after many long seconds, he began to slowly push and pull his hand back, to rotate his fingers, to lift her and let her down. With every single act, her breathing and cries reacted. Finally, he settled into something that appeared, from my angle, to be him lifting her a half inch and lowering her back while waving his hand back and forth about the same measurement. Every rare moment, he would slap her on the ass, hard, with his bare hand.

She slowly began to lose her mind.

"You said you were a good girl," he said to her.

"Yes," she replied, desperately.

"Is that still true?"

"I swear. I am."

"Show me."

After that I couldn't make out what he was saying to her. He was too close to her ear and speaking too quietly. But his lips continued to move, as did his hand. She squirmed, moaned and called out. Finally, she came and it was loud.

He held her tight and delivered sweet kisses all over her face, neck and shoulders as she did. When it all subsided, he slowly pulled his fingers from between her legs and placed them in her mouth where she hungrily sucked on them.

I should have brought a notepad, I thought to myself. *This is quality.*

It was at that time that I felt a little anxious, almost like *I* was on display. I looked to my right and noticed a middle aged man staring at me with a lascivious smile. I swallowed and nodded an acknowledgment. He nodded back.

"Fascinating, isn't it?" he said to me quietly.

"It is," I replied.

"Arousing too."

I suddenly noticed that I was erect when he said that. Had I not however, it would have become very clear to me a moment later, because he reached over, no ceremony, and stroked the front of my pants.

My hand went straight to his and pulled it off. "Do you mind?" I said, shocked and irritated.

"Not at all," he grinned.

I decided that I didn't want to wait around to see what he might do next and left the room. I found a place to stand along the wall in the hallway and tried to catch my breath. However, he was next to me again and still smiling.

"Look, dude," I told him, "I don't know what your game is, but I don't swing that way. And even if I did, you would at least have to buy me a drink first."

He got in front of me. "Well, allow me to then." He pressed himself very near, almost against me.

Before I could shove him away however, someone caught his attention, an arm to his chest.

"Irving," Mac said in a stern voice off to my right. "Leave that boy alone. He ain't interested in you."

"I suspect he doesn't know fully what he's interested in yet." Irving smiled grossly.

"I know I don't want you touching me," I told him firmly.

"There," Mac said as he got right up next to my assailant. "He just gave a very clear, 'no'. Now, you leave him alone, old man."

"I'm just playing," Irving said to him, almost nose to nose.

Mac continued. "That's D.C.'s new protégé you're harassing. That means, he's under D.C.'s protection. You want to get up in that kind of mess?"

The old pervert got a more concerned look on his face and backed up a step.

"Uh huh," Mac said. "Walk away."

The man paused and looked me up and down again before heading off downstairs.

"Thank you," I said earnestly to my rescuer.

"It's all good," Mac said with a huff. "I hate that old fag. He don't know how to keep his hands to himself and he don't know how to take no for an answer. He pulled some similar shit with me early on and I finally had to slap him in the side of the head. I was not having it, especially after one other person who used to be around here sexually assaulted me."

"What?"

"Um hm. Just cause everybody likes to preach consent don't mean it's always practiced. Like Christians talking about love and shit."

I was a little stunned and uncomfortable. I finally managed, "I guess I'm lucky I have you here and D.C. as my mentor."

"Oh, yeah. D.C. would not have been pleased," Mac assured me. "He gets real territorial and he don't like that pervy, little bitch any more than I do. I've only seen him get up in someone's face twice and one of those times was with Irving. I learned then that your mentor is not to be messed with. He may be a small man, but he stands his ground and he can be very, very intimidating when he loses his temper."

"That," I replied, "I am aware of."

Mac nodded. "Come on. Let's go downstairs and out of this crowded-ass hallway. You need some space and I need a cigarette."

We made our way to the first floor where Mac headed for the backyard. I scooted into the kitchen looking for that drink that my mentor had mentioned earlier. Next to the microwave I found a series of decanters of liquor that seemed oddly untouched. I opened one that, I'm pretty sure, contained rum, poured a shot into a glass that I pulled from the cabinet and swallowed it quickly.

"You know, alcohol and rough play, like ours, do not mix so well," I heard a female voice say in a Russian accent.

I turned to see, in all of her naked glory, the gangbang queen from upstairs. She was sweaty, but otherwise no worse for the wear.

"Uh," I managed as I tried not to stare at her tits...or anything else for that matter.

She walked over next to me, grabbed another glass from the cabinet and took the bottle from me. She poured a shot and took a big sip. "It thins the blood," she informed me, "alcohol, it does. And it compromises your judgment. You must be careful."

"Sage advice," I said with a forced smile.

I then got another surprise as there was a body next to me on the other side. After Irving's weirdness, I actually started a little.

"Hey," Jenny said to me happily. "Did I scare you?"

"Oh, just a bit," I said with a grin.

Jenny took notice of the naked woman I was talking to. I couldn't tell if she was jealous or curious. "Hi..." she said. "I'm Jenny."

"Hi," the woman said, all traces of any accent gone. "Nice to meet you, Jenny. I'm Tanya. I was just talking to your friend about the dangers of alcohol." She gulped the rest of her shot.

"Uh, okay," Jenny said with a furrowed brow. She pointed to Tanya's chest, just above her left breast. "You have a little something..."

Tanya and I both looked and realized that there were a couple of drops of semen there. The naked woman said nothing, but only wiped it up with her finger which she stuck in her mouth.

"Well, I gotta move along," Tanya said plainly. "There's still a bunch of dicks upstairs that aren't going to fuck themselves. Nice to meet you both." She smiled and walked off.

"Okay..." Jenny said. "That was actually a little weird."

"Just a little?" I replied.

Suddenly, Lady Nessa walked up. "Ignite, who is your friend? I haven't met her yet." Her tone was courteous, though it did seem that there might have been an underlying message wondering who this stranger was in her house.

"Forgive me, Lady Nessa," I said. "This is Jenny, she's..." I looked over at her and smiled. "She's under my consideration."

"I see. Nice to meet you, dear."

"You as well, ma'am," Jenny smiled. "Thank you for having us. Your home is lovely."

"Ah, thank you, Jenny."

"It's very lavish," my potential new sub noted. "May I ask what you do?"

"I'm in real estate," Lady Nessa told us generously.

Jenny nodded. "Well, it certainly seems to be paying off. And you have wonderful taste."

"Thank you." The very formal woman then informed us that we were not the only ones that she was approaching. "I just wanted to let everyone know that we are about to have a little ceremony in the living room. Please join us, if you'd care to."

"Oh," Jenny and I said simultaneously.

"Of course," I completed.

A few moments later, everyone was gathered together, filling the furniture and lining the walls in the living room while Lady Nessa stood with a man and two other women.

"Everyone," the hostess began. "Thank you all for coming. I hope everyone is having a wonderful and safe time. We have something special this evening. Sir Blacksky and Thylora have recently acquired a new pet, and after several weeks of negotiations and exploration, they have all decided to formalize the arrangement. They are honoring us tonight by allowing us to witness and take part in Maxie's collaring ceremony. So please, let's all send positive energy towards them to bless this joining, shall we?"

There was a short and quiet patting of applause.

Two of the people at the center of attention, a large man in dark jeans and a black polo shirt and a tall, buxom woman in a corset and heels, both about my age, pushed a younger, more petite woman, also in a corset, but barefoot, in front of them. The taller woman put a crop against the other's shoulder, urging her to her knees. The man pulled out a piece of paper and read from it.

"Maxie, you have, after sober reflection, offered yourself to Thylora and myself and requested to join our house, to submit to us and to our needs. Is this true?"

"Yes, Sir," the woman on her knees replied.

"Recite your oath."

She obeyed. "I pledge my devotion and worship to my Sir and Ma'am, Blacksky and Thylora. I will honor them and afford them all that I am for their needs, whatever they may be. From this moment on, Sir and Ma'am, I am yours."

Thylora placed a silver hoop collar, a large metal ring, around Maxie's neck. She began to fasten it, somehow, in the back. It took a while and I whispered to Jenny, "That seems like it's going to be hard to get off."

A man standing next to me apparently overheard and clarified. "It doesn't come off."

"Hm," Jenny mumbled. "That's commitment...and an inconvenience at the airport."

Thylora spoke next. "Maxie, you are ours now. You are our property, our prize possession, ours to love, to cherish, to mold, to teach, to discipline and to derive satisfaction from."

"Rise, Maxie," Blacksky continued. "Rise and be counted as one of our house."

Maxie stood and dropped her head. Everyone in the room, including her new owners applauded.

"That was pretty interesting," Jenny said.

"Agreed," I replied.

The applause died down and everyone went back to mingling. Jenny turned to me, "So, what's been going on up to my arrival?"

I chuckled nervously. "You wouldn't believe me if I told you." I considered where we were and what circumstances had brought us together. "Actually, that's ridiculous. You probably would because we are living in the land of the depraved. Despite that, let's just say that it's been eventful and leave it at that."

Suddenly, Tinkerbrat was in front of us with eyeliner still on her forehead and Posie behind her. She addressed my date. "Hello, Jenny."

"Hey, Tink."

"I have been instructed to apologize to you both for setting a bad example for all the other subs and slaves here. I was bad."

Jenny glanced at me and then back at her. "O...kay."

"Tink," I said soberly. "It's okay. You don't have to do this for us."

"I do, Mr. Ignite," she said. A look of frustration filled

her eyes as she looked into mine, but she was still respectful.

I sighed. "Well, we appreciate it. Understand that we don't hold it against you." I looked at Jenny. "Right?"

"Huh? Oh!" She looked back at Tink and shook her head. "No. No, of course not."

Tink let out a sigh and leaned into me. "Thank you, Iggy." She sighed again and moved on.

"What the hell was that?" Jenny asked me.

"It's...a long story."

"Okay."

"Come on," I said. "Let's mingle."

We made our casual rounds, looking at the place and making courteous hellos. Finally, we went upstairs after Jenny expressed interest in a bit of voyeurism. We squirmed into the increasingly crowded hallway, glancing into the first two rooms where little of interest was currently taking place. After that, she moved straight into the far right room, inching in aggressively with me behind her. Within was pure debauchery.

The gangbang queen was at it again, this time offering up everything she had as two men double penetrated her and another fucked her mouth. Not to be sold short, she was also manually stimulating two other men with each hand.

"Oh my." The quiet exclamation came from Jenny, who was fixated on the scene, an astonished grin on her face. While I found the spectacle excessive, I did allow the both of us to stay there for a couple of minutes since she seemed so fascinated.

Finally, I started getting tired of the one sided orgy and tried to direct my date to the other room.

"Just...just... Let's just..." she said, not taking her eyes off of the sex. "Another couple of minutes."

I sighed internally, but didn't give any obvious reaction. After a while though, I put my hand on her arm and began moving her towards the door. She relented and allowed me to guide her to the room across the hall.

I maneuvered Jenny in where we found something much more my speed. There, Thylora was putting the finishing touches on some very complex rope restraints on her new pet, who knelled, whimpering and playing out, what I would later learn from her profile page, was her favorite game.

As Thylora ran a hand down the girl's face, from her blindfold to her chin, Maxie jerked away and gave a very convincing, "Stop it!"

Thylora pulled Maxie to her by her new collar. "Behave, you little bitch. Don't make me hurt you."

Her sub acted unimpressed. "Get your hands off of me!"

This was met with a fist in her hair that pulled her to her feet. Thylora tied the rope around Maxie to the bed frame. All the while, Blacksky just sat calmly in a chair, watching.

"Don't pretend you don't like it," Thylora said.

"I don't," Maxie insisted.

Her new Domme slapped her before beginning to lick and nibble and touch her naked body all over.

"Stop! Don't! Let me go!" What appeared to be actual tears crept from underneath her blindfold.

Thylora halted the tongue bath just long enough to slap her again and say, "Shut up! You're mine now and I'll do whatever the fuck I want with you. I'm going to touch you and then you're going to eat my pussy. Do it well and I might even fuck you."

Maxie's breathing continued to increase. Every few seconds she would twitch or pretend to struggle more.

Finally, she began to protest again with a series of "No's" that culminated in her demanding, once again, for her new Domme to stop, even calling her an, "evil cunt."

Suddenly, Blacksky got up. He quickly moved to her and grabbed her face, squeezing until her lips puckered out.

"That is your Mistress, you ungrateful little whore. You will respect her and do as she commands you to or *I* will punish you. Understand?"

After a couple of brief seconds and several desperate breaths, Maxie nodded as best as she could. He let her go and went back to his seat. Thylora stood in front of her and began pinching the girl's hard nipples and rubbing her pussy. Then, while keeping her right hand at work between her new possession's legs, Thylora reached around and began massaging her rectum, perhaps trying to push a finger up inside.

"Protest all you want, little slut. You're getting so wet, I know you're full of shit." She kissed her hungrily before untying her from the bed frame and putting her on her knees. She let her own panties drop to the floor. "Eat me."

Maxie grimaced and shook her head.

Blacksky thundered from the chair, "Do it!"

Maxie started and then slowly, tentatively, began to inch her face towards her Mistress' crotch.

Thylora wasn't impressed and pressed the girl's face in, grinding her. "Lick it, slut." This continued for a minute or two before she pulled Maxie up and shoved her at the bed, bending her over. "Now, you get my cock."

Suddenly, Thylora pulled, from seemingly out of nowhere, a large, black strap-on dildo. She cinched it around her waist and rubbed it against the girl's opening.

"Don't you put that thing in me, bitch!" Maxie

screamed.

This seemed to really piss Thylora off. She produced a genuinely evil looking paddle from the same nether realm that her rubber dick had come from. It was small, stiff and had leather flaps on either side of it. A series of round holes were cut into the leather. Thylora pulled Maxie's head back by her hair roughly before beating her many times...hard.

Maxie cried out, more like screamed in agony. Her ass immediately turned bright red, with a series of marks that mimicked the holes on the paddle.

"Stop! God, please, stop!"

Thylora's grip in her hair tightened as she said, "Maybe I'll let your Master beat you for a while. How about that?"

"N-no," Maxie stuttered, sounding genuinely scared. "No, please. I'll do whatever you want just..."

Thylora laughed and pushed her back to her knees. "That's a good girl. Now suck my cock."

This, I found curious as there was no way for the Domme to gain any physical pleasure from it. I whispered something to that effect to Jenny.

"It's just another way to subjugate her," she whispered back, her eyes locked onto the scene. "Humiliation and forced obedience."

Thylora jerked the girl up and pushed her over the bed again with her red, blistered ass in the air. She ran a couple of fingers along Maxie's slit before inserting them. "You're so wet," she taunted. "I know you like it. And you're going to like this even more." She began to work the dildo into her, holding the base of it with one hand and Maxie's hair with the other.

Maxie grunted and groaned, sounding almost distressed, but it was also evident that she was pushing back a little too. Before long, she was getting a good, steady fucking.

And all the while, Blacksky remained motionless, simply watching.

"Whore," Thylora called out. "Nasty, fucking, dirty whore. You like my cock. Say it!" She slapped her subs battered ass.

Maxie wailed before obeying. "I like it, Mistress. I like your cock."

This went on for a while until it was obvious that Maxie came with loud screams. Once she was done, Thylora pulled out of her, put her on her knees and pulled off her blindfold. That's when Blacksky finally stood, went to where his partner in sin was holding Maxie in place, opened his pants and began jerking off. In a surprisingly quick time, he came all over Maxie's face.

Thylora let her go and she collapsed, breathing heavily looking completely used up, degraded and...satisfied.

Jenny turned to me with a giddy grin. She spoke quietly. "I want to do something like that."

I led Jenny outside, saying that I needed some fresh air. The rooms where everyone had been playing were hot and stuffy for obvious reasons. She followed happily, but she did begin pestering me to play there at the party.

"I don't think I'm ready for that, Jenny."

"It doesn't have to be really extreme," she told me. "Just a beating, maybe." Her tone was eager and begged me.

"I didn't bring any of my toys."

"Did D.C.? Maybe he or someone else would let you

borrow some." Before I could shake my head she said, "Or, we don't have to use toys. I'm open to lots of things, really."

"I'm not at the moment," I insisted.

She looked disappointed, but still conceded.

"Did I over hear that you were looking for some play tonight?" The question originated from a man that I didn't know. He was tall, mildly attractive and dressed in a black shirt and a kilt. He carried a drink of what smelled like scotch. "I'd be happy to oblige."

"Oh..." Jenny said. She suddenly looked hopeful. She looked at me, but immediately recognized my disapproving expression. She became resigned and looked back to him. "No. Thank you, though. That's very kind."

"Are you sure? I don't mind at all." His smile was eager and a little dirty.

"I mind," I said. "No offense, but she's under my consideration and we're still getting to know each other. I'd like to do so more completely before we engage in public encounters or even consider inviting others into our play."

"I understand," he said magnanimously. "Let me know if you change your minds." He smiled at Jenny and walked away.

"Tink and Posie were involved in our first play," my date mumbled.

"What was that?"

"Nothing."

I smiled a bit wickedly. "Alright, dirty girl. Keep it up and you may get your wish. Only the play will be strictly punishment."

"Sorry, Sir," she grumbled, yet with a reluctant smile.

"Ignite," I heard a familiar voice say as it approached.

I turned to see Purrterra there. She was followed by Greta and her new Dom, as well as another man. "How are you tonight?"

"Oh, hey, Terra. Good."

"Who's your friend?"

"Purrterra, Greta..." I looked to her Sir, "AmericanDom, this is Jenny. Sermonette on the website."

"It's nice to meet you all," Jenny smiled.

"Well," Terra purred. "Allow me to introduce my new Dom." She curled up next to a man of about thirty with slicked back, dark hair. He was very handsome and dressed in a black suit and black shirt. "This is Jackson. Consummate Tormentor."

He presented me his hand. "Pleasure."

"You as well."

I couldn't put my finger on it, but there was something very dark, almost sinister about him, even as he smiled and spoke in a friendly tone.

"This is quite a party," he said. "I didn't expect this many people."

"Yeah..." I replied as socially as possible. "I was a little surprised myself. There weren't even this many people at the Scene Shop's anniversary."

"You went to the Scene Shop for its anniversary?" Jenny asked.

"I did." I smiled as I suddenly felt more traveled and proud. "That's where Purrterra and I met."

"Yeah. That was a fun night," she said with a tint of naughtiness.

"I thought Xina was going to seriously mess you up," I told her.

"Nah. I'm tough," she replied.

"I can attest to that," Tormentor nodded an arm

around her neck. "This girl here likes pain and has been able to take everything I've thrown at her so far and I'm a pretty hardcore sadist."

"He is rough," Terra grinned, the lust still in her voice.

"I like pain too," Greta volunteered, as she nuzzled AmericanDom, who remained silent.

"What about you, Jenny?" Jackson asked. "You like it rough?"

She smiled. "I like mental domination more than physical. But pain can be nice."

Greta suddenly looked around. "Hey, have you two seen Lolly Popper? She was supposed to be here."

"Yeah," I replied. "She and Killer Rabbit were in the house last I saw."

Greta let out a grunt. "She can do so much better than that asshat."

"Uhh...no comment," I said.

Tormentor spoke up. "I think that I'm going to go find a beverage." He turned to Purrterra. "Would you care for anything, my dear?"

"No, I'm good. I shouldn't have any booze if we're going to play latter."

"Oh, we're going to play later," her Dom said with a kiss to her forehead. He went into the house.

"He's so good looking," Jenny noted. "You're very lucky."

"Thanks," Terra beamed. "I could say the same for Ignite. He scored himself a total babe."

Jenny smiled big and I agreed with a swat to her rump. "Yep. And, if she's good, she might get some play when we get home, too."

"Gretaaaaa," a voice sang. We all turned to see Mac approaching to hug her. "How are you and yours tonight?"

"Good. You?" she asked.

"I'm okay."

"Good," she repeated. "Because I never see you."

"Yes, well..." Mac began. "I don't do the munches anymore."

"Oh..." Greta gave an uncomfortable pause before glancing towards Terra. "Right. Sorry."

Mac shrugged. "It is what it is." He turned his gaze to Jenny. "Ignite, is this lovely little thing here the one you have under consideration?"

I smiled. "Mac, this is Jenny."

"Hi," she said.

"Hello, yourself. I see now that, even if I did have a chance of turning him, it wouldn't have worked with you in the wings."

Jenny chuckled and blushed a little.

Mac then asked Purrterra how she was doing. Her response was as elated as it had been since she arrived. "I'm excellent."

"Well, good," he said, seeming sincere. "Last we spoke you were not in a very happy place. What changed?"

"She met someone," Tormentor said, as he walked up, beer in one hand and the other claiming Terra's waist. "Hello, Mac."

Suddenly, Mac looked frightened. Considering his size and the way he'd stood up to Irving earlier, it seemed really odd and unsettling.

"Jackson," he said, clearly uncomfortable. "What are you doing here?"

"I'm back in town," he said in a not-unfriendly tone.

Mac didn't respond to him. He simply addressed us all with an, "Excuse me," and walked away.

Jenny and I exchanged confused glances and I told her to give me a moment while I went after him. I caught him over on the right side of the yard.

"Hey. You okay?"

"No, I am not okay," he replied, clearly distraught. "I'm pretty fucking far from okay."

"What is it?"

He took a few deep breaths, trying to regain some composure. "Remember I said that I got assaulted last year? Well, that is the mother fucker who did it."

"Oh, my god," I exclaimed.

"Yeah."

"Well...should we tell Purrterra?"

Mac shook his head. "It won't make any difference. Mistress Xina will just convince her that it's not true. Jackson has a way of making people think that he's a standup guy, trustworthy. In fact, that's why I don't go to the munches anymore. Xina told me not to come back after I told people what he did. She accused me of making it up, trying to start trouble."

He continued to breathe heavily. Suddenly, there was commotion over by the corner of the house. Killer Rabbit and Lolly were having some sort of disagreement and he was yelling at her. He took hold of her wrist and she tried to pull away. Then...he backhanded her.

You could hear gasps from all over the yard. Rabbit continued to yell, but he didn't get much more out before he was pulled off of Lolly...by Jackson. Rabbit spun around and swung a fist, but Jackson leaned back out of the way. The douchey Dom prepared to throw another blow, but was unsuccessful before he began as AmericanDom caught his arm, pulled it behind him, lifted him up by his collar, marched him to the driveway and shoved him out into the street. We didn't see him after that.

People went to check on Lolly while others thanked AmericanDom and Jackson. I looked over at Mac, who wore a pained expression. He let out an injured grunt and walked off. I wanted to catch him, to say something reassuring, but I didn't know what. That's when Jenny walked up.

"Is everything okay?" she asked, obviously shaken and concerned.

I sighed. "No. Things are just getting weird. Maybe we should get out of here. Go home and find something more pleasant to occupy our time."

She smiled warmly. "Okay."

We made our rounds, saying goodbye to the people we knew and left the party behind us.

When Jenny and I got back to my place, I shut the door behind us and went to the stereo where I cued up an especially passionate Saeta. After that, I didn't stand on even a fraction of ceremony.

"Take off your clothes," I commanded with a hand on her face. She wanted to play, she was going to get it.

She struggled out of her simple black dress, her breathing beginning to increase. Once she was naked, I had my fingers tangled in her hair and her pulled up next to me. I considered what to do next. She wanted to be used, but the overshadowing violence at the party had left me slightly out of the mood for that sort of thing.

"What are you going to do to me?" she gasped, yet with a smile.

It was good question. The lesson in sensuality played in my head.

"I think maybe we need to start basic," I said. "I'm going to command you and I'm going to beat you some, but it's just going to be to sensitize you. Understand?"

Her smile developed some confusion. "Not really."

I exchanged hands, putting my left one in her hair and my right one between her legs. I pressed up with my fingers and she gasped.

"We're going to make your body sensitive in order to amplify everything."

"How are you going to do that?"

I gave her a devastating grin. "First, say that you're willing. Say you're mine at the moment and that you are at my service."

She complied. "I am, Sir. I'm willing and at your service."

"Very good...dirty little thing."

She chuckled lustfully. I turned her towards the bedroom, marched her in and pushed her onto the bed. I began undressing. Once I was done, I tossed a blindfold towards her.

"Put it on," I ordered. She cooperated, happily.

Next, I cuffed her to the head board. I pulled my crop from where it hung on the closet door knob and my belt from my pants, feeling that it was time to test my theory about the stamps on it, as well as my new sub's limitations. With each in my hands, I stood there looking down at this beautiful woman who had granted me dominion over her and I breathed.

I studied her perfect body and her expectant smile. Then...I beat her.

It wasn't vicious. It wasn't sadistic. It was just a series of lashes that heightened the sensitivity of her smooth skin and caused a series of gasps and grunts from her. There wasn't a single inch of her flesh that I left untouched by my leather. And, once she was properly sensitized, still squirming on the bed, I dropped both of my battering toys and picked up the feather duster and began gliding it all over her, now incredibly delicate, body. I also touched, licked, caressed, blew on and rubbed all of it. She continued to squirm.

"Are you enjoying this?" I asked.

"Yes, Sir," she gasped. "But..."

I waited. "But?"

"It's not my pleasure that matters, Sir. It's yours. I'm yours."

Topping from the bottom, eh? We'd see about that.

I went to the kitchen and filled a glass with ice water. Next, I went to a drawer in the bathroom where I'd stashed some new items that I'd purchased just for such an occasion. I returned to the bedroom, to find Jenny breathing long and hard, but otherwise motionless.

"We need to tenderize you a little more," I said. I reclaimed my belt from where I'd dropped it and began spanking her all over. Again, it wasn't terribly hard. It was more like aggressive patting, just enough to sting a little. Once I had her extra sensitive again, I pulled a large makeup brush out of the bag. Slowly and softly, I guided it all over her pink skin as her breathing increase and she squirmed a little.

Next, I reached over to the glass that I'd placed on the nightstand and pulled out a couple of pieces of ice. I caressed her with them and she moaned. As the ice began to melt, I picked up the glass and dribbled small amounts of cold water onto her. The drops would hit her warm flesh and run off of her onto the bed, leaving little trails and glistening almost as much a her sweat.

But that wasn't the temperature extreme that I was mainly planning to expose her too. The next thing that I produced from the bag was a white paraffin candle. I lit it and waited as it began to melt. Slowly, I let some tentative drops fall onto her skin. This she responded to even louder, her moans beginning with grunts and then ebbing into sighs. As each drop hardened, Jenny would open and close her restrained hands and arch her back. But she said nothing.

Finally, I set the make shift toys aside, pulled on a condom and crawled on top of her. Grabbing a fistful of her hair, I whispered in her ear, "Are you ready, you dirty little girl?"

"Yes!" she called out. "Yes, Sir!"

I guided myself into her slowly. She moaned. I began moving back and forth as I continued to whisper to her.

"You're nasty for liking this. It's filthy what you're letting me do...hoping I'll do. You're going to be mine. I'll own you and I'll make you do whatever I want. Do you understand?"

"Yes, Sir," she replied happily. Then she asked, "Sir?"

"Yes, dirty girl?"

"Are you going to degrade me?"

I was a tad confused. "What do you mean?"

"Are you going to really use me?"

"That's what I'm doing, you filthy thing," I murmured. "You serve no purpose but to give me pleasure."

She gasped. "No, Sir. I don't"

"You're a thing that I fuck."

"Just a thing that you fuck," she repeated.

I started to hammer into her a few times as she called out. Finally, I eased off of her and went to retrieve more things to pleasure her body with: more ice, the feather duster, the satin pillow case, a recently purchased spiked wrist band that I dragged by the points across her flesh...

I ran them all over her skin, and while she panted and squirmed, she eventually begged me to fuck her again.

"Make me your fuck toy," she whimpered. "Use me."

I climbed back onto her and did as she requested, as best as I understood. This beautiful woman underneath me, allowing me to fuck her... I looked down at her, considering her to be mine. I owned this gorgeous thing and she responded, cooing out thanks and moaning as I shoved myself into her again and again and again. She was so sexy and so permissive, I couldn't help but feel proud and honored. I pounded into her until I could take it no more and came hard into the condom that I was wearing. I grunted and wailed as she moaned and called out. At the end, I collapsed on top of her, holding on for dear life.

A few moments passed before I eased off of and out of her with a loud gasp. I rolled over and began setting her loose before pulling her to me. I kissed her.

"Did you like that?" I asked.

"That was nice," was all she said, with a pleasant smile as she curled up next to me.

We fell asleep.

CHAPTER EIGHTEEN

The following week I was having lunch with Momma C. After taking time to catch up and bitch about our respective workplaces, I decided to get her opinion on my mentor's actions.

"Do you think it's acceptable to punish a sub when you're angry?" I asked her.

"I would never do it myself," she replied, "but, different people have different ideas about it."

"Seems to me that it borders on abuse at that point."

Cathy thought for a moment. "I think it depends. If the sub's really masochistic, I suppose it might be okay. Or maybe if they just aren't getting the picture."

I shook my head. "I don't agree with it. I'm thinking of saying something to D.C. about it."

Momma C. whistled at my bravado before saying, "I've only seen him punish one of the girls when he was angry once, but he didn't hurt her."

"I'm assuming Tink."

"How'd you guess?" she smirked. "It wasn't terribly different from what you described. She embarrassed him and he humiliated her."

"What did he do?"

"She had to take her panties off and hold them in her mouth while she sat with her nose in the corner at the Scene Shop for an hour. Nothing physical."

"He told me she was getting a beating when they got home."

Momma C. shrugged. "He didn't do it right then. Hopefully, he had calmed down by the time he wore her out."

I considered what she was saying, but I still couldn't fight the feeling that he'd been wrong. "I never thought I'd ever agree with Batlash about anything."

"Making you uncomfortable?"

I sighed.

We were both quiet for just a bit before I asked her about my other concern with my new mentor. "Do you know Master Jon?"

"Of course."

"He was there the other night."

"Was he?"

"Yeah..." I paused.

"Why do I get the feeling that there's more coming?" she asked.

"D.C. told him a little about my job," I informed her.

"He what?" She seemed extra surprised.

"Yeah."

"That's not like him," she scowled. "He's super concerned with discretion."

"Is it possible he more concerned with social climbing?" I asked, feeling bad about my supposition and worried about its possibility.

She pondered hard. "May I asked what he shared?"

I thought for a bit before telling her, "I have access to some information at City Hall. I discovered that someone there is aware of the Scene Shop and its location and may want to bring it to the public's attention. D.C. told Master Jon this and urged me to share whatever I learned with him and the board."

"Oh," Momma C. said, the look on her face seeming more understanding. "That's a little different. That's a little more like a superhero sharing their secret identity to save others."

"Yeah, but it wasn't his secret identity that he was exposing," I pointed out.

She nodded. "That's true." She was pensive for a bit more before finally shaking her head. "Still, it's important. He should have discussed it with you first, but it is important. There are too many people with too much to lose and the only person he told was Master Jon, who literally keeps secrets for a living."

"Do you think D.C. is a social climber?"

She pursed her lips and looked up. "No," she finally said, before adding, "and, yes. D.C. already has respect, but I think there's a part of him that wants to have it reinforced to him that he deserves it, wants to be reassured that it's not misplaced. When the higher ups grant him respect, I think he feels like it might be a lark sometimes. Does that make any sense?"

I nodded slowly, trying to believe it. It sounded similar to some of the things he'd said about Tink, making me wonder if it was something they had in common.

"He's not a bad guy, Iggy. He's a really good guy, actually, one of the best I know. Plus, he's awfully secretive. There may be something that he knows that the rest of us don't. That being said, while I urge caution in approaching him about how he handles his girls, you should talk to him about what he said to Master Jon. He needs to know how you feel."

"Don't worry. That's definitely getting discussed." I sighed. "Anyway..."

"Well, let's talk about something more pleasant," she suggested. She smiled. "How are things with Jenny?"

"Mmmm..." I scowled.

"Uh oh. What's that about?"

"I don't know. I'm having a hard time keeping her interest...or maybe just keeping up with her."

"What do you mean?"

"She wanted to play at the party. I didn't feel ready for something so public." I paused for a sip for my drink and to collect my thoughts. "Anyway, she accepted it, reluctantly. But then, some guy offered to step in and provide what she was asking for."

"He started hitting on her?" she asked.

"He wanted to borrow her," I clarified.

"I'm going to assume that you weren't down with that."

I shook my head. "No. I'm not that open minded or daring or whatever is required to go along with that kind of sharing. Besides, we just got together. I'm still exploring what it is that we are trying to create here. I took her home and showed her some things that I had learned, some more sensual stuff, which she seemed to enjoy, but..."

"But?"

"She wants more excitement. She wants to be taken, used, to feel like it's fast, hard and degrading. I can do that. I don't mind claiming her, but I want to do more than just smack her around and force fuck her."

Momma C. nodded. "Understandable." She thought for a bit. "Have you considered introducing her to pursuit, take down and capture?"

I was confused. "No. That's a new one on me. What is it?"

She smiled wickedly. "Oh, I think you and she will love it. You go out into the woods or a huge field and you chase her."

"And when I catch her?"

She cocked her head for a second. "That's up to you. But if she's the type to have rape fantasies or who likes to be treated as a thing to be used, it could be an idea."

I considered the suggestion before asking, "Where is there to go to do that around here? I mean, some place where we would be safe and wouldn't be caught? I don't want to go to a public park or anything?"

She continued to smile. "I have just the place. The Scene Shop uses it for this very thing on occasion."

I leaned in, now very interested. "Do tell?"

My next visit to the White House had my stomach in knots. I wasn't at all certain how my mentor would react to my concerns. I wasn't even certain what I would be walking into. Would he still be mad? Would the girls still be in trouble? Would I find Tinkerbrat hogtied in the middle of the floor with a severely bruised ass, a gag in her mouth and a violet wand duct taped to her vagina?

I approached their door and knocked with a trepidatious hand. After mere seconds, the door was opened by Posie, who smiled big.

"Hey," she beamed. She turned towards the couch where D.C. was seated with Tink in his lap. They were laughing even as Posie told them, "Mr. Ignite is here."

"Hey, my friend," D.C. said cheerfully, as he began tickling his sub, who squirmed.

"Stop it! Stop it! *Stop it*!" Tink yelled, before slapping him in the chest. The two continued to laugh.

"What can we do for you?" D.C. asked.

"I was hoping to have a word in private."

"Oh. Okay." He swatted Tink on the rear and instructed her and Posie to excuse the two of us.

"Yes, Sir," they replied. Tink took her sister by the hand and led her out, both of them still smiling and giggling.

"What's up?" my mentor asked.

"Well, uh..." I began as I sat. "Considering what I just witnessed, this may seem a little odd, but..." I hesitated.

"Don't be shy. Not with me. Spit it out."

I sighed and screwed up my courage. "I'm a little concerned about the girls after seeing you with them at the party the other night." I waited on him to become irritated or angry with me, but he just smiled.

"You're worried that I might have let my emotions make a decision for me and that I may have over reacted to Tink's clumsiness?"

I hesitated. "...Basically."

He sighed himself. "That's a valid concern," he admitted. "And I'm happy that you feel that you can come to me with it, as well as the fact that you care about my girls enough to do so. The fact is, Tink has been a bit of a handful lately. She's always rebellious and disrespectful, but she's been even more so and she's staying out after work more and more. It's been bothering me. So, the other day, she and I had a long talk about it. She agreed to try to be more restrained and to give Posie and I more of her free time. Before the party, I made her promise to be on her best behavior and not to embarrass me. Then..."

He didn't have to fill in the rest.

"I see. Well...I suppose that's mildly understandable. You weren't *just* punishing her for bumping into Master Jon."

"And I didn't actually beat her senseless. Although..." He paused. "I confess that, in the moment, I was mad enough that I wanted to take a cane to her for about an hour. I waited til we got home, we talked for a long time and she got five strikes from a strap. She now can't drink after work for the next two weeks and she has to come straight home. The last time we did this with her, her grades improved and she saved a lot of money."

"Oh, right. She's in school, isn't she?"

He smiled softly, almost condescendingly. "She takes classes online."

"What's her major?"

"English. She's toying with being a writer."

"Is she any good?"

His smile morphed into a smirk. "I'll let you know if she ever finishes something." He got up from his seat and went to the kitchen where he opened a bottle of Bourbon and poured himself two fingers. He offered me some, which I declined. He continued. "Tink needs structure. It's one of the reasons that she agreed to our arrangement. Now, I admit that I can lose it sometimes with her. But it's only after she continues to prod me and I usually try to stay my reaction until I can address it rationally. Most importantly however, we talked at length, really talked. I only like hurting her when we're playing. Punishment is never fun or arousing for me. I'm not like that and she knows it. That's why she gets so upset. She's mad at herself."

I was silent as I considered what he was saying.

"Look," he went on, as he sat. "I know arrangements like ours can seem unhealthy from the outside. But, just remember, it's all *consensual,* which means we all want it and enjoy it. It makes us happy and fulfilled." He sat his drink down and pat my shoulder. "Tell you what. Why don't you stay for dinner? We never get to just hang out unless it's at a munch or a party where we have tons of distractions."

"Actually, that sounds nice. Thank you."

"You have any special dietary restrictions?"

"No."

"Well, that makes it easy."

He turned, like he might call the girls, but I stopped him. "There is one other thing."

"Oh?"

"Yeah." Again, I summoned courage. "The stuff you told Master Jon about me—"

He held up a hand. "You are one hundred percent correct. I apologize profusely. It's just that the conversation came up and I felt that it was important, important enough to dive into without discussing it with you first. I know now, that was wrong. Please, forgive me. It was never my intention to put you in that position. I know better. I just let the situation get away from me."

I sighed and smiled. "It's okay."

"It's not actually," he told me. "However, I will add that, there are a few extenuating circumstances that you aren't privy to, and in that light, I can only ask you to trust me, even if I did act like a dick."

I considered what he was saying and nodded.

"Okay. Good. I still owe you one. Let's start with dinner." He called the girls who walked in with quick reverence. "Mr. Iggy will be joining us for dinner. I'm going to run to the store to get us something nice."

"I want to go," Tink piped in.

D.C. smiled at her. "You just want to make sure I come home with more alcohol."

"Yep," she laughed. Her tone then turned slightly affectionate. "But that's not the only reason I want to go with you."

He smiled. "Okay, kiddo. Come on." He stood and put an arm around her before directing his attention to his other sub. "Pos, would you be so kind as to entertain our guest while we're gone?"

My mentor and his alpha sub left. Without even a beat, Posie turned to me and asked, "So, what sounds entertaining? A strip tease?"

I was stunned. "A...what?"

"I'm kidding, Mr. Iggy." She said with a dry smile that made me feel a little dumb.

"Sorry, Posie. I just rarely ever hear you make a joke."

"I make jokes," she replied, sounding mildly defensive. She went to the kitchen and opened a bottle of wine. "Would you like some Merlot?"

I pondered the offer a moment before saying, "Well, I guess I'm not driving right away, so sure."

She poured us each a glass and we sat at the kitchen table where we began to talk.

"So, let me ask you, Posie, why do you do this? Live as a submissive, I mean?"

"It's fun," she grinned. "And it's enlightening."

"In what way?"

She took a sip off her wine and thought for a moment before telling me she loved being reminded that things as simple as having a roof over her head and being allowed to sit on furniture are why she's blessed.

"Blessed," I repeated with a chuckle. "Odd choice of words.

"Old habit, I guess. I was actually raised very conservative Christian and made a sharp reform. Sometimes enlightened people are born into shattered ranks, you know? Some of us make it out alive with nothing but the positive aspects of it still making our decisions. The rest is just a tragic reminder of how many mistakes you can make trying to be a 'good' person.

Church life is filled with drama." She made a brief, sour face. "Anyway, my current lifestyle keeps things simple. I think maybe I treat my sub life like that of a monk. And..."

"And?"

She blushed slightly and smiled. "I'm just a really, really horny person. I mean, I think about sex constantly and I get plenty of it here, any kind I want with two wonderful people."

"Tinkerbrat said something similar. I guess you two aren't as different as you appear."

"Two sides of the same coin, in a way."

"Does her acting out ever annoy you or scare you?" I asked, curious to try to gain a fuller version of what the punishment dynamic was like in the White House.

She laughed. "No. Not really. I mean, I get a little frightened when she makes Sir mad. I never know what's coming. His punishments can be pretty creative sometimes."

"For example?"

"For example..." She thought briefly. "Tink went through a period where she wouldn't always answer her phone. She'd hit ignore if he called and she was engaged in something else, shopping or hanging out with friends. She never put him off for long, but he didn't like it. So, he tied her up, had me hold a vibrator to her pussy and spanked her while she moaned and cried out. She also had to recite her name, her position as a sub, who she was the property of and that she enjoyed kinky sex, along with a list of her fetishes. Sir recorded it and set it as her ringtone."

"Jesus!" I remarked in amazement and some shock.

"Yeah," Posie giggled. "Forever after that, she picks up her phone right away."

"I would think so."

"Overall though, it doesn't really frighten me when she's irreverent. I actually think Tink is kind of funny. In fact..." she paused.

"...Yes?"

She leaned in, as if there were a need to whisper, like D.C.'s aura over his home might hear her. "I actually find her a little thrilling when she acts out. Tink gets to test the boundaries for both of us. I don't know. Maybe I like having my curiosity over such situations satiated. But I'm not one to act out. It's not part of my nature. With Tink, it's like having a big sister who makes all of the mistakes and gets in trouble, so I don't have to, you know? Plus, it's kind of funny sometimes. Scary, others, but funny some."

"*Big* sister," I repeated. "But she's younger than you. By, like, three years."

She smirked. "Relative. We have fifty year old people in our community who want to literally be treated like infants."

"That's a good point," I said as I remembered some posts on line about adults in diapers who longed for their pacifiers. In the lifestyle, everyone got to choose who and what they were regardless. I let it all sink in before asking, "You're not usually this forthcoming. Why are you being so casual and upfront?"

She simply smiled and said, "I have permission". And then she toasted me.

I tapped my glass with hers.

"So," I began again, "you like being subjugated?"

""Oh, God," she replied and tossed her head back. "It makes life so much simpler."

"How so?"

She rested her chin on her knuckles as she collected

her thoughts. "I guess, it's like a job, you know? I mean, at many places of employment you have a uniform. You don't have to think about what you're going to wear every morning. I don't have to debate with myself over that too much. I'm only allowed to wear certain things."

"He picks out your clothes for you?" I asked surprised, but hoping I didn't sound appalled, much less as intrigued by the idea as I actually was.

"Sort of. He makes me get rid of things that don't flatter me and puts restrictions on what I can wear certain places. I mean, I don't have to worry about my shoes in the condo because I'm not allowed to wear them."

I suddenly realized that I'd always witnessed her barefoot and Tink in socks in their place. "Go on."

"If we go out to a nice dinner, Sir just picks a dress and puts it on my bed. He only lets me wear perfume he likes and can stand because he's allergic to most of them. They make his skin itch and his eyes burn. When I come home at night from work, I have a strict list of things I have to do: laundry, exercise, make dinner..."

"They never cook?"

"Oh, Sir does," she assured me. "He's actually decent at it and likes to make food for us. But he and I trade off. Tink never does because her cooking is terrible." She snickered. "We just make her do the dishes afterward."

"Okay."

"Anyway, I have a regiment. And once I'm done with my work and house duties, I have to work on my own business for an hour or two."

"What does that mean?"

"I sell knitted stuff online. Scarves, mittens and things. Some sewing. I wanted to do it, but I could never stay motivated enough to really get it together. Sir made it a requirement and now I have a decent side business and savings because of it."

Interesting. I was seeing more real world practicality in this whole fetish.

"After I'm done with that each day, I get to relax however I want. I can watch TV or play video games or read or whatever. I don't do that much though."

"Why?" I asked.

"Well, because I only have so much time left in the day and I usually want to end it having sex."

I was a little stunned, though not as much as I would have once been. "You're a very unusual Christian, Posie," I said.

"I'm a Unitarian Universalist, now," she smiled.

"I see. And D.C. and Tink?"

"Sir is also a Unitarian. Tink is atheist. And I think she's probably going to hell even if it doesn't exist."

I paused, and then started to laugh.

"See," she said. "I told you I make jokes."

CHAPTER NINETEEN

"Where are we going?" Jenny asked from the passenger seat for about the third time.

"I told you, you'll see."

It was about that time that we turned onto the road that we needed to be on. The houses and businesses began to disappear and we approached a heavily wooded area, the only thing nearby being a small, lonely fire station. I slowed down just enough to confirm that the lights were on and that there were a couple of firefighters present. Then I headed a block down the road, eased off to the shoulder, put the car in park and turned it off.

"Here we are," I told my dirty girl.

"Where?" she asked confused. "We're literally nowhere."

"Actually, no. If you were paying attention then you know that we're only a few blocks from a residential and commercial area. However, the land next to us is about ten to twelve acres of woods." I pointed. "If you look close, you can see faint hints of light. Those are lanterns, electric ones that give just enough light to help you see for short distances."

"What are they doing out there?" Jenny asked.

"I put them out there."

"Why?" Her intrigue seemed to be growing.

"Because, I don't want you to hurt yourself."

The look on her face expressed confusion. "We're going out there? What? We're going to do it in the woods?"

"Not 'it', necessarily. That is..." I smiled. "Not if you can escape me."

"Escape you?"

"Yes. You get a two minute head start. I'm going to chase you after that. If you can make it to the other side of the land here, there's a purple scarf hanging from a tree limb. You find it, grab it and make it back to the car without me catching you and you win."

A nervous, excited grin grew on her face. "And if I don't?"

I shrugged. "Who knows? All kinds of terrible things can happen to a girl in these woods."

Her mischievous smile grew. She started to open the car door, but I stopped her.

"Hey, before we do this, there are just a few things that you need to know. First, the lanterns...there aren't many. So, it's still going to be dark. The faster you run, the more chance you have of hurting yourself. Second, there are a couple of first aid kits out there and I have another here in the car, as well as a small one on me. If things go really south, remember, there's a fire station down the street. And finally..."

I paused.

"Finally?" she asked.

"I have a pocket full of rope and rubbers and I'm not afraid to use them."

She smiled again.

"You have two minutes," I told her, starting the countdown on my phone.

She bolted. I sat there with a particularly rhythmic and primal tune playing on my iPod to get me in the mood.

After a very long two minutes, I got out, locked the

car and headed off into the woods. I knew where she had entered and had a small flashlight with me, so I quickly found her tracks before turning it off. My eagle scout training came into play, but mostly, I just listened and followed the noise.

The faint rustling of leaves could be heard from off in one direction. A few moments later, I saw the wavering of light, like she had moved one of the lanterns, probably to get a better look at the trail in front of her. I zeroed in on it and followed quickly. As I had already canvassed the area a bit, I had that as an advantage. I did notice that she was headed in the vague direction that I had put the scarf, but knew she would never find it, not before I found her. While it wasn't out of reach, it also wasn't near a lantern.

This was going to be fun.

"I'm coming to get you, dirty girl!" I called out, little concern that anyone might hear us, that far out.

I was returned a playful, yet careless, squeal that gave her position away even more.

"I know where you are!" I cried.

After another couple of minutes, I could tell that I was closing in on her. I used my flashlight periodically, but there was also more desperate movement up ahead, through overgrowth, not necessarily on the trail itself. She was getting lost. I followed her for a good bit more, careful not to catch her too soon and cut our game short.

But then the movement ahead stopped and there was only silence. I slowed my approach, turned off my flashlight and listened calmly. She had stopped and was, likely, hiding somewhere, hoping that I might pass her or go another direction. I looked around for any signs of movement. The lanterns were still, the trees were quiet. I crouched and waited.

After a pretty long time, maybe a good ten minutes or

so, I began to hear movement up ahead and to my left. It was slow and careful. It seemed to continue on deeper into the woods, towards the other side where I had placed the scarf. Then one of the lanterns far up ahead displayed her shadow.

I carefully rose. I calmly, but quickly, followed with a plan. I could tell that she had returned to the trail and could even hear her boots as they hit the dirt. I pursued at the same pace that she was moving, adjusting my angle just enough to take an adjacent trail.

Once she reached the far end of the woods, she began searching for the scarf. I could see her silhouette as she scoured the trees and bushes. The one lamp that I had out there was far away. I let her search near it and then move back my direction. All the while, I made my way to where the scarf really was and waited behind a large, nearby tree.

Eventually, she approached, out of breath and moving with urgency. She kept reaching into all of the tree limbs, bushes and along rocks, hoping her hands would run across fabric. Finally, she stopped. He breathing eased a tiny bit as she approached the limb that I had hung it from. It was just above her head and it looked as though she wasn't completely certain that she could make it out in the dark. Finally, she jumped with a grunt and pulled it down. The leaves on the branch rattled and she froze, after looking around anxiously. It was now obvious that she couldn't see me and I continued to wait.

She slowly began to ease back into the woods and search for a trail. As she carefully wandered, I let her pass me, moved around the tree and got behind her. I barely made it a step before she stopped.

I paused.

Her breathing increased again.

She slowly began to look around.

I remained where I was.

Eventually, she turned to look behind her.

"Boo!" I said.

She let out a short scream, and then took off. It was hard to see though and she was clearly afraid to run pell-mell into the trees. I found it easy to grab her and wrestle her to the ground.

As I straddled her, with my arm across her chest and my hand over her mouth I told her, "Careful, dirty girl. That field on the other side of those trees belongs to someone. They may hear you screaming and come to investigate. And you're not going to want them to find us doing what we're about to do."

I slowly let my hand off of her mouth, just enough for her to gasp, "What are we going to do?"

I laughed. I stroked her hair. "Something wicked," I said.

I grabbed her by the hair and pulled her up, her legs wobbling and feet hitting the ground hard as she struggled upright, grunting, laughing and whimpering. I muffled her emoting by taking the scarf that she had found and gagged her with it. Next, I pulled the rope from my pocket, tied her wrists with one end and wrapped the rest around a tree. During all of this she pretended to struggle, but only a little, tugging one way and the next, but ultimately letting me win. Finally, once I got her restrained, I pulled her boots and pants off, rather forcefully. If that didn't get the point across enough, I literally ripped her panties off of her, splitting the undergarment at the side and crotch. What was left of them, I tied in a sloppy bow around her neck. After that, there was little ceremony...if, in fact, the rest could have been considered such.

I pulled out a condom, dropped my pants, put it on and proceeded to fuck the ever loving shit out of my prey, right there against the tree. It was fast, hard and carnal. With each thrust, Jenny's muffled moans forced their way out of the gag. The wild smells all around us seemed to christen our act, making our play something natural. Despite that, I wanted to take it further, pulling her hair, biting her shoulder, at one point, hard enough to make her cry out.

"Shut up, bitch," I warned her. "Don't make me hurt you, not until I'm finished getting what I want, what you're going to give me." Her reaction was a delirious, muffled chuckle and eyes that rolled back in her head.

I slapped her, grabbed her chin and reminded her that we didn't need to be heard before biting her again. Eventually, though, neither of us cared how much sound we made or who might discover us as we slammed into each other harder and harder, building to a steady pulse, like the rhythmic vibrations of a steel refinery, until we came in succession, her first, then a couple of minutes later, me.

As we rested there, catching our breaths, I comforted her, pulling the gag off, bringing her down, stroking her hair and face, giving her water that I had in small bag. I kissed her sweetly, though she remain tied to the tree.

"What did you think of that?" I asked.

She laughed. "That was an interesting, horror movie experience. I can't say that that one ever crossed my mind."

"I'm glad you enjoyed it. You seemed remarkably comfortable, in your element."

"Perhaps." She continued to smile.

"Well, that's good," I said as I fixed the gag back on her mouth. "Let's hope nobody finds you here."

The look in her eyes changed. Suddenly, it was one of distress. I hadn't even put her clothes back on her. She began to mumble through the cloth, desperately.

"Relax," I finally said. "I'm just going to go collect the lanterns and first aid. If you're lucky, I'll be back before the people who own the neighboring property or Leatherface show up."

I winked and walked off.

"God damn, that's rough, Mr. Iggy!" Tink exclaimed after I told her what I had done to my sub.

I chuckled from my stool at the bar at Norman's. "Yeah, well, she wanted things to be more exciting."

Tink laughed. "You're a butthole. I'm glad you're not my Dom. I'd have kicked you in the balls when you finally untied me. Is she okay?"

"She's fine," I assured her. "She was a little freaked out when I came to retrieve her, but she also thought it was a little funny. Plus, she seems to get turned on by extremes." I smirked. "And I seriously doubt that, if D.C. did that to you, you would kick him in the balls."

She pressed her lips together in a tolerant smile. "No. But he's different."

"I'm her D.C., remember? I'm her, Sir."

"True."

Suddenly, a tall guy in a band shirt walked up. He was in desperate need of a haircut and he smiled suggestively at my friend, the bartender...my sister, you could now say. "Hey, Britt," he said. "You doing okay?"

"Hanging in there," she replied with a friendly smile.

"What ya' doin' after work?"

She took in a long breath, smirked and glanced over at

me before telling the dude, "I gotta go home."

"Really?"

"Yeah, really."

"Okay," he nodded. "Let me know if that changes. Okay?"

"Will do."

I examined her as the guy walked off. "Your customers really seem to like you," I noted.

"They're dogs," she quipped. "But they're nice...most of them."

"'K."

"So, what else have you been up to?" she asked me.

"I got a new television," I told her with a proud smile.

"Really?"

"Yep. It's nice. Seventy-five inches. LED, high def, smart TV... The thing is sweet."

"That's awesome," she exclaimed. "You should have a movie party."

I was suddenly interested. I hadn't actually had people—people other than Sluttypixie and Jenny—over to my place. I immediately considered the possibilities.

"You can have a night for kinky movies like *Secretary* or *Rocky Horror* or something. That would be awesome. I'd actually take the night off work for something like that."

I pressed my lips together and nodded as I thought. "That actually sounds interesting," I told her. I then asked, "What's *Secretary*?"

"Yeah," she chuckled. "You definitely need a kinky movie party."

I grinned. Then I moved the conversation to her. "So, D.C. told me that you weren't allowed to drink after work or stay out. How's that going?'

"Meh. It's going."

"You okay after...I don't know...whatever he did to you for punishment."

"Yeah," she said with the dismissive wave of a hand. "I mean...I got into *a lot* of trouble. But you saw the worst of it. The rest was really just a lecture and a lot of questions. Honestly, that was almost worse than the humiliation."

"Really?"

"No. But it seemed like it at the time. I don't like getting a talking to. I don't need to feel like I'm dating my dad."

I smirked. "Are you sure about that?"

She took a breath and raised a finger. It was clear that she was about to return a catty remark, but she stopped. Finally, she slowly waved the finger at me and said, "Don't get cute. You don't know that much about me. Even if..."

I waited before asking, "Even if...?"

"Even if you can, obviously, kind of, extrapolate a good bit."

I snickered.

She replied with a muttered, "Asshole."

Suddenly, the dude in the band shirt walked back up and handed her a piece of paper. "Hey, Britt," he began. "Just in case you can get out tonight, there's a party at this address. There's going to be music and a keg. You should come."

She accepted the paper, but shook her head. "Believe me, Ken, I'd like to. But I can't."

"What's stopping you?" he asked with a smile.

She glanced over at me, and then back. "I just can't." She walked to the kitchen.

I looked over at the dude who I found scrutinizing me pretty intensely.

"You two friends?" he inquired suspiciously.

I slowly nodded after a sip off of my drink. "Something like that."

"Something, exactly, like what?" he asked.

I grinned. "Well, Ken..." I said. "I'd tell ya'. But then I'd have to kill ya'."

He scoffed. I continued to smirk, but didn't waver. The reality of the situation made me feel like my comment was almost genuine.

He got a slight scowl on his face. "Man, whatever," he said before walking off.

I arrived at the munch a few minutes after it had officially started. Everyone had apparently all done introductions and were actively socializing. Jenny had beaten me there and turned to see me walk in after D.C. and Posie, who sat across from her, waved. She smiled big and rose.

"Hello, Sir," she said reverently.

I kissed her on the mouth and forehead. "How's my girl?"

"Good, especially now that you're here."

We sat and I exchanged greetings with the rest of my house. "Tink's at work, I take it?"

"She is," her Sir told me.

"That's kind of a shame, because she gave me an interesting idea that I wanted to run past everyone."

"What's that?" D.C. asked.

"Well, I just got a new TV, a really nice one that I've been wanting for some time. She suggested that we could have a kinky movie night, and seeing as how I never had a housewarming of any kind, I thought it might be fun."

"That could be interesting," Jenny said, sounding only

mildly into it. "Would there be play of any kind?"

"I don't know. I haven't thought about it."

"How big is your place, your living and dining area specifically?" D.C. asked.

I smirked. "Bigger than yours."

He gave me a tolerant smile in return. "Well, in that event, there is something else you might consider."

"And that is?"

"A high protocol dinner."

"Ooo," Posie beamed.

"What's that?" Jenny asked, her attention directed at me.

"I'm just as out of the loop on this one, baby girl," I was forced to tell her.

Posie addressed Jenny. "You'll love it. It's very formal and we would wait on them hand and foot. It's a whole different level of subjugation."

Jenny cocked her head as she pondered. "Sounds...intriguing."

"Are you sure you wouldn't just feel like you were at work?" I asked her.

She pursed her lips and continued to think.

"It's not quite like that," D.C. supplied.

"The subs could be naked," Posie suggested.

Jenny's expression turned a little more positive at that prospect. I, however, wasn't certain about that one.

"I don't know if I want nakedness next to my food," I scowled.

D.C. nodded. "I'm inclined to agree with that." He continued to try to sell the idea. "But there are all kinds of rules and formality. That does provide a power exchange atmosphere."

"Would we get punished if we messed any of them up?" Jenny asked.

"I don't know if I want someone's ass spanked next to my food either," I said.

"It doesn't have to be spankings," Jenny pointed out. "It could be all kinds of things."

"So, you're into in this idea?" I asked her. "You want to try it?"

She shrugged. "It might be interesting."

"Hey," my mentor said. "Why don't I send you some instructions on how to host one? You can look them over and if you two decide that it might be fun to try, we'll help in any way we can."

CHAPTER TWENTY

I got started right away with the planning. First, I designed a menu which focused on my cooking strengths and consisted of three courses and several choices of drink. Each would be served and offered by the submissives, who would tend to our every need, and only dine themselves, once we were done. Dress style for the Dominants would be as formal as possible. For the submissives, simple and elegant, without outshining any of the Doms or Dommes. Fine dining serving rules would apply and punishments would be allowed when subs made mistakes, as long as it wasn't too disruptive. The Dominants would be addressed, by all, by the formal names and titles that they preferred. While the Dominants relaxed over coffee and drinks, the subs would dine and then clean up the kitchen and dining area. After which, we would cap off the evening with D.C. reading part of something new he was working on, which he had volunteered to share and had referred to as, mood setting.

As I studied my plans, I had to admit that it did sound like fun...for the Dominants, certainly.

I dry cleaned my dinner jacket and even bought a new tie, a bow tie. Something about the way an untied one hung seemed sexier to me than the traditional ones, and that could make the end of the evening interesting. I also got something special for Jenny to wear. She and I cleaned and decorated the apartment meticulously. Halloween was just around the corner, so we were able to acquire a few interesting things to give the place a slightly more dark appearance easier than we might have been able to any other time of the year, such as a stone gargoyle. Though, I did avoid anything that appeared cheap or hokey in favor of lots of candles and a nice, silver candelabra that I got from a pawn shop.

Jenny happily helped me prepare the place and the food, which we left warming in the oven. Once we were done, I felt that it was time to reward her.

"I appreciate your help, baby girl," I said to her, followed by a kiss.

"Of course, Sir." She smiled.

"To show my gratitude, I got you a couple of things."

She beamed a bit, but still said, "You didn't have to do that."

"You earned them," I replied.

I went to my closet and retrieved a large, unwrapped box which I handed her.

"Oh, my," she said. "Don't I feel sweet sixteen? What is it?"

"Open it."

She placed it on the bed and pulled the top off and the tissue paper out of the way to reveal a cream colored, satin dress. It hung from the neck and was backless, with a tapered waist and broadly pleaded skirt that stopped at the knees.

"Sir, it's beautiful," she exclaimed.

"Try it on."

She pulled off her tank top, jeans and bra and started to pull the dress over her head.

"Aren't you forgetting something?" I said.

She looked down at her panties.

"Yeah," I told her. "You won't be needing those tonight."

She giggled and pulled them off before slipping into the dress. My hopes were immediately confirmed. The way it clung to her in some places and dangled in others, she looked like a privileged, Grecian slave, especially in her bare feet.

"It's soft," she noted as she stroked it.

"It's missing something." I reached back into the closet and pulled out another box, a smaller one, and held it out.

Jenny pulled the top off to reveal a sturdy, yet attractive, suede day collar with a bronze, heart shaped lock on the front. She paused and examined it, before looking up at me. "Really?" she asked, seeming both excited and uncertain.

"Really. If you're ready and willing, I'd like to claim you."

She thought for another couple of seconds before stepping closer. "Are we going to celebrate if I say, 'yes'?"

I smiled deviously. "We still have over an hour before the guests arrive."

Her lips parted to show me her perfect teeth. She turned around and lifted her hair. I pulled a small key from my pocket, unlocked the collar, placed it around her neck and locked it back. She turned back around to me with her hands tracing the bronze heart.

"How do I look, Sir? Pleasing?"

"You look immaculate," I murmured. "Except..."

She got a concerned look on her face. "...Except?"

"It's not time for that dress yet. And we don't want to mess it up. Not with the wicked things I'm about to do to you."

I put my hands on the hem of Jenny's skirt and peeled it off of her. She raised her arms to allow me to and then stood there smiling at me.

"What does my dirty girl do first?" I asked, lowering my gaze and giving her a diabolical grin.

She smirked, blew a raspberry and crossed her eyes.

"Seriously?" I replied.

She giggled. She then became very serious, though she still smiled. Reverently, she dropped to her knees and placed her face to the floor. She leaned up, biting the side of her lower lip. "Does, Sir desire anything?" she asked softly.

I brushed a stray lock of hair out of her eyes. I reached down, hooked two fingers in her collar and pulled her to her feet. "Yes, I do. You. Every bit of you."

Her smile was excited and nervous as she lowered her eyes. She seemed to shake a bit with anticipation, even as I laid her back on the bed. I returned to the closet where I retrieved several yards of nylon rope, dropped it next to my new treasure and leaned over her. I lifted her knees up to her shoulders and instructed her to grab the inside of her ankles. She did so with heavy breath and I began to tie her wrists to her legs, using a square knot and wrapping the rope around in a two column tie, and a lark's head knot to connect another piece of rope, which I looped behind her neck. I allowed her hands to remain free to move. As I did, I explained some things to her.

"We're using the stop light system. Do you understand?"

"Yes, Sir."

"That's something else. Your vocabulary is restricted to, 'Yes, Sir', 'No, Sir' and 'Sorry, Sir'. Understand?"

"Yes, Sir."

I rolled her over onto her face. With her knees up and arms down, it left her with her ass positioned in the air. I slapped it hard and she let out an exclamation somewhere between a grunt and a trepidatious moan. Reaching next to my nightstand, I picked up my crop and spanked her repeatedly in broad, slow, hard strikes. She let out more grunts each time it connected with her flesh. As her ass cheeks flushed, I pulled off my belt, ready to explore its relevance again.

I swatted her with it, hard. There was a piercing, loud "slap" and I watched it curve tightly around Jenny's pale bottom, followed by her crying out and squirming.

Again, I hit her. Her yelp was louder and she continued to move around on the bed, best as she could while so awkwardly restrained. I grabbed her by the hair and pulled her head back.

"Hold still, you little slut!" I commanded her.

"Yes, Sir," she managed.

I beat her in succession, seven or more times. Jenny buried her face in the pillow as she wailed. She never called "yellow", but the last couple of strikes were so hard, I became slightly concerned that I might hurt her. I pulled her head back again.

"Does the dirty, nasty, little whore like that?" I asked as a way to check on her, while still staying in the game and moment.

"Yes, Sir!" she gasped, while still sounding a bit frightened and uncomfortable.

"Really?"

"Yes, Sir," she assured me between pants. "It's my purpose to please you. You should use me as you see fit."

I hit her several times more, while holding her by the hair. This time, her cries rang out through my apartment. Once I relented, she whimpered. Still, no "yellow" or "red", though her ass was now shining with the later color. I flipped her over. Her smile was happy, though she breathed heavy, whined and moaned. I moved her legs apart as much as they would go, picked up my crop, placed the keeper about an inch from her clitoris and began patting it, fast. The tiny little slap sounds were quickly drowned out by Jenny's wailing.

"I *do* want you to tell me if you're about to come. So...are you?" I demanded to know.

"Soon, Sir! Soon!"

I stopped. I grabbed her by the collar and shoved two fingers into her drenched pussy. While digging inside of her, I said, "No, you're not. Not until I give permission. Understand?"

"Oh, God! Please, Sir!"

I slapped her lightly in the face and took her by the collar again. "Only one of those words are on your vocabulary list, you disobedient bitch."

"Sorry, Sir."

"The only thing that was included was that you're allowed—no, instructed—to tell me when you feel an orgasm coming on. Understand me?"

"Yes, Sir! Sir...I'm about to come soon, Sir!"

I stopped. I put my fingers in her mouth and ordered her to lick them clean, which she did eagerly. Next, I buried my face between her legs and began eating her out like a starving dog over a plate of meat.

I had read an article, a few years prior, about how to go down on a woman. It stressed that one should focus on all of her pussy, not just her clitoris. I took it to heart and received some praise over the years. I demonstrated my ability to Jenny by licking the inside walls of her vagina, the edge of her opening, outside, everywhere. Her taste and aroma was surprisingly pleasing, a bit sweet even. She went nuts, moaning, writhing and trying to grab my head. But I eventually began to focus on her clit. The same article had recommended using your tongue to spell out the alphabet. I did this, while stopping to suck and nibble every few letters. I made it to "L" before she started calling out again.

"Sir! I'm going to come!"

I stopped immediately and slapped her swollen, sore ass. "No coming. Not yet."

"Please, Sir!" she begged.

I spanked her again, noticing as her ass cheek shook just how intensely red it had become. "What did I say?"

"Sorry, Sir," she whimpered.

I went back to work. M, N, O, P... Back to sucking. I tormented her in such a manner, all the way through the alphabet. At the end, I leaned up, pulled my clothes off, rolled on a condom, climbed on top of her and slid in. She called out and I placed a hand on her throat and my tongue in her mouth, biting and sucking her lips and chin.

I grind into her with her pushing back, urging me with her body to go faster, harder. I decided to grant her that particular wish this time. I pounded into her and watched her face, her eyes fixed on me, her open mouth, smiling and moaning loudly.

Finally, she told me again, "Sir, I'm going to come!"

I stopped. She protested with a gasps and a few desperate, disappointed moans. That's when I decided to try something else. She wanted to be totally used, so I placed my cock at the entrance to her ass.

The one successful time I'd done this, the girl was willing, but not necessarily eager. I had to go incredibly slow and it took forever to build up any sort of rhythm. However, my new sub was, not only eager, but hopeful and I slid right in. I began to fuck her slowly, but steadily. I leaned up, onto my knees and put her's closer together so she could reach her clit. I told her to touch herself and reminded her to tell me when she was approaching orgasm. As I sodomized her, feeling her narrow entrance grip me like a wound rubber band, I allowed her to get close before I stopped her one final time.

"Please, Sir!" she begged. After I grabbed her face, she amended her comment to a desperate, "Sorry, Sir."

I resumed fucking her ass, that feeling of going into a large room through a small door and the sheer dirtiness of our act consuming me, making me feel like a sexual conqueror of the forbidden. I made her return to rubbing between her legs. She reached out with her middle finger, touched the very tip of her clit and began rapidly rubbing back and forth, barely an inch. After a minute or two, I could tell that she was getting close again. She confirmed this.

"Sir, I'm going to! I feel it..."

"Then do it," I ordered.

She continued to touch herself delicately, yet frantically. About five seconds later, she let out several short gasps. Next, she became quiet, her mouth still open, before letting out a long, piercing wail.

"Thank you, Sir! Thank you, Sir! Thank you!" she punctuated her orgasm with.

I was worked up enough, by this point, that I was able to get off too. I pulled out of her, ripped off the condom and covered her chest and face in my semen, which I rubbed into her skin. I even shoved some in her mouth.

"Thank you, Sir!" she gasped, at first. "...Thank you...for your cum..." she continued, more quietly as she sucked my fingers.

I leaned down and kissed her forehead before untying her while she panted. She relaxed and let her tired limbs drop onto the bed. I lay down and pulled her into my arms, where she nuzzled into my chest.

"Sweet, pretty girl," I whispered. I kissed her head

again. "You make me so happy."

"Thank you," she managed gleefully, before gasping lightly, "Sir...may I speak freely?"

"You already have been," I pointed out.

She giggled. "*That* was exactly what I want."

I smiled. "Only the best for my prize possession."

"Ignite, thank you so much for having us," Mistress Xina smiled as she walked in. She and Wired arrived promptly at six thirty.

So did everyone else, as punctuality was imperative for one of these events. Right behind her was D.C. with Tink and Posie following him on his left and one step behind. Momma C. was pulling up into the parking lot with Scott.

"Mistress," Jenny said to Xina, very formally. "May I take your coat?"

"Thank you, dear," Xina turned her back and let Jenny remove her wool overcoat to reveal a beautiful red gown.

"James," I said to her sub, who simply wore black pants and a black shirt. "How are you?"

"Well, Sir Ignite. Thank you for having us."

Next, D.C. entered looking appropriately dressed for a fine dining experience as only he could, in an actual tuxedo. Tink and Posie were in simple, yet nice, black dresses and flats. They looked like hostesses at a quality restaurant. As the three walked in, the girls took his over coat and handed it to Jenny.

"My friend," D.C. said to me with a broad smile.

"Good to see you," I smiled back. We shook hands. "Momma C. is on her way up as we speak. The subs can all go with Jenny to the kitchen in a moment. In the meantime, we can all adjourn to the balcony for a drink if you'd like."

"Sounds good," D.C. nodded.

Jenny smiled hospitably and asked, "What would everyone care for?"

"Well..." Xina pondered, "I don't normally imbibe in alcohol, not regularly. But this is a special occasion. So why not? What do you have?"

"A couple of decent wines, bourbon and gin. We also have some beer," my new girl said.

"Oh, just a glass of wine."

"Red or white?"

"Red. Cabernet if possible."

"Will Merlot be acceptable?"

Xina smiled pleasantly. "It will."

"Bourbon," D.C. said. "On the rocks."

"I'll have the same," I told her, "but, with some lemon lime soda in it."

"That's disgusting," my mentor teased.

I smirked at him and then nodded at Jenny who nodded back. She turned to get us our drinks, when Momma C. walked in. She was slightly out of breath.

"Your stairs suck, Iggy," she laughed.

"Ma'am," Jenny smiled, may I take your coat.

"Of course, darling. Scott."

Scott pulled off her overcoat to reveal a classy, maroon dress and handed it to Jenny. He, like Wired, was in a black shirt and slacks.

"Would you care for a drink before dinner?" Jenny asked.

"Whatcha got?" the Domme asked.

"A selection. The Sirs are having bourbon and the Mistress is having Merlot."

Cat pointed at the last option. "There you go. I'll have some of that."

"Cathy," I said happily. "Welcome."

"Thank you." She gave us all hugs and we all went to sit on the balcony.

"I have to say, Ignite," my mentor began, "Your place is really nice."

"You've never been here before?" Momma C. asked him, somewhat surprised.

"Never had reason to," he replied.

"Oh, you know, Sir D.C.," Xina said with the wave of a hand. "He never goes anywhere unless he has to."

"Or unless there's sex or booze," Cat kidded.

"Speaking of which," he said.

Jenny came out and handed us all our drinks. She turned to me. "Sir, the other submissives need to be oriented."

"Of course," I said. "We'll be fine until then, angel."

Once she was inside, Xina began to praise her. "Ignite, she is positively gorgeous. You are a lucky man."

My grin actually hurt my cheeks a little. "I am. In fact, as of an hour or two ago...she is completely mine."

"Is she?" Momma C. asked with excitement.

"Good job, my friend," D.C. smiled.

"I thought that collar looked new," Xina noted. "You have very good taste, in apartments, in women, in accessories..." She had a sip of her drink. "Oh...and wine." She nodded more of her approval.

We all relaxed and chit chatted for the next half hour or so. At one point, the Mistress asked if she could smoke and I obliged. That was why we were on the balcony instead of the living room, in fact. That, and the weather was still just hospitable enough that we could enjoy it. Finally, Jenny came to get us.

"Mistress, Ma'am and Sirs, we are ready for you now."

We all got up and were seated by our respective submissives. Jenny asked what we would all like to drink with dinner.

"I'm actually fine with water," D.C. said.

"Once again, I concur," I said.

"I think I'll do the same," Cat said. "I plan to have more of this..." She held up her half full glass of wine, "later."

When I looked at Mistress Xina, she was swallowing the last of her glass. "I would like some more of it as well. But I'll have mine now."

"Mistress?" Wired asked hesitantly.

"Yes. Come on. Chop chop."

Each of our respective subs did the honors of serving us. When the appetizers came—mushrooms stuffed with cream cheese, parmesan and garlic—they each served us on the left, with the exception of Xina's wine, which Wired poured for her on her right. Once we had everything that we needed, the subs stood behind us until we needed something else or until it was time to prepare the next course. It was very pleasant, very formal and gave us all a bit of the feeling of royalty.

Of course, the thing about royalty is, they occasionally think that they can do whatever they want, especially after imbibing in a little libation. By the time the main course arrived—baked salmon and asparagus—Xina was nearing the end of her second glass of wine. We began to eat and Xina began to get more and more obnoxious.

"I like the new editions that Scene Shop has made," Momma C. said. "Those straps with the o rings that run down the wall next to the St. Andrews cross? Those are surprisingly handy."

"Are they?" I asked, trying to imagine what all they could be used for. Before I could ask for examples, Xina broke in.

"Oh, please. That whole thing was Batlash's idea and he practically forced it down the board's throats. The man is such a bully."

"Mistress," D.C. began reasonably, "with all due respect, I think we might want to try to refrain from gossip tonight. We're here to share some dignity. Am I right?"

"Right you are," she smiled back before demanding another glass of wine from her sub.

"Mistress?" he asked again, more concerned this time.

"Come now, James. One cannot dine without something to wash it down."

He glanced up and our eyes met. He looked worried, but still said, "Yes, Mistress." He retrieved the bottle and poured a small amount into her glass. As he started to return it to the counter in the kitchen, she stopped him.

"'Tut tut,'" she said. "If that's all you're going to pour, you might as well keep it nearby."

"Yes, Mistress." He held the bottle.

"Well," she continued. "I, for one, still think that the Scene Shop could use some improvements. That old swing they had broke months ago. And those metal, folding chairs on the smokers' deck have got to go. I despise them."

"Well, they're good if it starts to rain," D.C. pointed out. "We can't really put recliners up there."

"Build a canopy," she suggested.

"Still, humidity," he said. "And more relaxing chairs would be a pain to get down if a major storm hit. The metal ones are much more practical."

"I suppose," she sighed as she had another hearty sip. "James, rub my shoulders, please."

He looked around for a place to put the bottle he was holding, but there wasn't anything near. Posie, who was standing silently next to him, offered to take it from him. The Mistress polished off her glass and held it out for more. Posie looked at her Sir, who gave a disapproving smirk, but still nodded. Posie poured, with Xina waving her hand to keep going. Once it was over half full, she allowed her to stop. All the while, Wired kneaded his Mistress' shoulders.

We managed to get through the main course in a similar fashion and Jenny announced that it was time for dessert. I had selected, and she had helped me prepare, a fantastic bread pudding with a Bourbon sauce. However, I was beginning to doubt that Xina needed it. I was inclined to suggest that she skip to the coffee at the end.

"All I'm saying," she slurred, "is that we shouldn't worry about what the city thinks about where we're located. They'll never build that school there."

"What makes you say that," Momma C., who had abandoned her wine after three quarters of a glass, asked.

"Well, I probably shouldn't say, but, Master Jon hinted to me that we have people on the inside. They'll look out for us."

I glanced over at my mentor who sighed through his nose and graced me with a regretful look, though its origin being the fact that he told Master Jon about my job or the fact that he had convinced me to invite Xina over Mac and a new Dom that he was courting remained unclear.

Xina leveled a naughty look my direction and then up at my submissive. "So, Jenny," she said, "it's my understanding that you are no longer under consideration, but fully owned."

"Yes, Mistress," she replied politely.

"I do hope the two of you celebrated." Her tone was incredibly suggestive.

"Uh..." Jenny began.

But I cut her off. "We had what could be considered a moment to christen the joining. We'll just leave it at that."

"Kind of a shame," Xina grinned. "I thought maybe we might get some entertainment tonight."

I returned a smile, though mine was more tolerant than wicked as I told her, "I'm a bit tapped out for the moment," in an attempt to put the idea to rest.

"Well, I could just have James do it. They can perform for us."

I glanced around at Jenny, who was now staring at him, a faraway look in her eyes. Suddenly, she looked back down at me. I said, "We're going to have to decline."

"...Right," my sub agreed, though it seemed slightly forced.

"Really, Ignite, you can be such a prude sometimes," she scolded with a chuckle. She drained her glass again. "James," the now drunk Mistress demanded. "Where is that Merlot?"

He suddenly looked beyond worried and embarrassed. Leaning down to her ear, he whispered something to her. Whatever it was, it was not taken well.

"I don't give a shit," she shot back. "Do your duty, boy."

He stood. He looked down at her and remained motionless.

"Well?" she demanded.

He was still motionless. "Mistress, I think perhaps we

should consider heading home. It's getting late."

"What? We haven't even had dessert."

"Well, perhaps you'll speak to me outside for a moment?"

She sighed heavily and accompanied her breath with an equally heavy eye roll. "Fine."

The two walked out, James humbly behind her and Xina as best as she could manage.

The rest of us, the subs included, exhaled hard and long.

"This has been interesting," I said.

"The Mistress doesn't drink much," D.C. informed us all. "Obviously, her tolerance isn't that great."

"I guess, next time we'll just have tea and coffee," I suggested.

"Or milk and cookies," Momma C. joked.

Suddenly, there were loud voices outside. We all got up and ran to the front door. When I opened it, I found my two guests down the breezeway, arguing hotly. Xina was raising hell and Wired was trying, desperately, to get her to listen to reason.

"Don't even suggest such things to me!" she yelled.

"Would you just listen to me for a minute? Please?"

"I will do no such thing! You are being very insubordinate and I will not tolerate it."

"Xina—"

"No!" She slapped him.

James' frustration started to mutate into something that looked more like anger. "Okay," he insisted, "timeout!"

"I don't want to hear anything that you have to say right now," she snarled back at him. "I just want dessert." She started to stomp back our way but he caught her arm. That seemed to really piss her off as she turn back and began slapping him repeatedly while struggling to free herself of his grasp. "Let go! Never grab me! You never grab me!"

That's when a body darted past me. It was D.C. who intervened. He got right up in her face and called her name, firmly and with a tone of astonishment.

She stopped. James stopped trying to wrestle her still. There was a standoff for a few seconds as my mentor looked at her like she was crazy and she huffed. Finally, she jerked her shoulder loose from D.C's hand, stood up straight and adjusted herself in an attempt to regain what composure she had left. She took a deep breath and slowly exhaled.

"James," she said with an authoritative calm. "Get my coat. We're leaving."

James hurried back in the apartment, handing me a quiet apology as he passed. Xina and D.C. just looked at each other. Once her sub quickly returned and put her coat on her, she turned to me and tried to sound rational.

"Ignite," she said. "Thank you very much for your hospitality. I...apologize for our course behavior." She took James' arm and allowed him to lead her out.

We all stood there for a few moments in silence before going back inside. Once I shut the door, Jenny said, with no formality whatsoever, "So, can we assume that dessert is off?"

"Well, that didn't go very well," I complained, tugging loose my tie.

"No," Jenny agreed.

The two of us were cleaning up dinner ourselves as we talked.

"I'm sorry you had to be present for all of that," I told her.

"Yeah, well," she began in a frustrated tone, "it's my duty and all."

I paused. "How did you mean that?"

"It's..." She bit her lip and shook her head, eye staring off and hands on her hips. "You know what? You were right. This was a lot like bringing work home with me and I didn't really get off on it at all."

I nodded slowly. "I'm sorry. We won't do it again." I went to hug her, but she moved away from me. "Are you okay?"

"No. I'm not. This..."

"What?"

"I'm not finding this as fulfilling as I had hoped."

"We just got started. What do you want?"

She finally looked at me. "You know what I want. And when you don't, it would be nice if you asked."

"What the hell are you talking about?"

She looked away again. "Nothing." She resumed cleaning.

"No," I said, taking the dishes out of her hands and setting them down. I pulled her in front of me. "Tell me what's on your mind."

She thought for a moment before coming out with, "Why didn't you get my input on her offer to play with Wired?"

I was taken aback. "Seriously? You wanted to fuck him?"

"No," she said, though it didn't sound entirely sincere. "I just... You just made that decision. You didn't negotiate it with me."

"I don't have to in cases like that. You're mine," I pointed out. "That's the arrangement we have. That's the deal we made."

She sighed and rubbed her face. "I know. I know. It's just..." She trailed off again.

"Tell me what is going on in your head, right now. Talk to me. What is it that you're unhappy about? What is it that you want?"

"I want out," she said plainly. She looked sad as she said it. There was a long pause. We stood there, quiet. "I can't do this," she finally completed.

I was surprised. "Already?"

She nodded with her head down. She looked back up at me. "I'm sorry, Kelly. You're a great guy and you're going to make someone a wonderful Dom. It just won't be me. I thought that I could be happy just being owned and fucked really dirty, but...I want more. I want to play at parties and explore. I'm still learning about myself and it's becoming clear that what I desire is more intense than I realized."

I huffed a little. "To be *totally* objectified?"

She looked off to the side and simultaneously gave a shrug and a slight nod.

I stepped back from her and paced a little, stopping to point at her and say, "You want to be the gangbang queen."

"What?"

"That woman we saw at Lady Nessa's party. That's what you want. Not just to be conquered and objectified, but to be passed around like a joint."

She still had trouble maintaining eye contact as she weakly said, "Maybe..."

"Well," I grunted, "forgive me if I think of you as more than a video game that I can play with my friends. Forgive me if I think of you as more than just a series of moist holes."

"Kelly, stop!" she begged. "I get it! I get why you're disappointed. I'm a little disappointed too. But I can't change how I feel or what I want. I don't necessarily need to be gangbanged, but I need something more exciting than a feather duster on my skin and cleaning up after your friends. I need to explore myself more and I was so hoping that you'd be able to help me." She walked over and put her hands on my cheeks. She smiled softly, a tear dripping out of her eye. "And you have. But this isn't going to work. And I think it's better that we accept that now, before we spend a year trying to force it."

I pulled her hands down and held them. Now, I was the one having trouble making eye contact. Finally, I nodded. "Okay. Okay, we will..." I struggled. "...We will set this bird free. You go. I'll...I'll clean up this mess."

She repeated that she was sorry before asking if I could, please, unlock her collar. I pulled out the key and released her.

"Thank you." She paused before leaning in to softly kiss me one last time.

She left.

CHAPTER TWENTY-ONE

I made plans to go to the Scene Shop later in the week which was hosting a very basic D/s night, with the exception that it was encouraging unattached Doms and subs to attend. A kink speed dating night, if you will. Couples and people in open relationships were welcome, but mostly, it was for people like me.

Or, like I suddenly was.

I told my mentor about my break up the next day, as we sat in a restaurant near City Hall discussing Xina's obnoxious behavior. He was majorly appalled, more than I ever remember seeing him and apologized for convincing me to host the dinner, especially in light of the demise of my relationship.

"Not necessary," I said after a sip from my cocktail. "If anything, it ended up exposing the inherent flaws between Jenny and I before things went too far. Like you said, better to waste your time looking than..." I swallowed before continuing. "...To waste your time having. Besides, this event is this weekend. I'll find someone else."

"Are you sure you're ready for that?" he asked.

"Yeah. I'm...I'm good."

"Okay," was all he said.

I stared at him. "Are you alright?"

"Yeah. Just disappointed in Xina."

"For getting drunk?"

"For not respecting Wired's time out, more than

anything."

"Is that all?"

He was silent for a moment. "Mostly. There's also some stuff going on at home. But that's another matter"

"What is it?"

"Honestly? I'm not entirely sure. Just...something seems odd. I can't really put my finger on it." He gulped the rest of his drink.

"You want another round?" I asked him.

He shook his head. "No. I have to drive. And after watching Xina the other night..."

I suddenly felt a little put off by the cocktail in my hand. "Yeah, I guess we want to keep it to one."

He stood and dropped money on the table.

"Hey," I said. "I got this."

"You got the dinner party," he pointed out.

I smirked. "Yeah. I guess there *is* that."

He returned a smile. "Tell you what, Iggy. I'll tell Tinkerbrat to find someone to cover her Friday night shift. The girls and I will go to the Scene Shop too. And, if you can't find anybody there that night, I'll let you beat the crap out of Tink." He smirked and winked.

It felt good walking into the dungeon without anyone else's aid. I had been a few times since my first visit, but always with a sponsor. Never mind that this particular night was actually open to vetted nonmembers, I'd proven myself enough that the board had let me have a full membership. I had originally planned to bring Jenny once instated, but this would have to do.

Besides, I looked really good. I had bought a new suit and a new shirt for the occasion and they fit better than anything I had. As I was buzzed into the hallway by the gatekeeper, I felt like a force to be reckoned with.

The single subs of Clinton needed to watch out. Ignite35 was on the prowl.

"Mr. Iggy," Wired said as he turned to find me behind him in the hallway. "It's good to see you." He offered a hand to shake.

"You as well, James." I pointed to his hand as I shook it, confused.

"Ah," he began with a disheartened smirk. "Xina and I are no more."

"Oh," I said with genuine empathy. "I'm sorry to hear that."

"I'm the one who's sorry," he replied. "I'm sorry that we ruined your party. Also, I noticed on the website that your relationship status changed as well. I hope that we didn't have anything to do with that."

I granted him a dismissive wave. "It wasn't meant to be. No big deal."

"Still, I'm sorry, for everything."

"Don't sweat it." As we resumed walking to the main room, I noticed that his dress was very nonkink. His black polo shirt had an emblem on it that said, "Dungeon Monitor." "Working tonight, I take it?"

"Yeah," he said. "Until I find another Domme, I figure I can still participate by contributing. You know what I mean?"

I smiled. "That's very enlightened."

We reached the dungeon door and he held it open for me. I thanked him. Then he went to work. So did I. I glanced around, standing up straight, yet with my hands casually in my pockets. My eyes locked with a couple of pairs of others, both belonging to two attractive women that I'd never seen before. I smiled and it was returned to me by one of them with deep dimples. I considered introducing myself. However, someone approached from my other side and stopped me.

"There he is," I heard them say.

I turned to see my mentor there with his girls, both in matching gray dresses.

"Hey," I said cheerfully.

"Uh..." D.C. began cautiously. "How are you doing?"

"Me? I'm good. Ready to mingle," I said, glancing back at the woman who had smiled.

"Well, you look really good," he told me. "Doesn't he?"

"Yeah. You do," Tink said reassuringly.

"Very handsome," Posie added with a nervous smile.

Their demeanor was odd, like I had just lost a loved one in a car accident and they didn't know what to say.

"What?" I asked. "I didn't get a terminal diagnosis. I just got dumped. I'll be fine."

They all had trouble making eye contact.

"What?" I asked again.

D.C. cleared his throat and looked towards the back of the room. I followed his gaze and got a shock. There, next to the pummel horse, was Jenny and she wasn't dressed or alone. The Dom who'd asked to borrow her at Lady Nessa's party was behind her. He had her arms tied behind her back and was holding her by her elbows and hair. If that weren't enough, he was presenting her to a couple. Both of them were smiling wickedly, even as the woman pinched Jenny's nipples and grabbed her face.

Jenny just smiled in ecstasy.

"I'm sorry, Iggy," D.C. said to me as my smile faded.

I looked away from the scene and gritted my teeth. I took a deep breath and forced a smile back on my face. "Not important anymore."

"Iggy," my mentor said. "You don't have to do this."

"Nonsense," I replied as casually as I could. "I paid my money. I'm here. Besides, the reason that I am is to meet new people, not to worry with those I already know." I looked back at the woman I had planned to speak to when I entered. "If you three will excuse me."

I walked over to where she was standing, hands behind her back, watching the scenes that were going on. She was petite, pretty and around thirty, with light brown hair that had a ribbon in it. She wore a very tasteful version of a schoolgirl outfit. As I approached, she noticed me again and rewarded me with another view of her dimples.

"May I speak with you?" I asked, trying to establish if she was owned.

"Sure," she replied, beaming suggestively.

"My name is, Ignite. Who are you?"

"Offering," she said.

"Offering," I smiled. "Nice. So, are you here to meet someone?" I asked.

She shrugged. I smiled.

"Tell me about yourself," I said.

"What's to tell? My husband's a musician on tour and I have free time to even out the arrangement we have. Thought maybe I'd find someone else...powerful to fill that time." She smiled. I didn't.

I stood silent for a moment. My eyes hit the floor and then diverted around before finding hers again. "I hope you find what you're looking for," I managed. I walked away.

As I did, I couldn't help but look back towards Jenny. Her new Dom had her on her knees. He was trading his cock in her mouth with the other man's and the woman's pussy. He shoved her face into the woman hard. I couldn't hear them over all of the noise, but the woman enunciated so well that it was easy to read her lips as she said, "Oh. She's nasty, isn't she?"

I couldn't take anymore. I had to walk out. The night had barely even begun, and already, I needed a break.

I stepped out onto the smoking deck in a rather anxious state. I stood there a moment, eyes closed and breathing heavily, trying to steady my heart beat. If this was what a break up was like in the kink community, I thought frantically, I may remain single indefinitely.

"Hey, handsome," a voice called out.

I opened my eyes to see Sluttypixie, seated by herself in the smoking pit. She was bundled up tight in her leather jacket and with a blanket over her lower half. Her legs bounced up and down fast, in an unconscious attempt to generate heat.

"Oh," I said. "Hey, Megan. I've never seen you here before."

"I've never had the extra cash to drop in. But I got some birthday money, so I figured I'd splurge." She exhaled smoke that seemed to billow out extra thick as her breath froze in the chilly air. "You here with your new girl?"

"Well," I said as level minded as I could manage, "I'm here. So is she. But...not together."

"You two break up?" she asked with a confused expression.

"Yeah, I guess that's what normal people call it," I grumbled. "She's downstairs right now getting worked over by three people. I had to come up here."

"Shit. That's sucks," she said with only a little trace of

empathy in her voice. Her eyes turned a little naughty. "Does that mean you're free to play tonight?"

There was an interesting idea. I could have a little fun, while I reminded myself that I was still viable. Of course, the notion of sceneing in front of Jenny to get the inconsiderate little bitch back wasn't a motivating factor at all.

"You know what, Megan? That sounds like a fabulous idea."

Megan and I strutted back into the main room where we found Jenny in the same spot being screwed hard by her new Dom as the other two shoved their private parts in her face. I wasn't prepared to let that be the spectacle of the night, however. Megan and I were going to do a scene of our own.

I looked around until I saw a free fixture, a red one that looked like a ladder doing a backbend. It looked like something that might be put in a city park as art. But I decided that it needed to be used for something more sinister.

I didn't even look at Megan. I just put a hand on the back of her neck and dragged her towards it. "Come on."

We reached the fixture and I shoved her up against it, a little harder than I normally would have considered doing to someone. She grimaced, but regained her wicked smile once I said, "Take off your clothes, all of them." In seconds, she was naked and I had both pairs of my hand cuffs in my palm. I shackled her to the bars of the piece and grabbed her by the face. "This is going to get rough," I told her.

"Wouldn't have it any other way, cowboy," she

smirked.

I circled her as I spun my crop in my fingers. I reared back more than I ever had and delivered a sharp blow to her hip. She hissed through her teeth and contorted her face, but said nothing. I grabbed her by the hair.

"You want to see what I've got? Well, you're about to." I turned the crop around in my hand, so that I held the tight end and the handle was dangling. I hit her with the hard, ribbed grip.

"Ughhh!" she exclaimed, as she tugged her leg up from the blow. I'd hit myself with the handle a few times and knew it genuinely hurt. But she didn't call, "red."

I pulled back and hit her on the side of her ass with the keeper end, really hard and several times. But she didn't call, "red."

I pulled her back by her hair again, hard. She laughed like a defiant interrogation victim. I slapped her. She laughed a little. I grabbed her by the throat.

I squeezed.

Over my shoulder, in the back of the room, Jenny had some guy slapping her in the mouth with his dick while her Dom continued to fuck her.

I focused back on Megan. "Sluttypixie," I mused viciously. "Such an appropriate name, because you are a little slut, aren't you? A dirty, nasty, filthy little thing."

She smirked. "Yes, Sir," she managed, with a sarcastic drawl.

I squeezed.

Megan chocked a little. I hit her, my open palm stinging a little from the impact. I hit her again and I squeezed harder.

Out of the corner of my eye I saw Wired walk up close to us, his arms crosses, and a severely concerned look on his face as he observed our play.

I held that girl so tightly by the throat until...

 I squeezed...

Until...

Wait... I thought suddenly. *What the hell am I doing?*

I let go. She coughed and choked and leaned over as much as she could. I held my hands up.

"Is that..." She coughed a bit. "Is that...all you got?"

I stood there gasping and feeling like I had found a crazy person in the mirror. I felt terrible and uncuffed her.

"Megan, I'm sorry," I said desperately, as I tried to hold her.

She shoved me away, even as she choked. "What is your problem?" she asked.

"I'm sorry. I didn't mean..." I didn't even know what to say.

"Mr. Ignite," Wired said as he stepped up next to us. "I think maybe you need a timeout."

I walked out of the main room, into the entrance hallway. I began to pace. I rubbed my face hard as I tried to regain composure, all the while trying to give myself an internal beating that topped the one that I'd just given Megan.

The door to the dungeon opened and D.C. walked out.

"Hey," he said with excessive concern. "You okay?"

"Am I okay?" I shot back anxiously. "I'm not the one who just had their boundaries crossed."

"Megan's fine," he assured me. "I mean, she's still choking a little and she's frustrated, but she's tough and she doesn't feel violated. ...Even if that was your subconscious intent." He tread carefully with his tone. "That little girl will pass out before she taps out."

I gave him a dissatisfied look. "That doesn't excuse

what I just did."

"No, but—"

"But nothing!" I shot back. "I lost it in there. I'm not that guy. But the darkness took over and I was ready to do some horrible shit to—"

"Jenny?" my mentor questioned.

I paused. I thought about his accusation. "No," I said. "I wasn't looking to hurt Megan and I wasn't looking to hurt anyone else. I just freaked the fuck out for no—"

"Kelly! Kelly. Kelly..." my mentor said soothingly. "Look..." he paused and took a breath. "Why don't you tell me where your head was back there? I mean, I know. But it might do you some good to say it out loud."

I actually found myself angry with him. I didn't feel like being handled at the moment. And yet, as I paced and breathed, I began to calm. I shook my head. "It's obvious, right? You're right. I was mad at Jenny and I took it out on Sluttypixie. I was..." I trialed off.

"But you caught yourself," he pointed out.

"That's completely irrelevant!" I shouted. "I hurt somebody!"

"You didn't, actually," he insisted. "You got lucky." He put his hands on my shoulders and stopped my pacing. "Hey! ...I asked you if you were okay and you said that you were. Obviously, that isn't true. So...what did you learn?" His question was soft and understanding.

I took another deep breath and slowly let it out. "I'm... I'm not as enlightened as I want to be."

He returned a comforting smile. "You're not as dangerous as you could be either. And you're human. You also need to face and address these feelings when they come up instead of trying to...I guess...fit in. You have nothing to prove to the rest of us and it's okay to feel hurt."

"I hurt that girl," I pressed.

"You didn't," he assured me in a soft voice. "You could have," he clarified, "if it had been anyone else. You did cross a line. But you got lucky, in the respect that you picked a super masochist and you stopped yourself." He rubbed my shoulders and sighed hard. "Why don't you go home?"

I looked down. I paused. I nodded.

He pat me. "We'll talk tomorrow...if you want to."

I started to walk out. Then, I felt a sudden need, the kind that wasn't normal to me. I grabbed him and hugged him. He hugged me back even harder.

"What the hell happened to me?" I asked as I fought tears.

"Hey," he said sharply. "It's okay. You let your heart have control over your libido. You know you fucked up and you stopped." He squeezed me even tighter. "I've got you..."

I grunted, still trying not to cry. "I..."

He pulled me up by the face to meet his gaze. "You're stronger than this, Kelly," he insisted.

I gritted my teeth and then pressed my lips together. "Megan..." I struggled.

"She's going to be fine," he told me, again. "I will personally make sure that she is. I know for a fact that Wired has already checked on her and I will make my girls do the same. I will even check on her. But somebody had to check on you."

I suddenly felt a little better, more composed. I stood straight. I took a deep breath and exhaled.

"I should go home," I told my mentor, basically repeating his recommendation.

"Yeah."

I breathed again. "I will speak to you later."

He smiled at me and pat my shoulder. "Drive safe, brother," he said.

I left.

CHAPTER TWENTY-TWO

I laid low for the next couple of weeks. I didn't go to the next munch and I didn't take advantage of my new membership at the dungeon. I barely looked at the website. I just went to work, came home and did my best to recover from the heartbreak that I was feeling. I also spent a lot of time punishing myself. More than not wanting to face everyone in the community, it was like I was denying myself the lifestyle for a bit. I had been bad and I wasn't allowed to indulge my desires, not until I could come to terms with what I had done.

What few times I did get on the website, I noticed a continual series of conversations originating from Purrterra's page. She was becoming completely wrapped up in her new relationship with Tormentor and constantly posted status updates and photos related to their play.

"Last night, Sir pierced my tits thirty times. Then he tortured them by poking and pulling. It was unbelievable!"

This was accompanied by pictures of her bloody breasts, full of long needles. It was freaky beyond belief. There were also pictures of her ass so bruised that her skin had turned an entire rainbow of colors. If that weren't enough, there were more shots of other marks he'd left on her, including on her throat where he'd choked her during sex.

Jesus, I thought. *That's definitely got to be abuse.*

But she never cited it as such. Instead, she praised his

prowess and virility. Obviously, her frenzy was leading her to allow her limits to be tested to their maximum.

I breathed deep and scowled. I could, at least, take some comfort in knowing that I hadn't gone that far. Also, just because I could lose it, didn't mean that I had actually violated Megan. I mean, I knew I had, even if she didn't see it that way. I had let myself travel to a dark, dark place, to look off into the abyss and consider leaping. However, like D.C. said, I had stopped myself before it went too far. I had learned a valuable lesson and suddenly knew where the line was.

I clicked on another picture that Terra had posted. In it, she was tied up on the floor, gagged and blindfolded, bruised and had things like "Whore", "Fuck slut" and "trash" written all over her. It began to make me a little sick and I clicked off of it.

I began to believe that, just because a sub liked something, didn't always make it okay. While it was widely accepted that limits needed to be pushed to constantly find new forms of ecstasy, one could also be flirting with abuse. I always focused on the submissive's hard limits, never my own. Outside of not wanting to share, I'd never really gone through what I wouldn't do myself, or for anyone else for that matter. I decided that needed to change and I made a list.

No open relationships.

No playing while I'm angry.

Grabbing someone's throat is fine. Choking is not.

No drawing blood.

No marks or bruises that take longer than four days to heal.

No complete removal of a subs dignity.

No hard play without negotiations first.

No bathroom sports or rainbow play. (Pretty

universal.)

No calling a sub bad things when I might mean them.

I stared at my list, reading it over and over. I was sure that it was too short and that other things would get added as time went on, but it was a start. Somehow it made me feel a little better.

Suddenly, the chat bar on the website popped up. Much to my surprise, it was Sluttypixie.

"Hey, handsome," her message began. "Haven't seen or heard from you since the Scene Shop. You cut out of there pretty quick. You alright?"

I was completely taken aback. I typed a response.

"I just needed some time. I think I went too far with you and have been feeling pretty ashamed."

"Yeah, I heard," she replied. "D.C. told me. Just for the record, I'm fine. It was even a little exciting for a while."

I shook my head. This girl was crazy. "You may be okay with it, but I'm not. If it had been any other girl, I might have seriously hurt them. I lost control."

"Well, don't do it again, dumbass."

I didn't write anything back. I just sat there staring at her last message while the cursor blinked. Finally, she messaged me again.

"You're a good Dom," she told me. "You just made a mistake and now you know not to again, right?"

I sighed. "Right," I replied.

"Tell you what. Make me a promise. Promise that you'll only be the best version of your Dom self from now on and we'll let that be our contract. Deal?"

Interesting idea. I thought about her suggestion and agreed. "Deal."

"Good," she wrote back. "Now, stop being such a little bitch and get yourself together. Otherwise, I'm coming over there to beat *your* ass."

I smirked. "Yes, ma'am."

I logged off. I poured myself a glass of water and considered how I might hone my Dominant tendencies to their best form. I suddenly remembered Tink and Posie's declaration of submission. Perhaps one fashioned for my side of the dynamic could be helpful. I went back to the document I had listed my hard limits on and began to type underneath them.

I am Dominant. I am strong, assertive, creative, dependable and measured. I respect limits, while responsibly testing boundaries. I am educated, while continuing to learn, determined to be the best that I can be. I am a force to be reckoned with, as well as a gentle protector. I vow to care for any submissive that grants me the privilege of dominating them as much as I will entertain their desires. I will set the best example in my community that I can. I am Ignite35 and I am a powerful Dominant, a caring lover and a good person. That is what I am and always what I will be.

I read it a few times, memorizing it. I recited the words a couple of times, trying to feel and believe them as I did. From there on out, I would say them every night and every morning, like a prayer. This would be my mantra and I would never allow myself to lose control or feel that type of helpless again.

A couple of days later the weather took an ugly turn. It was sudden and snow covered our whole town. I was very concerned about driving in it, especially with some hesitant behavior that my car had recently displayed. Cautiously, I walked out to it in my parking lot and reached for the key in my pocket. Shoving it in through the ice that had covered the lock, I turned. After forcefully pulling the frozen door open, I climbed into the driver's seat and pulled the door closed behind me. I put the key in the ignition and turned it. There was a slow groan and then...it stopped.

I'd had a few problems with the car getting started, slow grinding until turning over, but nothing like this. Now, I was turning the key and getting nothing. I grit my teeth and gave up.

I considered my options. Not being familiar with the local bus system, I searched my phone for people who might be able to help me. After noticing Momma C.'s number, I remembered that she worked near City Hall. I sent a text, politely explaining my situation and asking for a ride. I then contacted AAA and asked them to tow my car to the mechanic's.

I waited.

Finally, I got a ping on my phone. It was Cat.

"Hey, bud," it read. "I'm about to leave my place. I'll be at yours in about twenty minutes. I can take you to and from work until you get this problem fixed. No worries."

That was a relief.

Not long after that, a tow truck arrived. I waited in the cold as it hitched my car up. No sooner than they began to pull away than Cat eased into the parking lot and over next to me.

She rolled down the window. "Hey, good looking," she said with a smile. "You lookin' for a wild time?"

I smirked back as she opened the door. "I appreciate this," I told her as I crawled into the passenger seat.

"Not a problem at all," she assured me. She then said, "So, I haven't seen or talked to you in a few weeks. You doing okay?"

"Yeah, I just had to work through some stuff."

"I heard. You want to talk about it?"

I sighed. "Not really. I formed an exercise to help me focus and I talked to Sluttypixie about it. We're cool and I'm getting my groove back, so to speak."

"Well, good. I'm pleased to hear it."

My response was a little unsure. "...Yeah."

She smiled. She could tell that I was still struggling a bit. "You know, there is no hard, clear line between consensual rough play and abuse. Different people want different things and it's impossible to know what they are and how to navigate them one hundred percent of the time."

"I know," I assured her. "I simply fucked up and I learned from it. Like I said, I'm getting myself back together. I think I'll be ready to play again soon. I've been trying to look at what happened as me actually injuring myself and the wounds are almost healed. I won't be hitting anyone in the immediate future, but I think I can be assertive enough to effectively top should the opportunity present itself."

She nodded. "That's good to hear. You're a good guy, Iggy, one of my favorite people. And I think the fact that you recognize the problem that you encountered and are dealing with it is a sign that you're a good Dom. You're going to make someone very happy one day."

I smiled a small bit. "I hope so. Thank you, Cathy. You're always such an enormous help, a great influence and a good friend."

"I aim to please."

It was a Thursday, towards the end of, what was

becoming, a very long week. I finished struggling to clean up, yet another portion of the city's warped computer system. It was five-thirty and I decided that it was time to leave, especially if I didn't want to make Momma C. wait on me. I disconnected and turned off my lap top, tucked it into my canvas briefcase, pulled my jacket off of the back of the chair and my overcoat from the coat rack by the door. After turning off the lights, I headed towards the elevators. There were a few people there waiting to get on. Among them was the pretty, young, freckled blonde from records that I kept seeing. Her usual, completely buttoned shirt and tight skirt, along with her nice heels and cold expression made her look as stiff as always. She seemed withdrawn and tense, like she was still trying to send a general, "fuck off," to the rest of the world. She carried a small stack of books and papers, which she clutched to her chest, as she walked in front of me and made her way to the back of the elevator.

In spite of my recent confusion, I couldn't fight the intense curiosity that I had about her. Now, more focused and feeling a bit brave—or, perhaps, like I had less and less to lose—I nudged my way to the back as well and stood next to her. I could barely take my eyes off of her, and in fact didn't, even when she glanced over at me.

I smiled. She just resumed staring straight ahead.

We began descending. However, at one point, the elevator suddenly jerked a bit and stopped. As this happened, the pretty blonde lost grip on one of the books that she had in her arms, the one that she was keeping closest to her chest, and it hit the floor.

I reached down to retrieve it for her and looked at the cover as I did. I was surprised to find that it was a reference book about sexual exploration aimed specifically at those interested in submission. Before I could give it back to her, she snatched it out of my hand. She gave me a quick, nervous look out of the corner of her eye and hid the book underneath the rest of her things before muttering a quick and cursory, "Thank you."

Oh, my. This was too good to be true. Was it?

The elevator began to move again. At that point, I couldn't help but to continue to stare. I found the whole thing amusing and began to study her. She kept trying to see me out of the corner of her eye and eventually turned to get a better look at me. I smiled again. It wasn't the smile of a lech salivating, but rather a curious and entertained one. She began to breathe a little rapidly, pressed her lips together and returned her gaze to the front of the elevator. I could almost hear her thoughts telling me to leave her alone, to forget that I had ever seen her, much less the book.

Yeah. That wasn't going to happen.

The elevator came to a halt on the bottom floor and everyone exited. I walked behind her. Finally, I decided that I needed to say something.

"You know," I called out, "if you really want to learn about that sort of thing, there's a much more practical way of going about it."

"Not interested," she shot quickly over her shoulder.

I caught up with her and walked at her side. "I don't mean to sound fresh, really," I assured her. "What I mean is, there are plenty of people who can explain these sorts of things, make them more applicable."

She didn't respond.

We exited the building and were approaching the cars in the parking deck as she pulled out her keys, hitting the electronic lock and opening her vehicle with a chirp. I pulled out one of my cards and quickly wrote the name of a neighborhood restaurant on it.

"If you want to talk to someone who knows a fair amount about this sort of thing, no strings, no funny business, meet me here at six o'clock, Sunday evening."

I handed her the card. She hesitated, her free hand on the handle of her car door. Eventually though, she reached out and took my information.

I smiled again and nodded a polite good bye. "Think about it," I said.

<h1 style="text-align:center">CHAPTER TWENTY-THREE</h1>

The following day was crazy. It started reasonably enough, with Cat picking me up at my place. The mechanic had said that my car needed a new starter, which wasn't a huge deal. However, they had to order the part and so, I was left to inconvenience my friend for a bit longer. I felt a little bad about it and told her so.

"Don't be ridiculous," she said as she pat my hand. "I don't mind. It's not really all that inconvenient for me and it gives us a chance to hang out a little."

That made me feel a little better.

She adjusted the conversation away from my current predicament with my transportation. "So, anything new in your world?"

"Uh," I chuckled. "Yeah, I bumped into a baby kinkster yesterday."

"A what?"

"A newbie. I don't think she's in the community, but she's...curious."

Momma C. gave an interested grin. "I see. Planning on initiating her?"

I thought hard. "Maybe. I don't know. I'm just trying to get her to talk to me first. We'll see."

"The student becomes the teacher," she mused.

I laughed again. "Like I said, we'll see."

Suddenly, her cell phone rang. She answered. "Hello," she said into the receiver. "Hey, I—" There was a brief pause before Momma C. started trying to calm the caller.

"Wait. Slow down. Slow down, Greta! What are you talking about? When? Oh, Jesus! Where is she now? Alright...alright. We're on our way."

She hung up and began to make an immediate u-turn. "Sorry to tell you, Iggy, but you're going to be late for work."

"Where are we going?"

"The hospital. Terra's there. She's been assaulted."

We marched into the hospital and went straight to the front desk. Momma C. began trying to find our friend.

"We're here to see Michelle Li," she told the woman behind the counter. "She was most likely admitted early this morning."

"Who are you?" the woman asked.

"We're who she has," Momma C. replied.

"Okay. Well, if you aren't family we can't—"

"Where is Dr. Amato?"

The woman froze and gave a look that asked why she needed to know.

"You page him or call him or whatever and tell him Dr. Cathy Altermann is here and wants to see Michelle Li. Do it now."

The woman asked us to wait.

"That was impressive," I said.

"His wife was a client of mine."

"What were you seeing her for?"

"That's privileged. But let's just say that he owes me one."

A few moments later the receptionist came back and gave us a room number. We went straight there and headed in where we found Purrterra in bed with an IV and multiple bruises and abrasions. She seemed asleep. Cat walked to her, leaned over and whispered her name. Terra opened her eyes.

"Hey, Momma C.," she managed. "What are you doing here?"

"Greta told us you were here."

Terra glanced over at me and said, in a weak voice, "Hey, Iggy."

I smiled sympathetically.

Cat continued. "Tell us what happened."

"It was Tormentor. We were playing and things got a little out of hand."

"What did he do?"

Purrterra struggled to respond. She was weak, traumatized, and it seemed, medicated. "He had me shackled to a grid at his place. We were just fooling around. It started to get pretty rough, which was okay, but I started getting a little...I don't know, anxious, I guess. I asked him to slow down, but he didn't. When I called out 'red,' he gagged me. He..." She started to tear up a bit. It was clear that she was trying to be strong, but she was also hurt and very upset. "He fucked me pretty hard and hit me a lot."

Before either of us could reply, a doctor came in to look in on her. As he checked her pupils, heartbeat and IV, he asked who we were.

"I'm her therapist," Momma C. said. "Can you tell me the extent of her injuries?"

The doctor was surprisingly frank. "She's got trauma all over her body, two fractured ribs, anal tearing and a possible, slight concussion. Whoever did this messed her up pretty good."

"Who brought her in?" I asked.

"She apparently drove herself. She managed to walk

in on her own two feet. She got dizzy shortly afterward, though."

"What do you have her on?" Momma C. asked.

"Anti-inflammatories and a mild sedative. Nothing else. We're still trying to establish the extent of her injuries."

"I see," Momma C.'s brow furrowed as she looked down at Terra in the hospital bed. "Is she going to be okay?"

"Most likely," the doctor said, "physically, anyway. She's probably going to need your help a great deal in the foreseeable future though." He scribbled something on her chart before hanging it back on the foot of her bed. "Are you two going to stay with her for a while?"

"Is that alright?" Momma C. asked.

"Of course. Someone will come and check on her periodically."

He started to leave, but I stopped him. "Thank you," I said sincerely, trying to cover his honesty, patience and understanding.

He nodded once and walked out.

Momma C. leaned down to Terra again. "We're here, baby girl. You just feel better, okay?"

A few hours later, I went to get Cat and I some lunch. Purrterra had insisted that she wasn't hungry vehemently enough that we were forced to respect it. I walked back into the room and handed Momma C. a bag from a burger joint down the block.

"Thanks," she said. "Sorry to keep you away from work."

"They'll manage for a day without me," I told her.

"How's Terra?"

"She's resting. She fell asleep right after you left." Momma C. reached over and stroked the girl's hair.

That's when a nurse entered the room rather rapidly with a new bag for her IV. She changed it out while asking us if, "the patient," as she put it, had had anything to eat.

"No," Momma C. informed her. "She said she wasn't hungry."

"Well," the nurse began in a snide tone, "he'll need to soon. We can't have him getting worse because of malnutrition."

"*'She'*," Momma C. corrected sharply.

"Whatever," the nurse scowled.

"Not 'whatever'," Momma C. insisted. "You will respect her choice of identity."

"I don't have to respect someone who mutilates their body and engages in cheap, dangerous sex acts with sketchy people. What is *he*? A gay prostitute?"

Momma C. became even more incensed and stood. "Lady, she is a sweet girl who trusted someone she was dating, someone who, as it turned out, didn't deserve it. Lots of of people make similar mistakes, for example whoever hired you for this job. I won't tolerate you being nasty simply because you happen to disagree with unrelated personal choices that *she's* made. So, adjust your attitude. Get me?"

The nurse snapped back. "Your condoning his behavior only makes the situation worse. In fact—"

"Do I need to speak to your supervisor?"

"All right," I said finally. "That's enough." I pointed at the nurse. "You. Beat it. Don't come back."

She huffed at us both, but walked out.

"Raging cunt," Cat hissed.

Before either of us could say anything else, someone else entered. It was D.C. He was silent and wore a deeply concerned look.

"Jackson," Momma C. told him. "Messed her up pretty bad."

My mentor clenched his fists and continued to scowl. He then turned on his heels and walked out, which I found confusing. I went after him, stopping him in the hallway.

"Hey. Where are you going?"

"Supposedly," D.C. began, "there are a couple more people he hurt out there. That's the rumor, anyway. I'm going to find them and convince them to press charges. Once Terra is better, we're going to get her to do the same and see to it that this asshole goes away for a long time."

"And how exactly do you plan to find these people, much less make them press charges if they already haven't? I mean, I haven't heard anyone use a name in connection with any of Tormentor's more brutal, alleged acts."

"We can't tolerate this kind of thing in the community," he shot back.

"I understand that and can see that you're desperate to do something about it. But do you really expect to just charge to the nearest computer and start interrogating everyone on the website for information about other victims?"

He paused. He closed his eyes and took a deep breath. "Of course not," he said more rationally. "But I will certainly do everything that I can. I can discreetly ask around. Maybe somebody in his last community knows something. In the meantime, I can ask Xina to talk to Jackson. They're tight. Maybe he'll confess something to her.”

"What makes you think that?”

"Damn it! I have to try!”

I considered what he was saying and finally conceded. I nodded. "Okay.”

"Stay here with Cat and Terra,” my mentor ordered. "Let me know if anything changes.”

"You got it.”

Cat sat in a chair next to Terra's bed, waiting and watching. I leaned against the door frame, arms crossed. We were both quiet.

Suddenly, Mistress Xina marched in. She stopped a few steps beyond the threshold. She looked at Momma C. "Is she okay?” she asked desperately.

"Of course not,” Cat said with steel eyes. "That bastard hurt her.”

Xina looked downwards and had a mournful expression. She glanced over at me. "Ignite,” she said seriously, "I'd like to apologize again for my behavior at your place.”

I leaned off of the wall. "Appreciated. But we have more pressing matters to concern ourselves with at at the moment.”

She nodded.

There was silence. Finally, Momma C. said to Xina, "Let's talk outside in the hallway.”

"I'll watch Terra,” I volunteered.

They exited to just outside of the room, the door still open. I leaned back against the wall and eavesdropped without really trying.

"This is unfortunate,” Xina said.

"Unfortunate?" Momma C. shot back. "Are you serious? Jackson is a psychopath."

"He's not," Xina insisted. "He's extreme, but he's decent."

"He hurt her!" Momma pointed out sharply.

"...Yeah."

I heard Cat sigh hard. "Look," she said, "we all know that Terra is probably in frenzy and that means she needs us to protect and guide her. She struggles emotionally and she's not in the right head space to make rational decisions about such things. And putting her together with someone like Jackson isn't the best idea. We have a responsibility to her and others in her position. Otherwise, they get in over their heads."

"Absolutely," Xina agreed urgently. "I thought she could handle him, but I misjudged, largely based on her eagerness."

"No one can handle him, Xina," Cat declared. "He's dangerous."

"He's not. He's just—"

"He is!"

There was a moment of silence. Finally, I heard Mistress Xina sigh and ask, "Is she going to be okay?"

Momma C. returned the sigh. "She'll recover...eventually."

"Okay," Xina replied.

They both walked back in and the Mistress walked over to the bed. She put a hand on Terra's and paused. She fought a couple of tears before, finally, taking a deep breath. "Let me know how she progresses," she said to me.

She left.

When I got home and logged onto the website, the homepage was blowing up, as was my inbox. Pretty much everyone in the local community had an opinion to express and, almost unanimously, they were calling for repercussions for Tormentor.

"When you violate consent, you sacrifice your privilege of being a part of this community!" Benji had written.

"Are we going to let legitimate crimes go unpunished? No!" Mac said. "Legal prosecution may be an unlikely road, but we don't have to allow you into our parties, our events or our lives."

Greta followed with, "Why can't we have someone's sorry ass arrested when they rape someone? Why is that so hard these days?"

"I say we beat the rattling shit out of him!" Batlash suggested.

There was only one post that had a different opinion. It was a blog that Mistress Xina had composed and, due to the continual negative responses it garnered, links to it appeared up and down the page.

It read as follows: "I feel that I need to clarify a few things, since no one else wants to express anything but panic and hostility. The person in question is being convicted with no trial whatsoever. Conclusions are being drawn based on hearsay and nothing more. And, while I don't wish to shield someone if they have truly done something horrible, I will neither join a frantic lynch mob.

"I know both parties very well. I do not believe that the 'victim,' in this case, would intentionally concoct accusations like this. However, as much as I do love her, I must realistically acknowledge that she does struggle with a variety of mental and emotional problems, ones that frequently compromise her grip of reality. We have a mental health professional in the community, one that you all respect, who can back me up on this and has already given me her opinion.

"As far as the 'accused' goes, I have known him for years, known him to be of upstanding character, as well as responsible. I know him as a person of integrity and cannot believe that he is capable of such acts of horror.

"I will admit that there exists a possibility that a miscommunication took place, one which would have been less likely if the 'victim' had made their feelings and thoughts more clear. Furthermore, the word 'frenzy' has been tossed out with regards to her multiple times and such behavior is bound to get anyone in over their head sooner or later. Also, if she really did feel violated, why did she not make this known with a safe word or through other means, which I know that the 'accused' employs? I am certain that he would have respected such an action and would have relented. More likely than not, the 'victim' simply thought that she could handle more than she really could and refused to confess her limitations.

"Let me conclude by repeating that I know *both* of these people very well. I cannot, in any world, see the 'accused' knowingly violating anyone. So, calling for his ostracization—much less, 'beating the rattling shit' out of him (which even suggesting is illegal, by the way) is out of line.

"If you're going to express opinions about such things, get your facts together and know who you're talking about first."

I sat there aghast. Did she really write such a horrible thing? What could possibly motivate someone, a woman no less, to ardently come to a rapist's defense? While I could comprehend, and even appreciate, not sentencing someone without a trial, I could not see standing between him and those who wanted to arrest him. This was certainly not a situation to take the 'accused's' side, much less attack the victim.

I opened my email box and was met with a variety of messages bitching, asking my opinion and proposing solutions. The predominant one concerned with the later came from Momma C. who was calling for a meeting at The King's Kettle to publicly and collectively address the problem. Conspicuously absent however, were any comments or messages from my mentor. I decided that that would not do and that I needed his input, if for no other reason than to know where he stood.

"Are you going to this meeting?" I asked in a text.

I received a quick reply. "Yeah. See you there?"

"Yeah," I said. "What do you think of this whole situation?"

His response took a while, almost a half hour. It took enough time that I was surprised by its brevity.

"We'll discuss it later."

His silence, coupled with all of the drama exploding on the website inspired me to hold my tongue as well. We would, indeed, discuss it later.

I was getting ready for bed when I got the text. It was from Momma C.

"Terra just cut her wrists," it said.

"What?" I replied, in shock.

I got a quick response. "She's okay. They found her quickly and have her on suicide watch. Obviously, Xina's note got to her."

I gritted my teeth. This shit was starting to get out of control.

CHAPTER TWENTY-FOUR

My car fixed, I drove myself to The King's Kettle. I walked into the restaurant and went straight to the backroom. The sense of responsibility was in stark contrast to the nervousness I felt during my first visit. When I entered, I had to look around to find an empty chair as the place was packed. Xina really had pissed a lot of people off.

D.C. and I looked at each other and he nodded, even as he continued to talk to Momma C. As I looked for seating, Mac caught my attention and pat the empty chair next to him. I crossed over, pulled it out, unbuttoned my coat and sat down.

"How's it going?" I asked as I offered him a hand to shake.

"Well, we're here to fuck this bitch in the a-hole, so I'd have to say, good."

I nodded.

"Alright," Momma C. announced as she stood. "I think everyone is here now, so let's get this meeting started."

"This justice squad," Batlash said proudly.

Many present agreed loudly, but Momma C. quieted them. "Let's not get out of control right away."

I looked across the room at D.C. who simply stared at the table in front of him appearing disappointed and mad.

Momma C. continued. "We all know what's going on. We've been passing tons of messages and emails back and forth, and obviously, we all agree that we have a problem."

"Damn straight," Batlash called out again. "Mistress Xina has got to go."

Everyone conquered and even began applauding.

"Well, then," Momma C. said, "let's discuss our options. Simply starting a new munch is easy. However, we are talking about ousting someone from the community."

"We did that with Killer Rabbit after he attacked Lolly," SeptemberSnowGirl said. Several people agreed.

"That was different," D.C. interjected. "He knew he fucked up and was afraid of our safety in numbers. Xina won't simply bow out like that."

"Just because you're crammed up Xina's pussy hole—" Batlash began.

"Fuck you, Jeff," Tink, who sat next to her Dom, shot back.

"Let's keep it civil," Momma C. insisted. "I know we're all angry, but we can't take it out on each other." She sighed. "Look, D.C. is right. As far as Mistress Xina is concerned, she has marked all of Clinton as her territory. It would not surprise me in the least if she were to continue showing up at events and treating us all like a bunch of unruly children."

"So, we beat her ass, throw her in a car trunk and drop her off at the mental ward in Jefferson County," Benji suggested with hostility.

"I'll drive," Mac volunteered with a raised hand.

Momma C. commandeered the floor again from all of the laughing and agreeing attendants. "Look, we can make nasty jokes all night, but it won't actually solve the problem. We are talking about telling someone, 'you're not welcome with us anymore.' We are setting a precedent. No one disagrees that we want nothing to do with her from here on out. But we are making it easier to toss people aside when we don't like them or something that they have said or done." She sighed and put her hands on her hips. "We have to really spell this out, identify the real details of what she did wrong, the actual violations, so that we don't start eating our own."

The room was quiet for a moment. When it seemed that no one had anything but nasty slurs to offer, I raised my hand.

"Yes, Ignite?" Momma C. said.

"Um, maybe we could make a very specific list of all the things she did that we feel were out of line and isolate the things that really were...well...violations."

There was a slow crawl of agreeable murmurs across the room. I looked over at D.C., who still looked unhappy, but did offer me a single, approving nod.

"Reasonable," Momma C. said.

That's when we all got a shock. The doors opened and in walked Master Jon. The room became deathly quiet as he entered, a small, but friendly, smile on his face.

"I hope I'm not interrupting," he said, sounding courteous and sincere, while still commanding respect with his presence.

"Of course not, Master Jon," Momma C. replied, obviously surprised. "Er...please join us."

"I just want everyone to know, I'm not here to get involved. Not really. Just observing." He went to the empty seat Momma C. had vacated and sat while greeting and shaking hands with D.C. He then looked back at Cathy. "Please, continue."

"Well, as Ignite35 suggested, maybe we should go through the transgressions."

Master Jon's presence made me wish she hadn't given

me credit for my idea.

"She got Purrterra hurt," Greta shot out hatefully. "And she made excuses for that rapist sack of shit that did it."

Momma C.'s response was quiet and reverent. "Yes. Yes, she did. That is obviously first and foremost."

There was momentary silence before Mac pointed out, "She barred SnowGirl just because the two of them didn't get along. And she barred me when I accused Tormentor of violating me."

"Yes," Momma C. agreed with a finger pointed his way. "True. What else?"

We all received another shock when D.C. offered a public critique. "She assaulted her sub after he called a timeout in front of several of us." His tone was dark and disapproving.

Then the floodgates opened.

"She tried to force Greta and Wired to have sex with each other when they didn't want to." That sounded familiar.

"She outed us to a couple of the waiters here."

"She showed up at a private party I threw without an invitation."

"She's a cunt!"

The accusations got louder and louder and elicited more and more cheers of approval.

Finally, Master Jon stood. "It looks like you all have a list of grievances that you can cite and a unanimous vote. I don't want to interfere. I just wanted to make sure this wasn't a witch hunt. I'll leave you to it. Thank you for allowing me to attend."

He shook Momma C.'s hand and excused himself. I looked at D.C. with concern, but he simply shook his head, the implication being that Master Jon really wasn't there to cause trouble, just to investigate.

"Alright," Momma C. said. "What else? And let's keep the critiques genuine. 'She's a cunt,' doesn't count."

The complaints continued. Nasty messages on line people had received were brought up, ones that took issue with irrelevant behavior or unimportant comments made, times she'd allowed bad behavior from some members that she shot down in others, lies she'd supposedly told about her past meant to make her seem more experienced than she really was... Everyone had something, even the people who hated her simply because they were assholes themselves. The list of community crimes grew.

Momma C. kept tally, actually writing them down. Then, as the venting in the room began to reach a fevered pitch, we all got another surprise in the form of another unexpected visitor. Most of us saw her coming through the glass doors. Those that did not, immediately grew quiet when the tall, blonde Dominatrix entered.

"Well," Mistress Xina said hotly. "Isn't this an interesting party?"

After a few seconds, Momma C. visibly screwed up her courage and took responsibility for the whole situation. "I felt that we needed to discuss the problems you've caused as a group and address them in an organized fashion," she said calmly and strongly.

"Problems I've caused?" Xina retorted. She then looked over at D.C. "Et tu, Brute?"

He sighed. He replied like it pained him, but with his disappointment obvious. "You fucked up, Christina." The way he said it, sounded like he was talking to a person, a former friend, rather than a respected Dominatrix.

She sneered. "Fuck you." She looked around. "Fuck all of you." She turned and charged out.

"Well," Batlash began, "I guess we don't have to

break news of the bad to her now."

There was a little bit of mingling after the meeting. D.C. stood with his hands in his pockets and nodding with one attendant, all the while with a concerned look on his face. As I approached my mentor, the other person walked off.

"Hey," I said in a brotherly fashion.

He offered me his best attempt at a smile while in, what was obviously a bad mood. He shook my hand and pat my shoulder. "Hey, Iggy."

"How are you?" I asked. "You seem upset."

He grimaced and slowly shook his head. "There's... There's just a lot going on."

"Aside from all of this drama?"

"Yeah."

"Like what?"

He sighed. "Well, for starters, Posie and I both have to go to the doctor."

"Is everything okay?"

He nodded. "Yeah. It's nothing serious. We just need some tests run."

"You sure?" I asked. "You seem awfully preoccupied."

He nodded again. "Yeah. I'm just..." The pause seemed long as he contemplated. "...really disappointed at the moment."

I took this to mean that he was consumed by his distaste for Xina and her actions.

"Okay," I said. "Let me know if you need anything."

"I appreciate it."

I cleared my throat and looked around. "So, where's Tinkerbrat?"

His brow furrowed even more. "She had to leave."

"Work?"

"Yeah," he said. "Work. Anyway, speaking of leaving, I should be as well."

He started to go, but I stopped him.

"Say, uh, do we have any idea what's going to be done about Tormentor?"

"It's been handled," was all he said.

"What does that mean?"

He sighed and pulled me aside, away from where we might be overheard. "I spoke to Master Jon about Jackson. He contacted some of our people in law enforcement—"

"We have law enforcement in the community?"

He gave me that look that said that I was asking too many questions again.

"Sorry."

"Anyway," he continued, "Jackson apparently had a couple of warrants in two other cities for assault. Officers picked him up this morning. That's one of the reasons that Master Jon stopped by, to fill me in."

"Well, good." I smiled. "I guess some things do work out."

He didn't reply. He just pat my shoulder again and walked out.

While the weekend was eventful, to say the very least, Sunday was also excruciating. I couldn't keep my mind from obsessing over the woman from city hall and wondering if she would actually show. I seriously doubted it and kept telling myself that she wouldn't, just so I wouldn't be disappointed.

I sat at one of the tables in the bar area of the restaurant that I'd chosen, the same one that D.C. and I had had drinks in after my disastrous dinner party, sipping a cocktail and trying to make myself examine the menu. I read the descriptions of each appetizer and entree, but little of it sunk in. My mind kept moving back to the blonde.

After about forty-five minutes and three brief conversations with the server about how I intended to wait for my other party before placing an order, I began to get frustrated. It was starting to become obvious that she really wasn't coming. Despite all the mental preparation for such an outcome, I was still pretty disappointed. I pulled some money out of my wallet, laid it on the table, collected my over coat and started to leave.

Much to my surprise, there she was, walking in the door. I felt a big smile inch across my face which I tried hard to control. I didn't want to seem too eager. As she looked around and saw me there, she took a deep breath and walked my way.

"I was beginning to think you weren't going to show," I told her as I directed her to our table.

"I wasn't certain that I was going to either," she said frankly. "But...I figured, it's a public place. It should be safe to...talk."

I offered to take her coat. She declined, taking it off herself and sitting down across from me.

"What's your name?" I asked.

She hesitated before finally telling me, "Mary."

"Mary," I repeated. "Well, Mary, I'm Kelly. It's nice to meet you."

At that time, the waiter approached and asked if we'd like to order. Mary quickly picked up her menu and began to skim it.

"Get whatever you'd like," I told her. "It's on me."

"I can pay for myself," she insisted.

She ordered off of the appetizer menu. I figured this was either due to a lack of funds or because she didn't intend to stay long. I ordered another cocktail and the same appetizer that she did.

"What would you care to drink, Miss?" the server asked.

Mary continued to look at me suspiciously as she told him, "Water is fine."

The server left and we continued to stare at each other, me with a slight smile on my face and her with paranoia.

"So, why did you decide to come?" I asked.

Mary thought long and hard. It was pretty obvious that she was trying to select which answer to give, the truth or something that would keep me at a distance.

"I guess, I was just curious," she bravely confessed.

I continued to smile. Mary seemed to grow more and more uncomfortable and frustrated, even a little irritated.

"Look," she said, "I'm not here to hook up with some strange guy from IT, certainly not under the circumstances that we...encountered each other last. Let's just get that straight. I also have my car right by the door of this place, so I will be getting into it directly. I'm going to head straight to my sister's place and my brother-in-law is a cop. So, don't get any weird ideas, okay?"

I actually started to chuckle a bit. "You've got this all figured out, haven't you?"

Mary said nothing.

Our drinks came and, the second the server walked away, I asked her why she was reading the particular book that she had with her on the elevator. She said that it was just something that she was interested in learning more about.

"Kinky sex?" I asked.

"Sexual intimacy," she snapped back.

"Is that what we're calling it?"

"Look, why did you ask me to meet you here, anyway?" she demanded.

I stared at her for a few moments, looking over her face, trying to determine how direct I could be with her, what she would listen to and what would scare her off, what would intrigue her and what would offend her. Finally, I decided that none of it mattered. What mattered was that I wanted to know more about her and that was what I was going to pursue.

"Tell me about yourself, Mary," I said calmly.

She hesitated and did her best to study me. I remained motionless and continued to smile as politely as I could. However, I'm sure that some of the thoughts running through my head couldn't help but make it appear, at least a little, suggestive.

"I work in the records department and I go to school at night," she said.

"What are you studying?"

"I'm getting my masters in criminology."

"That must be taking a while."

"It did," she confessed. "I'm finishing my thesis now though."

"Do you have any friends?"

"Of course." Her answer, like most of them, sounded defensive.

"Are any of them aware of the...subject that you're interested in?"

She lost eye contact for a brief moment. "Not really."

"Do you live alone?"

Her eyes turned to steel as she met my gaze again. "Why is that important?"

"It's not, actually," I assured her. "Just a question. More curious how self-sufficient you are than anything unseemly." I realized that my tone and demeanor were becoming more and more like my mentor.

Mary took a deep breath and relaxed her shoulders. "I do, for about a year now. I had a roommate up until then."

"How old are you?"

"Twenty-nine."

"Do you like your job?"

She got an uneasy look on her face, one very different from the discomfort that she displayed concerning my questions about the book she had been holding or any personal matters. "It's okay. Some of the city officials and police officers can be..." She trailed off.

"What?"

She fixed me with a defensive, almost accusatory gaze again. "Invasive. Creepy."

"That's unfortunate," I said sincerely. "Are you single?"

"At the moment."

"That must make any advances they send your way feel even more threatening."

"What makes you think that they're making advances?"

I grinned. "You're an attractive woman and they're...politicians and police officers. Authoritarians often seem to think they can have whatever they want."

"Mmm," she said with a nod and a factious grin that leveled a similar assessment at me.

"Hey, I'm not like that," I assured her. "Like you said, I'm just an IT guy. And I have no illusions about getting what I want. I just investigate what interests me. If I can..." I motioned genuinely toward her, "help someone else do the same..."

Her arms remained crossed and her body language protected as she showed a suspicious and apprehensive smile. "So, you're not looking to have sex with me?"

I shook my head sincerely. "I barely know you. I'm just trying to change that."

She nodded like she was trying hard to believe me.

"When was the last time you had sex?" I asked.

She looked appalled. "None of your business."

"Was it disappointing? Is that why you're reading that book? Or are you just naughty?"

"That's also none of your business."

"So, you are naughty?"

"I'm going." She grabbed her coat and stood.

"Sit," I told her a bit sternly. I didn't mean for it to come out as an order, but it did. Maybe it was me being desperate. Or maybe, I was instinctively responding to something inside of her. Whatever the case, Mary paused...and then sat back down.

"Look," I began calmly, "I meant it when I said that I'm not trying to get into your pants at the moment. I'm just trying to talk. If you can bring yourself to read a book like that, to be that interested in the subject of BDSM and submission, then you should find it in yourself to be able to talk about it. If you can talk about it then you can understand it better and you can learn… about yourself more than anything."

She stared at me. Her breath was picking up.

"Do you trust me?" I asked.

"Of course not," she replied.

"Try," I insisted. "In fact, let me just clear a few things up. I promise that, unless you specifically ask me to, I will never lay a hand on you. Even then, I might not. All we're going to do is talk, okay?"

Mary sat there.

"Okay?" I asked again.

Finally, she nodded.

"Good. Answer me honestly. You want to learn about submission, about control by being controlled?"

Mary swallowed and then nodded.

"You want to just read about it and hope that you can talk your next boyfriend into it, hope that he can comprehend it and do it properly? Or would you rather meet some people..." I hesitated and then clarified. "...Someone...who actually knows a good bit about it and has some legitimate experience?"

She continued trying to look into me, clearly trying to see how sincere I truly was. I didn't display any kind of tell. For the first time, I really did feel that I held all the cards, as well as the reins, that what I was saying was on the level and that I had earned the confidence that I was displaying.

"I, uh..." she began quietly. "I'm not really sure. Are you...experienced at this sort of thing? Really?"

I nodded slowly.

"How experienced?"

"I'm a member of an online and local community of people who explore BDSM very extensively. I have been studying under a highly experienced Dominant. I have experience with subs. I have a membership at a sex dungeon, have been to multiple play parties, hosted a high protocol dinner... I have some very nice toys that I know how to use very well."

"What kind of toys?" I could clearly see her pulse throbbing on her neck and it was increasing.

"Various things," I told her. "But of course, the most

effective thing to bring into a BDSM experience is one's imagination. I have a lot of that." I felt my smile grow.

She swallowed. "So, you're interested in me because I'm curious about...that sort of stuff."

"Why wouldn't I be?" I replied. I had a sip from my drink before continuing with, "But, to be honest, I've been interested in you for a while. I just didn't explore it because...well, people like me, we tend to make others...apprehensive, let's say."

"How did you get into this?" she asked.

I sighed. "It's a long story. The short version is that I broke up with someone, moved here and needed to make some friends. Having had one D/s experience and wanting more, I decided that this was the way to proceed."

"So, you're a Dominant?"

"That's right."

"And you have training?"

"Yes."

"And you hang out with a bunch of other people who do this and go to dungeons and sex parties and high...whatever?"

"I do."

She swallowed. "Well, I have no interest in doing anything like that," she insisted. "Public sex and group sex and whatever else... I mean, I have a job with the city. My career—"

"It doesn't have to be like that," I informed her. "There are plenty of people who conduct their kinks strictly in the privacy of their own homes."

"So, you're not necessarily saying that you're interested in me for yourself. You just want to find out what I'm looking for and talk about it."

"Oh, I already told you. I'm interested." My tone was

solid and I kept my body language still and controlled. "But yes. I do want to find out what you're looking for."

She was quiet.

"Perhaps I can provide it," I said. "If so, I can teach you a lot of things. I don't even have to touch you right away. If I'm not what you're looking for, then I may know someone who is. Regardless, I'm here, telling you who I am, what I can offer, completely in truth and trying to see what the possibilities are. I am outing myself, offering you *my* trust, for your benefit, in the slim, possible hope that it's also mine. But not completely. Ultimately, I'm just reaching out."

Suddenly, our food arrived. We both jerked out of the fantastical world that we were discussing and tried to appear normal, whatever that was.

For the remainder of the meal, I insisted that we just talked about more mundane stuff. She asked me about my job and my non-deviant hobbies and I was honest, explaining my work with the IT company, my simple apartment with the big TV, where I was from and what my formative years had been like, as well as my passion for Latin music.

"Really?" she asked with sudden interest. "Do you dance at all?"

"It's been known to happen."

"That's actually kind of cool, because I take salsa dancing."

"Really?" Okay, now I was super intrigued.

"Yeah. It's frustrating though, because we never have enough guys in there."

"Well," I grinned, "I am a guy."

She actually laughed a little. It made my smile grow.

"Why Latin music?" she asked. "I mean, I figured you'd be into industrial metal or something like that."

I felt my brow furrow as I laughed. "Latin music is fun. And it's very emotional. It's playful and sensitive."

"Not really the best choice to have sex to, is it?" she asked as she chewed her food.

"I guess it depends. It can be very dramatic, though. And sensual."

She nodded her concession, still with a mouth full of food. She finished chewing enough to ask, "So...do you beat women?"

"You mean, do I strike them appropriately to elicit the right kind of adrenaline rush during intimate moments? Or are you asking me if I'm abusive?"

Mary looked a little embarrassed and shrugged.

"I can be a bit aggressive." I paused, trying to decide how much to share. "I actually almost hurt someone once, but I caught myself. It taught me where the line is. Still, that's not what it's really all about."

"What is it about?" She seemed to sincerely want to know.

I stared off for a bit, collecting my thoughts. "It's about exploring the senses, finding the kind of mythical world that we indulged in as kids, I think. When you're little, running around the yard, chasing dragons and saving a princess..." I looked at her and smiled, "...or being saved...it's all fun and exciting. But as adults, we're expected to leave that behind. In my lifestyle, we don't accept that. We still want the fantasy. And as adults, the way we indulge, the forces that motivate us, are often sexual. It's one of the main things that separate us from children." I clarified. "One of the things that isn't steeped in everyday responsibility, that is." I then added, "Of course, we have people who think that that's part of it too, conditioning and structure and sexualizing them."

I looked back at her and she was just staring. She

seemed to have let her defenses down and was genuinely listening.

"Anyway..." I said.

"Okay, I'm interested," she suddenly admitted.

"Really?"

"Yes. I want to learn more." She folded her napkin and put it on her plate and her elbows on the table. "Look, obviously this whole thing had me pretty freaked out. I mean, a guy that I don't really know, finding out something very intimate about me, pouncing on it, something sexual no less..." She paused and put her hands between her knees. "I am interested though. What can you teach me?"

I didn't smile any more than I already was. I just asked, "Do you really want to learn?"

"Yeah. Yeah, I think so."

"Really?"

"Yeah. Nothing too invasive, though. Like you said. No touching or getting creepy. Just..." she trailed off.

"You have to offer me some trust, okay? That's part of the power exchange."

"Power exchange," she repeated with a nod. "They talked about that in the book."

"Mary..." I began, "do you trust me?"

She looked nervous, but slowly nodded.

"Fine," I said. "Go into the bathroom, take off your underpants and bring them to me."

She looked appalled. "I'm not going to—"

"Do it." I didn't raise my voice, and my tone was soothing, even if my delivery was frank.

Mary sat there staring, almost falling back into the defensive facade that she walked in with. For a moment, she looked like she might want to slap me. But that faded and her body relaxed again, while she still met my gaze.

Her eyes drifted down for a moment, but she looked back up at me, like she was trying to determine if I was serious. I said nothing, merely held my ground. I meant what I had said. And if she really wanted to play this game, then I fully expected her to cooperate.

"Go," I calmly insisted.

Mary pressed her lips together. She didn't say anything. She simply rose, and to my amazement, walked towards the ladies room. A couple of minutes later she emerged and made her way back to where we were sitting. She took a brief moment to, clearly, consider what she was doing and then quickly handed her panties to me under the table.

I looked down into my palm at the small, plain, pink, cotton garment. "Cute," I smirked.

Mary visibly blushed.

"Alright, Mary, here's the deal," I said as I shoved her underpants into my coat pocket. "You and I are going to meet here again at the same time next Sunday. In that time, you are not allowed to masturbate at all."

"What?" she asked, rather concerned. It was difficult to tell if the distress was from the declaration that she would meet me again, the restriction that came with it or just my sheer audacity, but it was definitely there.

"You heard me. Not even a little," I told her.

I stood and collected my over coat while adding that my assignment for her may seem easy enough, but that she'd most likely find it very frustrating. I tossed some money on the table, bid Mary goodnight and told her that I'd see her in a week.

CHAPTER TWENTY-FIVE

I made it a point to check on Terra after work, the following day. She only had a couple more left in the hospital and I felt that she needed to know that there were some of us who cared and made her a priority. This seemed to boost her spirits some, as did the many get well baskets and cards from other community members.

"I shouldn't have let all of this get to me," she grieved. "I don't know. I just got really depressed. Momma C. says it happens to rape victims."

"Rape survivors," I corrected with a smile.

Suddenly, there was someone else at the doorway. "Knock knock," they said.

I turned to see Cat there.

"Speak of the devil," Terra smiled.

"You two weren't taking my name in vain, were you?" she teased.

"Now, why would we do that?" Terra replied.

"How you feeling?"

Terra grinned and sat up a little. "I'm better. I was just telling Iggy that I was silly to get so overwhelmed."

"It's understandable," Cat said. "Have you thought anymore about what we talked about yesterday?"

"Yeah."

"And..."

Terra sighed. "I think you're right."

I broke in. "What exactly was it you discussed, if I may ask?"

Terra continued to try to sit up in bed and Cat helped her. "I think..." Terra began, "I'm going to move back home to be close to my parents."

"Really?" I asked.

"Yeah. Momma C. made me consider that I might have some work to do, getting them to understand my situation better, understanding them better... We need to heal and I need to take a break from the community for a while."

I thought and nodded. "Not the worst idea I've ever heard."

She smiled and took each of our hands. "Thank you both for being there for me."

"Of course, kiddo," Cat said. "This community may have its heaping basket of problems, but I like to think, that when it really matters, we're there for each other."

"Amen," I agreed.

A week went by and I did not run into Mary. On Sunday, I waited at the same restaurant, at the same table. After thirty-five minutes, she arrived.

"You like to keep me waiting, I've noticed," I said to her.

"I came right after my dance class. It just takes time to clean up and get here in all the traffic," she informed me.

"I see."

I took a sip off of my cocktail while the server took her drink order. Again, she got water. Once he had gone I asked Mary how her week had been.

"Fine," was all she said.

The server returned with Mary's water and took our

order. This time she got a regular meal and I decided to do the same. We ate and talked. I deliberately kept the conversation polite and just tried to learn about her.

She was from a big city in a neighboring state and had migrated to Clinton for college. She worked forty hours a week and paid the rest of her way in student loans. She was, despite her original assertion of having a sister, an only child and her parents were strict Catholics. She was agnostic and at a point in her life when she was really beginning to feel independent. She would be graduating shortly and then she had no idea what she would do. Her degree was starting to feel foreign to her, really just a goal that she had set and was determined to finish. She'd had a string of short, unfulfilling relationships during her undergraduate years and had been, mostly, single while getting her Masters.

"What about you?" she asked. "What haven't you shared yet?"

I grinned big. "I was born to a couple of billionaire parents who got gunned down in an alley, which inspired me to don a cape and cowl and fight crime in a never-ending attempt to bring meaning and justice to the world."

"You're an asshole, you know that?" she said between bites and with a smirk that wasn't nearly as amused as I had hoped for.

"I am kidding," I confirmed, "but, not entirely. I have a pretty boring daytime life and spend my nights in a world of mystery and intrigue."

"No hobbies other than that?"

"I read a good bit," I told her. "I like going to the movies—"

"What do you read?" she broke in.

"I like Chuck Klosterman a lot. I recently finished the

Harry Potter series."

"Oh, I love J.K. Rowling," she emitted.

"Really?"

"Yes. Have you read her other stuff, besides the Harry Potter books?"

"I haven't," I confessed with a shake of my head.

"You have to. It's *so* good. She is so talented." She seemed genuinely engaged in our conversation, even as she scooped her Cajun pasta into her mouth.

I grinned. "What do you think about Hitchhiker's Guide?"

"Oh," she began, "you mean the book that everyone should be forced to read their freshman year of high school?" She suddenly adopted a poor British accent. "'You know, it's at times like these, when I'm trapped in a Vogon airlock with a man from Betelgeuse, and about to die of asphyxiation in deep space that I wish I'd listened to what my mother told me'."

"'Why?'" I returned with a smile. "'What did she tell you?'"

"'I don't know, I didn't listen'."

We both laughed.

We continued to talk in this manner, sharing the kind of information that most people consider important, but that is really just used to make each other feel at ease enough to talk about real things.

"So, you said your week was fine. Was it frustrating?" I finally asked.

Mary blushed a little. "Maybe," she said.

"Did you touch yourself at all?"

Mary blushed more. "No," she insisted.

"Are you sure?"

"I didn't."

"Well," I raised my glass. "I'd say that's progress."

I smiled at her and Mary started having trouble making eye contact.

"Why is it difficult to talk about these things?" I asked. "Sex is perfectly normal."

"Not all sex," Mary insisted. "Sometimes it's more…"

"Exciting?" I supplied.

Mary still didn't look at me. She suddenly wasn't looking down either, however. She just seemed to stare off in the distance like she was trying to put together a puzzle without a complete picture of what it was supposed to be. She didn't seem nervous or defensive. It was as if she had so much to say, but no way to say it.

"Was it hard?" I asked her.

"Was what hard?"

"Not touching yourself?"

Mary pondered a moment. Surprisingly, she was rather frank. She told me that it wasn't terribly difficult at first, but that it became so as the days went by. She mentioned that there were plenty of times when she had gone for weeks without masturbating with no thought or concern. However, now that she was forbidden to do so, it became all that she thought about.

I just smiled. "So, masturbation is an obsession now?"

"Sort of."

I continued to smile. Finally, I gave her my next set of instructions.

"Go to the bathroom, Mary," I said. "Bring me your underpants."

Mary hesitated for a bit. Then, she stood up and marched to the ladies room. When she emerged she had another pair of panties for me. These were satin and a little nicer than the ones from the previous week.

"Good girl," I told her as I shoved them into my jacket pocket. "Now, put your coat in your lap."

Mary slowly pulled her coat across her legs and narrowed her eyes, perhaps trying to predict what I was going to tell her next.

"You get a reprieve, Mary. Your restriction is over and you are now allowed to masturbate again. So, do it."

Her eyes grew wide. Her breath picked up and she looked as though she might start shaking her head.

"Mary..." I said calmly. "Reach up under your coat...and touch yourself."

We stared at each other for a while, a long while. Mary was obviously trying very hard to wrap her mind around what was going on and to decide how to respond. I remained motionless, an insistent look on my face. I gave a slow, very small nod. Finally, she glanced around, carefully reached under her coat, raised her skirt in the middle and began to do as she had been told.

"Go slow," I told her. "But don't stop until you come."

She rubbed. She also maintained full eye contact, at first. The look on Mary's face became more and more distressed. She began to shake a tiny bit and her free hand clutched the table until her knuckles turned white. After only a couple of minutes, Mary let out a small, but desperate, whimper. She rocked back and forth slightly, her eyes now closed and a pained expression across her freckled face. Her breathing was heavy and she had started to visibly sweat.

Finally, she relaxed and stopped. She sat still, her eyes still closed, her breathing very slowly returning to normal.

"Good girl," I said.

Her next question was desperate. "What else can you teach me?"

I walked through the corridors of City Hall looking for someone that I could give my news to. Eleven grueling months and I finally had the computer system under control. I even spent a few extra days cleaning out non-printable characters from their database, just to make things go smoother. Jack Pierce wasn't in his office, so I was forced to seek out Mike Underwood. When I found him however, he was talking to the City Planner, in his office.

"What makes you think this is a real place?" he asked Jack. "And what makes you think that what they're doing there is so bad?"

"It's real. A swingers club or something. And that's not something we need across the street from a school, Mike. Isn't that obvious?"

Mike Underwood sighed before looking up to notice me. "Can we help you with something, Mr. Ferrall?"

"Uh, yeah," I began. "I just wanted to let the two of you know that you're all set. You shouldn't have any more problems. You're cleaned up and completely up to date. All your information is intact, too."

"That's great news," Jack said.

"Took you long enough," Mike tacked on.

I gave a patient laugh. I then decided to try to get more information about the situation with the Scene Shop. "So, what's this you two are talking about with a sex club or something?"

"Just something that we're looking into," Jack told me dismissively.

The City Chair however, was more than willing to share. "Jack here is concerned that there may be an adult club in one of the buildings on Truman Street. He wants to build a new elementary school there and is having a little bit of a panic over it."

"Mike, it's not appropriate to have a bar five hundred feet from a school, much less whatever this place is. There's no telling what they do there."

"Well," I said, "couldn't you just build the school somewhere else?"

The City Planner shook his head. "We need it in this neighborhood."

I pretended like I was offering understanding with a nod before asking, "You said it was on Truman?"

"That's correct," Mike said.

"I know that area. There's a huge tract of land, several acres, in fact, a few blocks away. It's just woods at the moment," I told them, referring to the area that I had chased Jenny in.

Jack shook his head. "That's the problem. There's nothing there. We'd have to run electricity and that would be one more thing we'd have to—"

"No, actually. There is something out there, just at the edge of the property. It's a fire station."

Mike held a hand out to his work partner. "That sounds like a much better thing to be next to a school."

"But we don't know if the property is available or—"

"What?" Mike asked. "You're the City Planner and you don't know? Well, I happen to remember this land that Mr. Ferrall is referring to and I'm pretty certain I know who to ask about it." He picked up his phone and dialed. After a few seconds, he gave a warm greeting. "Vanessa. Good afternoon, it's Mike Underwood. I know, it's been forever. Good. Good. You? Excellent. Listen, we're curious about some property on, Tiffany Avenue, I think it is. It's several undeveloped acres next to the fire station. Jack Pierce wants to build an elementary school on Truman, but we think that the property on Tiffany might be a far better place for it. That is...if it's available. Would your office happen to have any information on it?"

There was a long pause. No one in the room said anything. Mike sniffed once. Finally, he became animated again. "Yes, I'm still here. Yes, that would be the land. Interesting. Excellent! That is wonderful news. I appreciate it. Of course. We definitely will have to some time. I can't wait. I have to get back to work, but I will call you this weekend and we'll set up a date for it. Thank you so much, Vanessa. Bye bye." He hung up and told us, "The property is available, it's cheap and it is zoned for commercial and city business. I'd say the problem is solved."

Jack began to speak up. "Yeah, but, Mike, if—"

"The problem is *solved*, Jack. Now, do us all a favor and make the changes in the plan for the school. Otherwise, we'll have to take it to the mayor and you know how much she hates complications."

Jack Pierce got a frustrated look on his face, but then got up and left.

Mike offered his opinion. "That should keep that little mongrel busy for a while."

I smiled. "I'm glad it worked out. But why would he want to pursue trying to put the school on Truman if there is something...I don't know, decadent there?"

"Oh, old Jack just likes to frighten the public every once in a while. If he can look like he's then solving the problem, it makes him seem valuable. And since I'm pretty sure he has his eye on the Mayor's office when she finally gets out, something like exposing a 'sex club' and protecting the children would look really good on his resume."

I slowly nodded as I took it all in.

Mike continued. "Politics is a dirty, dirty business some times." He rose and offered a hand to shake. "Thank you, Mr. Ferrall, for all of your hard work. I'm sure it couldn't have been easy."

"Ah, it wasn't bad. Just very involved."

"Yes, well, thank you anyway. Will you be doing our regular diagnostics and handling any future problems?"

"That's the plan."

"Well then, I'll see you again. Thank you also for the suggestion on where to locate the school."

I shrugged. "Just trying to help." I started to walk out, but he stopped me.

"Oh, and, Kelly..." he said. His face took on a strange, knowing look as he said to me, "I've never told you this, but...nice belt."

I froze. I looked at him and he grinned a small amount. He then sat back down as he said. "Have a good day."

CHAPTER TWENTY-SIX

After getting home, I sighed out what felt like a year of responsibility. And, I guess, it was. I plopped on my couch. Then I picked up my phone to check the website for whatever new bullshit was on it. Was Xina gone? Was Tormentor?

I got a surprise, however. The people who were gone where, apparently, me and Tink. That is to say, when I looked at my page, I was no longer listed as D.C.'s protégé and looking at his, Tink was no longer his sub.

I messaged him.

No answer.

Well, what the hell was this about?"

I jumped in my car and headed straight to his place. This was something I wanted an answer for right away.

I knocked and the door was opened quickly. Posie was there looking very, very expectant and sad.

"Oh... Hello, Mr. Iggy," she said.

"Iggy," D.C. said over her shoulder, as he tugged his tie off, headed for the kitchen. "What brings you here?"

"What brings..." I couldn't even form a response as Posie allowed me in and shut the door. I forced one out. "What do you mean by that? I looked at the website and I am no longer listed as your protégé and Tink is no longer your sub." I glanced over at Posie, who looked like she had been crying for some time.

"You don't need me anymore, Iggy," D.C. said as he wrestled with a bottle of Bourbon that he was trying to open. "You've obviously come into your own and you can move on from here without me."

"Well," I began, "you could have discussed this with me before deleting me."

"There's nothing to discuss." He managed to open the bourbon and began pouring himself a shot, which he added ice to. "You graduate. Congratulations." He marched back to the couch where he sat down.

I was confused. "Wait. What are you talking about? You could have, at least, given me a heads up. Do you just spring graduation on your writing students?"

"It's not the same thing." He looked frustrated and mad as he sat swirling his drink and taking a tentative sip.

I was speechless. I slowly moved over to where he was on the couch and sat in the adjacent chair. "What's going on?"

He was silent for a while. Finally, he began to catch me up...slowly.

"Tink," he said. "...She's been...apparently..." He stopped again. He sighed angrily. He resumed with a new start. "Posie and I both have gonorrhea," he told me. "I haven't been screwing other people. Posie hasn't been screwing other people. Tink..." He gritted his teeth, but said nothing.

"She brought something home?" I asked, somewhat in shock.

"Yes, she brought something home," D.C. said with frustration. "It seems she's been fucking all of these people that she stays with and she caught the clap. Posie and I started having these burning sensations when we would pee. I confronted Tink about it and she lied. It went on and we all got tested. And..." He trailed off again.

I struggled with the information. "Jesus. So—"

"So, Tink is right back to where she was when I found her," my former mentor said. "Or she never left. She once told me that she liked bed hopping, but I thought we'd moved her past that. Obviously not. Nor have we taught her to give a flying shit about the people who care about her. So, I threw the little bitch out."

"You...what?"

"That's right. We got our test result back, I confronted her. After a bit of resistance, she confessed and so, I threw some of her shit in a suitcase and her out into the street. Good residence."

I glanced over at Posie who was fighting tears and looking at me urgently.

"Fuck her," D.C. said. He then stood and turned to me. "Iggy, if you never learn anything else from me, learn this: never be too trusting. I have been. I take people at their word. It's burned me. Xina burned me. Now, Tink has."

I looked at him with a reassuring, concerned strength as I stood. "I haven't."

He paused before saying, "All the more reason to set you free." He began to pace. "If you fuck up now, it's not on me." He started to march off to his bedroom, but stopped to speak over his shoulder. "Not that I think that ever you would." He then amended his tone to express the original disappointment he had. "But then...what do I know about people?" He went to his room and shut the door.

I looked after him and then at Posie. She was clearly falling apart, while trying, unsuccessfully, to hold it together.

I sighed deep and hard before asking her, "You mind telling me what the hell that was all about?"

She started crying harder and moved over to me where she spoke quietly, yet urgently. "Tink did," she sputtered. "She fucked up. She let her wild side get the better of her and she..." Posie fought her tears getting worse. "But...he threw her out. He... *He threw her out*!"

"Well," I began as reasonably as I could manage. "From what he said, she did cheat...a lot."

"So what?" Posie said desperately. "I mean, yeah, she fucked up, but..." Her tears and sobs increased while she still tried hard to quiet them. "He threw her out."

I sighed. "Posie, I—"

"This is bad. Like, *really* bad," she said, her blue eyes now very red.

"I'm sure everything will be fine," I lied to her and myself. "It'll just take time."

"No, Mr. Iggy!" she insisted. "You don't understand. Tink is out there with nowhere to go. Her family is far away and she doesn't have transportation. I *know* her. She'll do something irresponsible...possibly self-destructive. You have to find her. You have to find her and make sure she's okay."

"Isn't that a little co-dependent?" I offered.

"I don't give a shit," she urged. "I'm just worried."

"You're not mad at her, too?"

"Of course, I'm mad." She scowled, and because of her sensitive nature, it looked more serious than it would on most people. It grabbed my attention hard. She continued. "But she doesn't deserve to be homeless. And I don't want to see anything bad happen to her." Her tears kept pouring. "I just want her..." Her lip quivered and she struggled to form the word, "...back."

I told myself to hell with protocol and no touch

policies and whatever the hell else and hugged my, now former, sister while she did her best to quietly weep.

"Please, Mr. Iggy, find her," she begged. "At least make sure she's safe."

I pulled back from her and put a hand on her cheek. "You watch and work on him. I'll be back as fast as I can."

As I drove, my mind ran over the past year and how much everything had changed. When it began, I was unemployed, content in a vanilla relationship that I didn't even realize was failing and without direction or purpose. Now, I was an IT specialist for a major, metropolitan city and a graduated Dominant on a mission.

I had learned a lot, both about the lifestyle and about myself. Yet much of my experience involved a lot of drama. I had witnessed drama, I had been a part of it. I had even created some when I snapped on Sluttypixie.

...On a young girl named, Megan.

Of course, I helped prevent and address some too. But that didn't seem to matter now. Maybe Mary was right trying to learn on her own, avoiding the community and it's public entanglements. Maybe keeping all of this behind the closed door of one's bedroom was the way to go.

If I did bow out, I knew I would miss some things. The Scene Shop, with its exquisite equipment and festive atmosphere, was a great place to see new and unusual things and to learn. I had made friends at the munches and been afforded a place to go where I could relax, enjoy myself and socialize freely. I had been places and done things, exciting things that most people would never even dream of.

Still, there was the drama and there was the pain. There were old perverts to grab my crotch, ex-girlfriends screwing their new partners right in front of me, fights, abuse and broken trust. We all knew too much about each other right off the bat and that could become a weapon, or, at the very least, prove to be a delicate, priceless, personal item, belonging to someone else, that we were expected to care for and protect as we traveled over rocky and perilous terrain.

Perhaps, I just needed a break.

I turned the flamenco guitar up on my iPod to drown out my thoughts, other than those concerned with, what might be, my last mission.

Tink wasn't hard to find, not even a little. She was right where she had made all of her mistakes, building the possibility of new ones. As she sat at one of the taller tables in Norman's with a beer in front of her, the only things askew were that she was alone, she wasn't wearing her day collar and she looked really, really depressed. I walked over and sat across from her.

"Hey. How you doing?" I asked sympathetically.

She exhaled her cigarette. "Oh, I'm great," she said with sarcasm. "I mean, I completely fucked my whole life up. I hurt the two people who care about me more than anything in the world. I did it by being selfish, shallow, inconsiderate, irresponsible..." She began to tear up a small amount. "I don't even know where I'm going to sleep tonight. Things are just fabulous."

I sat there silently, listening. Tink just wiped her face and hit her cigarette again. That was when a thin guy with long hair walked up and stood behind her. He gave me a slightly dirty look before addressing her.

"Hey, Britt. I thought you wanted to be left alone."

"It's okay," she muttered. "He's a friend."

The guy gave me another look clearly meant to convey that he was prepared to meet whatever challenge I presented to his conquest of Tink...or rather, Brittany. He then sat in the chair next to her and asked what she planned to do for the rest of the night. "Someone mentioned that you might not have a place to stay."

She shrugged.

"She has a place to stay," I insisted. "She's going home. I'm here to make sure she gets there."

He glared at me. "Who are you exactly?"

"I told you," Tink said quietly. "He's a friend. And I need to talk to him for a little while. Do you mind?"

That seemed to really irritate the guy, who just got up and walked off without another word. Tink just sighed, seeming to have no emotion one way or the other concerning his feelings about the matter. "I can't go home. You know that, Iggy."

"What if I can convince D.C. to forgive you?"

She scoffed. "Yeah, right. Good luck." She put out her cigarette and took a swig of beer. "Once he's made his mind up..." She shook her head. "I don't need to be there anyway. I'm just going to fuck things up again. And again."

"Why do you think that?"

"Because I'm a stupid, selfish..." She paused and real tears started to pour. "...Whore. I'm a whore. I've always been a whore and now, I've proved it beyond a doubt."

I took her hand and stroked it. "You are a person who made some mistakes."

"I'm some ungrateful bitch who can't keep her legs

closed, who doesn't care who she hurts, who doesn't care about the people who care about me. You know that. You don't even like people fooling around outside of their relationships when it's consensual." She continued to cry. "I don't deserve to be allowed to come home."

She put her head on the table and I let her cry for a bit. I thought hard about what to say. Finally, I knew there was only one course.

"Stop feeling sorry for yourself, you child," I ordered her.

She looked up.

"Seriously," I continued. "Yeah, you fucked up. Based on what I've been told and seen it was probably all another way of indulging yourself to hide from the truth. D.C. and Posie both saw something worth caring about in you and you sabotaged it just to prove them wrong because you don't feel that you deserve their love. And now you're sitting here beating yourself up in an attempt to keep from admitting that." Her face contorted as more tears streamed down her face, but I didn't stop. "You were bad. But that doesn't mean that you can't be forgiven. Someone once told me that in our lifestyle, 'you don't have to do a whole justification dance. You just apologize in the right way, get a simple punishment and you're done. Your sins are washed away'."

She wiped her face as she thought before shaking her head. "I don't think that's going to work this time."

I sighed. "Listen, what do you want?"

She shrugged. "I don't even know."

"If you could go back to the White House, would you?"

She didn't respond.

"If a choice was right out there on the table, do your penance and go home or leave it behind and go on with this real world life that you have here, what would you do?"

She remained silent. I leaned forward.

"Who do you want to be? Brittany or Tinkerbrat?"

Her tears were beginning to diminish as she thought. "I want a little of both. But honestly, I don't know how much of Tink I can be any more. The community itself is so full of drama all the time. There are some days when Tink's life is fabulous. But there are others where I just want to be away from all of that."

"Did you ever tell D.C. that?"

She shook her head.

I sighed. "Okay, kid. Get yourself together. I'm taking you home."

"Iggy, I—"

"Let's go," I ordered. "Now."

She sniffed and nodded. Killing her beer and grabbing her suitcase, she followed me out.

I knocked on D.C.'s door. It was late and I was concerned that I might wake them, but I didn't have to be worried. The door opened quickly and Posie stood there, still looking sad.

She turned towards the couch, where D.C. sat, looking unhappy himself. "Sir," she said quietly, "Mr. Ignite is back."

D.C. didn't get up, but just waved me in. He had a drink in his hand and looked a bit disheveled. "What can I do for you, Kelly?"

"I need to talk to you about Tink."

His eyes flashed with anger. He got up and went to the kitchen where he refilled his glass with a double.

"Once again, there's nothing to talk about."

"I disagree."

"You disagree?" His tone was sharp. He walked back to the couch and sat down. He looked over at Posie who was just standing there by the hallway door and told her to find something to do. She went to the kitchen and began wiping down already clean surfaces.

I sat down in the chair next to my former mentor. "Yeah, I do. Look, I've been listening to you for months now. You've helped me a lot. Let me help you."

"I don't want your help, Kelly, not on this."

"Tough," I said flatly. "Besides, I think that's a load of crap. You're clearly miserable. Both of you are. Just take Tink back, punish her for what she's done, forgive her and move on."

"Not going to happen. She crossed a big line. Not only did she cheat, a lot, but she did it unprotected and she lied about it. She knows I don't tolerate that kind of shit. She did it on purpose."

"You're right. She did."

He looked up at me. It was clear he was confused as to why I would agree with him, yet still take her side.

"She was acting out. You said it yourself. It's what she does. She doesn't communicate well, so she does things to draw attention to herself. It's a character flaw. Absolutely. But that's why you have to open those doors of communication yourself. And you can't just talk. You have to listen. And remember, you still owe me one after outing me to Master Jon. This is what I'm asking for."

He sat there with his mouth closed and his brow furrowed, staring into his drink.

"D.C., why do you really think she did what she did?"

He looked very uncomfortable and shook his head. "I honestly don't know."

"Well, that's something you have to find out, so you can fix this." I reached over and took his hand, squeezing his fist. "I know you love her and want her back. You just want her back with her past erased. Since that's not going to happen, you have to try to move beyond it."

He didn't say anything, but rather continued to look sour. Finally, Posie walked in from the kitchen and spoke to him delicately.

"Sir..."

Nothing.

"Daniel..." she said more sternly and realistically.

He looked up at her. The anger and hurt on his face began to morph into wounded. His remaining sub walked over and knelt in front of him.

"We can address this," she told him. "You always taught me that we could address anything. We both miss her and want this to be fixed. Please?"

He thought a moment and gritted his teeth, holding tears in place so they wouldn't escape his eyes. He suddenly relaxed and set his drink aside. "Okay. We'll talk to her. She's got some really intense punishment coming if we do take her back, but we'll talk to her tomorrow."

"Why put it off?" I said. I got up and went to the door. I leaned out and looked to my car where Tink waited and motioned for her to come in.

A few seconds later, she crept into the condo, looking ashamed. D.C. got up and walked over to her. "You look like shit," he said quietly.

"Yeah," she whispered and sniffled, not making steady eye contact. "You too."

He cleared his throat a couple of times and began, "Obviously, if we try to put this behind us there would have to be some severe punishment and discipline. All kinds of new rules and stipulations..."

"I understand," she replied. "I, uh...I have a few of my own."

That caught him by surprise.

She continued. "Look, I miss you guys already, but I can't do this all the time anymore. I can't spend every weekend at the Scene Shop or hitting all the 'important' parties. I don't care about being a pillar of the community. I just want to be us." She paused to let her words soak in. "Outside of that, I'm willing to accept whatever you think is necessary."

D.C. thought for a while. Before he could say anything, Posie walked over and hugged her sister who whimpered. She turned back to address her Dom.

"We can talk about that," Posie said as she wiped a couple of tears from her eyes and a few from Tink's. She looked urgently at D.C. "We can. Please?"

He was still and silent for a while longer before letting out an incredibly long sigh. "Go to bed, you two. We'll talk tomorrow."

Posie smiled with immense relief and led her sister by the hand, towards the bedrooms. Tink stopped however, and threw her arms around D.C. for a tight hug.

"I am so, so sorry," she wept.

"I know," he replied, equally as emotional, but trying to keep it stern.

"I'm *so* sorry!"

"It's okay. We'll discuss it tomorrow."

The girls went to Posie's room and closed the door. D.C. looked at me with an odd expression. "I don't know if I should be irritated that you meddled in my business or thank you."

I smiled. "In this lifestyle, we have plenty of opportunity for both."

I picked Mary up from her small apartment on the east side of town at around six pm the following Sunday. We drove a few miles, most of the way with her asking me where we were going and what we were going to do.

"It's a surprise," I told her.

"You're not taking me out into the middle of nowhere to attack me, are you?" she kidded...sort of.

I laughed. "No," I said. "The last time I did that, it didn't turn out so well."

She was quiet and when I glanced over I found her staring at me nervously. "I assume that's a joke," she remarked.

"Not as much as you might think," I confessed. "But don't worry. Where we're going and what we're doing, you will be perfectly safe."

Ten minutes later, we were easing into the parking lot of the Scene Shop. The sun had already begun its nap and the parking lot was empty save one other car. I pulled up close to the door and turned my engine off.

"Where are we?" Mary asked me.

I smiled. "Some place fun. Come on."

We got out and went to the front door. I held it open for her and we went in where Wired was waiting for us.

"Good evening, Mr. Ignite," he said with a formal tone and a friendly smile.

"Good evening," I replied. I turned to my guest, who looked slightly amused.

"Mr. Ignite?" she smirked.

"Mary," I said to her, "this is, James. He's here to help you feel safe."

"How is he going to do that?" she asked a bit

nervously.

I simply smiled.

"Sir and Miss," Wired said politely. "If you will both follow me."

He led us to the door to the back, pausing only briefly to go behind the counter and buzz it unlocked. I pulled it open, but not fully. Rather, I waited for him to come back and take the handle from me and hold the door for both of us. I thanked him and entered with Mary, pausing again once we passed the threshold so that Wired could take his place ahead of us and continue leading us in.

As we walked down the long hallway, Mary continued to ask what the place was. I playfully scolded her for being impatient and told her that she was about to find out. Once we reached the door to the main room, Wired opened it slowly. He reached just inside and flipped a switch to turn on the lights as I lead Mary in.

The effect was instantaneous. Her jaw dropped and she looked around in shock and awe.

"You...you brought me to a dungeon?" she asked.

"This is the Scene Shop. I told you about the place." I then immediately tried to reassure her about any misgivings she might already be having about allowing me to bring her there. "James, here, is a certified Dungeon Monitor. He has emergency medical training, knows all kinds of safety measures, the rules of the place...and he's much bigger than me. If at any time you don't feel safe or something happens, he'll be right outside the door."

"Miss," he said with a nod. He then stepped out, closing the heavy, steel door behind him.

Mary began to appear very confused and unsure. "What are you going to do to me?" she asked hesitantly.

"Relax," I said as I took off my coat and made my

way to the sound system. "I didn't bring you here to beat you or fuck you, if that's what you're wondering."

"Well then, why did you?"

I cued up a mix of salsa music, the jaunty horns reverberating splendidly through the large, open room full of metal fixtures. I tossed my jacket onto the speaker and walked towards her as I rolled up the sleeves of my shirt.

"Mary," I said with a playful smile, "I brought you here to dance."

She looked surprised. Then she looked relieved. Then she looked amused.

I held a hand out to her. "What do you say?"

She actually began to giggle and took my hand. I tugged her forward and spun her at the same time, so that she connected with her back to me. And then...we began to dance.

For the next thirty minutes, we salsaed, sambaed and tangoed around the room. Mary beamed and I couldn't help but reflect her joy. Every step, every spin, every dip was an experience and both of us began to lose ourselves in the movement. With one hand on the small of her back and the other, confidently holding hers, I moved her though every inch of free space and she beamed and kicked, thrusting her hips in ways that didn't express sex, but passion and joy. Each of our smiles, especially hers, shined around the room.

It was exhilarating.

At one point, the music slowed and so did we. I pulled her close to me and our movements calmed.

"Having fun?" I asked.

"Yes," she nodded vigorously. "This is never how I dreamed I might spend my first night in a sex dungeon. Not that I ever considered actually going to one."

"Well, enjoy it and get as much as you can out of it. We only have the place for another hour or so."

"What happens then?"

"That's when the club's guests start to arrive and I don't think they'd take too kindly to us sliding around in between all of their Big and little play."

"What's that?"

I started to explain, but quickly thought better of it. "Some other time."

"So," she smiled before biting her lip. "Is this all we're going to do while we're here? Dance?"

"What else did you have in mind?"

She fought a growing grin and shrugged. I maneuvered her up against one of the metal, bar fixtures and eased her back just enough while she gasped. I reached into my pocket, pulled out a handkerchief, produced two pairs of handcuffs from it and held them up. She stared at them and then back at me for a couple of seconds, almost losing her smile.

"Don't worry," I said. "They have a safety on them. You can actually let yourself out of them if you feel the need."

Slowly, she leaned back against the fixture, held her arms up and out and grabbed a couple of the bars. I calmly reached over and cuffed both of her wrists to them. I then touched her cheek and ran my fingers down her neck, shoulders and arms. Her breathing increased.

I placed my hand back on her cheek, leaned in and kissed her as she reciprocated. Our tongues danced just as much as our feet had minutes before. Eventually, my lips moved from her mouth to her jaw, her cheek, her eyelids, forehead and temples.

"You are such a good girl," I whispered to her with cheerful sincerity.

She giggled. "I'm learning to be. I'm having a really good time."

"Yeah, that makes two of us," I said. Then I swatted her dense bottom, hard. She squealed. I smiled. "We, at least, know how to have fun together."

She breathed heavy and looked into me. That gaze she had that wondered if I was trustworthy was gone, dismissed by her joyful amusement and excitement. She laughed and moaned again. I squeezed her ass with one hand and pulled her face to mine with the other.

"I'm going to kiss you again. Would that be alright?"

"Yes," she began. She then tacked on, "Sir."

We smiled at each other and began to make out like drunk college kids in a closet. We continued to kiss and I touched her some, but that's all we did that night. The rest would wait. It would wait until we knew each other a little better, until we trusted each other more and until we both felt ready.

Eventually, we would establish a formal arrangement, one where I would be able to come home, most nights, to find her there, collared and presenting down on the floor, eagerly awaiting my arrival. We would have protocols and rituals that were specially ours. We would explore animal sex, dark fucking and passionate lovemaking. We would also watch movies, cuddle and laugh together. We would go on dates and vacations. We would build a world where she was my most cherished possession and I was her owner and guardian, yet where we were both closer than most people could ever imagine.

That night, the night of dancing in the dungeon, was just the beginning and it was marvelous.

The End